Harlem Renaissance

Harlem
Renaissance

Kelly King Howes

Christine Slovey, Editor

AN IMPRINT OF THE GALE GROUP

DETROIT · SAN FRANCISCO · LONDON
BOSTON · WOODBRIDGE, CT

Harlem Renaissance

Kelly King Howes

U•X•L Staff

Christine Slovey, *U•X•L Editor*
Carol DeKane Nagel, *U•X•L Managing Editor*
Thomas L. Romig, *U•X•L Publisher*

Margaret A. Chamberlain, *Permissions Specialist (Pictures)*
Tracey Rowens, *Cover Design*
Pamela Galbreath, *Page Design*
Kenn Zorn, *Product Design Manager*

Rita Wimberley, *Senior Buyer*
Evi Seoud, *Assistant Production Manager*
Dorothy Maki, *Manufacturing Manager*
Mary Beth Trimper, *Production Director*

Robyn Young, *Image Editor*
Pamela Reed, *Imaging Coordinator*
Robert Duncan and Dan Newell, *Imaging Specialists*
Randy Basset, *Image Database Supervisor*
Barbara Yarrow, *Graphic Services Manager*

Linda Mahoney, LM Design, *Typesetting*

Cover photographs reproduced by permission of Corbis (Fletcher Henderson's Orchestra), The Estate of Carl Van Vechten (portrait of Zora Neale Hurston), and the Gibbes Museum of Art/Carolina Art Association (portrait of Aaron Douglas).

Library of Congress Cataloging-in-Publication Data

Howes, Kelly King.
    Harlem Renaissance / Kelly King Howes; edited by Christine Slovey.
        p. cm.
    Includes bibliographical references and index.
    ISBN 0-7876-4836-1
    1. Afro-American arts–New York (State)–New York–Juvenile literature. 2. Arts, Modern–20th century–New York (State)–New York–Juvenile literature. 3. Harlem Renaissance–Juvenile literature. [1. Harlem Renaissance. 2. Afro-American arts. 3.Afro-Americans–History–1877-1964.] I. Slovey, Christine. II. Title.
NX512.3.A35 H69 2000
700'.89'9607307471–dc21   00-034364

Printed in the United States of America

10 9 8 7 6 5 4 3 2

Contents

Almanac

Biographies

Reader's Guide

Harlem Renaissance presents a comprehensive overview of the events and people that comprised this rich period in American history in the early twentieth century. Centered around Harlem, a section of New York City and a thriving center of African American life and culture in the 1920s, the Harlem Renaissance is generally recognized as taking place between the end of World War I (1914–18) and the beginning of the period of economic hard times called the Great Depression (in the early 1930s). This period was a time of blossoming culture and great creativity in the African American community. Black people had lived in the United States for several hundred years and had already produced art, music, poetry, and novels. But never before had they done so much, at such a fast pace, and with such confidence and enthusiasm. The period known as the Harlem Renaissance eventually came to a close, but even today it is clear that it had a profound impact on American culture. It gave African Americans something to be proud of, to learn from, and to build upon.

Format

Harlem Renaissance is divided into two sections: Almanac and Biographies. The Almanac contains seven chapters, which range from the pre-history and launch of the Harlem Renaissance to the end of this movement. Chapters also cover fiction and poetry, the performing arts, the visual arts, and Harlem nightlife. Placed throughout the chapters are primary source documents that showcase poetry (such as "The Weary Blues" by Langston Hughes) and other writings (such as "We Return Fighting" by W.E.B. Du Bois) by key figures of the Harlem Renaissance. In addition, several images of famous works of art appear in Chapter 5, The Visual Arts.

The Biographies section details the lives of fifteen people who had a strong impact during the Harlem Renaissance. Coverage includes poets Langston Hughes and Countee Cullen, fiction writers Jean Toomer and Zora Neale Hurston, musician Duke Ellington and singer Bessie Smith, visual artist Aaron Douglas, dynamic thinker and leader W.E.B. Du Bois, and others. Primary source documents are also found throughout many of the biography entries.

Each chapter and biography entry also contains photos and illustrations that enhance the text.

Harlem Renaissance includes a timeline of key events, glossary, research and activity ideas, general bibliography, and subject index.

Acknowledgments

A note of appreciation is extended to the *Harlem Renaissance* advisors, who provided invaluable suggestions when this work was in its formative stages:

Mary Alice Andersen
Media Specialist
Winona Middle School
Winona, Minnesota

Bonnie L. Raasch
Media Specialist
C.B. Vernon Middle School
Marion, Iowa

Paul P. Reuben
Professor of English
California State University Stanislaus

Comments and Suggestions

We welcome your comments on *Harlem Renaissance.* Please write: Editors, *Harlem Renaissance,* U•X•L, 27500 Drake Rd., Farmington Hills, Michigan, 48331–3535; call toll free: 1–800–877–4253; fax: 248–414–5043; or send e-mail via http://www.galegroup.com.

Harlem Renaissance Timeline

1890 Between 1890 and 1920, about two million African Americans migrate from the rural southern states to the northern cities, where they hope to find better opportunities and less discrimination.

1910 The National Association for the Advancement of Colored People (NAACP) is founded, and prominent black leader W.E.B. Du Bois becomes editor of the group's monthly magazine, *Crisis.*

1912 James Weldon Johnson's influential novel *Autobiography of an Ex-Colored Man* is published.

1917 Jamaican-born Marcus Garvey arrives in Harlem and founds the United Negro Improvement Association,

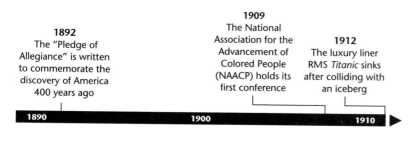

1892
The "Pledge of Allegiance" is written to commemorate the discovery of America 400 years ago

1909
The National Association for the Advancement of Colored People (NAACP) holds its first conference

1912
The luxury liner RMS *Titanic* sinks after colliding with an iceberg

1890   1900   1910

W.E.B. Du Bois.
(Courtesy of the Library of Congress.)

James Weldon Johnson.
(© CORBIS. Reproduced by permission.)

an organization that urges blacks to unite and form their own nation.

1917 Between 10,000 and 15,000 African Americans join the Silent Protest Parade, marching down Fifth Avenue in complete silence to protest violence against blacks.

1917 The politically radical black publication *The Messenger* is founded.

1917 Two of Claude McKay's poems are published in the white literary journal *Seven Arts*.

1919 The 369th Infantry Regiment, a highly decorated unit made up entirely of African American soldiers, returns from World War I to a heroes' welcome in Harlem.

1919 Jessie Redmon Fauset becomes literary editor of *Crisis*.

1919 During the "Red Summer of Hate," African Americans react angrily to widespread lynchings and other violence directed against them, with race riots occurring in Chicago, Washington, D.C., and two dozen other American cities.

1920 James Weldon Johnson becomes the head of the NAACP.

1920 Acclaimed American playwright Eugene O'Neil's drama *The Emperor Jones* opens at the Provincetown Playhouse with black actor Charles Gilpin in the lead role.

1921 Harry Pace founds the Black Swan Phonograph Corporation and begins production of the "race records" that will help to bring jazz and blues music to a wider audience.

1921 The musical revue *Shuffle Along* opens on Broadway, delighting audiences with its high-energy singing and dancing and, many believe, providing the spark that ignites the Harlem Renaissance.

1921 Langston Hughes's great poem "The Negro Speaks of Rivers" is published in *Crisis*.

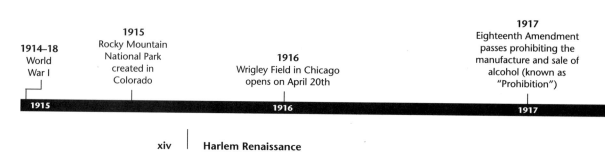

1914–18
World War I

1915
Rocky Mountain National Park created in Colorado

1916
Wrigley Field in Chicago opens on April 20th

1917
Eighteenth Amendment passes prohibiting the manufacture and sale of alcohol (known as "Prohibition")

1915   1916   1917

1922   Marian Anderson performs at New York's Town Hall, launching her career as a classical singer.

1922   The first major book of the Harlem Renaissance appears when Claude McKay's novel *Harlem Shadows* is published by Harcourt, Brace.

1922   Meta Warrick Fuller's sculpture *Ethiopia Awakening* is shown at the "Making of America" exhibition in New York.

1923   Bessie Smith records "Downhearted Blues" and "Gulf Coast Blues," soon becoming the most famous blues singer in both the northern and southern states.

1923   The National Urban League establishes *Opportunity* magazine, which will not only publish the work of Harlem Renaissance writers and artists but will help to support them through an annual contest.

1923   Roland Hayes makes his New York debut, singing a program of classical music as well as African American spirituals.

1923   Marcus Garvey is arrested for mail fraud and imprisoned for three months.

1923   The National Ethiopian Art Players produce Willis Richardson's *The Chip Woman,* the first drama by a black playwright to appear on the Broadway stage.

1923   Joe "King" Oliver's Creole Jazz Band makes a series of recordings with trumpet player Louis Armstrong.

1923   Pianist, composer, and band leader Duke Ellington arrives in New York with his band, the Washingtonians.

1923   Jean Toomer's innovative novel *Cane* is published and Toomer is hailed as one of the most promising young authors of the Harlem Renaissance.

1923   Harlem's largest and most famous cabaret, the Cotton Club, opens.

Bessie Smith.
(The Bettmann Archive. Reproduced by permission.)

1918
Daylight Saving Time first goes into effect in the U.S.

1918–19
Influenza kills between 20 and 40 million people worldwide

1919
Federal troops are called out to end Chicago race riots

1920
Nineteenth Amendment guarantees the vote to women

1918   1919   1920

1923 The Ethiopian Art Players perform Eugene O'Neill's play *All God's Chillun Got Wings* in Washington, D.C., while in Cleveland the Gilpin Players at Karamu Theatre present *In Abraham's Bosom* by Paul Green.

1923 Louis Armstrong joins Fletcher Henderson's orchestra, which—performing at the famed Roseland Ballroom—becomes the most popular dance band in New York.

1923 Kansas City-born artist Aaron Douglas arrives in New York and begins developing a new style that will make him the official artist of the Harlem Renaissance.

1923 *The Fire in the Flint,* a novel by NAACP leader Walter White, is published.

1923 The publication of Jessie Redmon Fauset's *There Is Confusion* marks the first Harlem Renaissance book by a woman writer.

1923 At the Civic Club dinner hosted by *Opportunity*'s Charles S. Johnson, promising young writers meet the influential editors and publishers who can boost their careers.

1923 Josephine Baker appears in *Chocolate Dandies* on Broadway.

1923 Roland Hayes performs at Carnegie Hall.

1923 Poems by Harlem Renaissance star Countee Cullen appear in four major white publications.

1923 Zora Neale Hurston publishes her first short story in *Opportunity.*

1925 The exciting new musical form known as jazz is showcased in the "First American Jazz Concert" at Aeolian Hall in New York.

1925 *Survey Graphic* magazine publishes an issue devoted entirely to the work of Harlem Renaissance writers and artists.

Jessie Fauset with Langston Hughes and Zora Hurston.
(Schomburg Center for Black Culture. Reproduced by permission.)

1921–23
Warren G. Harding is the 29th President of the U.S.

1922
Lincoln Memorial in Washington, D.C., is dedicated

1922
The *Reader's Digest* begins publication

1923
Yankee Stadium opens in New York City

1921   1922   1923

1925   Marcus Garvey is convicted of mail fraud and imprisoned in the Atlanta Penitentiary.

1925   Marian Anderson wins a singing competition sponsored by the New York Philharmonic Orchestra.

1925   Countee Cullen's first volume of poetry, *Color,* is published.

1925   Artist Sargent Johnson exhibits his paintings at the San Francisco Art Association, and Archibald Motley wins a medal from the Art Institute of Chicago for his painting "A Mulatress."

1925   Wallace Thurman moves from Los Angeles to New York and soon becomes a leader of the younger generation of Harlem Renaissance writers and artists.

1925   Zora Neale Hurston enters Barnard College on a scholarship, studying anthropology.

1925   Well-known white poet Vachel Lindsay reads the poems of Langston Hughes, then working as a restaurant busboy, to the audience at his own poetry reading, announcing that he has discovered a bright new talent.

1925   The *New Negro* anthology, edited by Alain Locke, introduces the work and ideas of the Harlem Renaissance.

1926   W.C. Handy's *Blues: An Anthology* is published, bringing wider attention to this unique African American musical form.

1926   Langston Hughes's first volume of poetry, *The Weary Blues,* is published.

1926   The NAACP-sponsored theatrical group the Krigwa Players stages three plays.

1926   White author Carl Van Vechten's controversial novel *Nigger Heaven* is published.

Langston Hughes.
(The Bettmann Archive. Reproduced by permission.)

Lafayette Theater.
(© Bettmann/CORBIS. Reproduced by permission.)

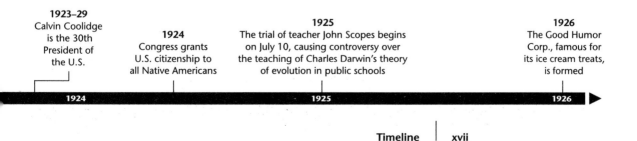

1923–29
Calvin Coolidge is the 30th President of the U.S.

1924
Congress grants U.S. citizenship to all Native Americans

1925
The trial of teacher John Scopes begins on July 10, causing controversy over the teaching of Charles Darwin's theory of evolution in public schools

1926
The Good Humor Corp., famous for its ice cream treats, is formed

1924   1925   1926

1926 The Harmon Foundation holds its first annual art exhibition of works by African American artists, and Palmer Hayden and Hale Woodruff win top awards.

1926 A daring new (but short-lived) literary journal called *Fire!!* appears.

1927 Duke Ellington begins a three-year stint at the Cotton Club, gaining fame and praise for his innovative style and compositions.

1927 James Weldon Johnson's *God's Trombones,* a book of poems modeled after sermons by black preachers and illustrated by Aaron Douglas, is published.

1927 Several young Harlem Renaissance writers and artists accept money and other help from wealthy patron Charlotte Mason, whom they call "Godmother."

1927 Langston Hughes's second poetry collection, *Fine Clothes to the Jew,* features blues rhythms and Harlem-inspired imagery.

1927 Ordered to leave the United States, Marcus Garvey returns to Jamaica.

1927 Wealthy African American A'lelia Walker, whose mother founded a successful black hair and skin care business, opens a nightclub and literary salon called the Dark Tower.

1927 *Porgy,* a musical play with black characters and themes, opens on Broadway.

1928 A number of important Harlem Renaissance works are published, including Rudolph Fisher's *Walls of Jericho,* Nella Larsen's *Quicksand,* Jessie Redmon Fauset's *Plum Bun,* W.E.B. Du Bois's *Dark Princess,* and Claude McKay's *Home to Harlem* (which becomes the first best-seller by a black author).

Nella Larsen.
(UPI/Corbis-Bettmann. Reproduced by permission.)

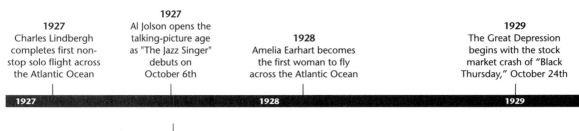

1927
Charles Lindbergh completes first non-stop solo flight across the Atlantic Ocean

1927
Al Jolson opens the talking-picture age as "The Jazz Singer" debuts on October 6th

1928
Amelia Earhart becomes the first woman to fly across the Atlantic Ocean

1929
The Great Depression begins with the stock market crash of "Black Thursday," October 24th

1927   1928   1929

1928 Poet Countee Cullen marries Yolande Du Bois, daughter of the great black leader, in an extravagant wedding that is one of the most memorable social events of the Harlem Renaissance.

1928 Palmer Hayden's work is featured in a one-man exhibition at a Paris art gallery, and Archibald Motley exhibits his paintings at the New Galleries in New York.

1928 Wallace Thurman edits another literary journal, *Harlem,* that is—like its predecessor, *Fire!!*—destined to appear only once.

1929 Wallace Thurman's play *Harlem* opens on Broadway, becoming the most successful production of its time by a black author.

1929 The Harmon Foundation sponsors an exhibition of black artists at the National Gallery in Washington, D.C.

1929 Novels by Wallace Thurman (*The Blacker the Berry*) and Claude McKay (*Banjo*) are published, as is Countee Cullen's *The Black Christ and Other Poems.*

1929 The Broadway show *Ain't Misbehavin'* features music by piano player Fats Waller.

1929 The stock market crashes, setting off the economic downturn known as the Great Depression.

1930 Marc Connelly's play *The Green Pastures,* notable for its African American characters and content, opens to great acclaim on Broadway.

1930 Langston Hughes's novel *Not Without Laughter* is published.

1931 Artist August Savage opens the Savage School of Arts and Crafts in Harlem.

1931 A'lelia Walker dies unexpectedly.

Harlem in the 1920s.
(© Underwood & Underwood/CORBIS. Reproduced by permission.)

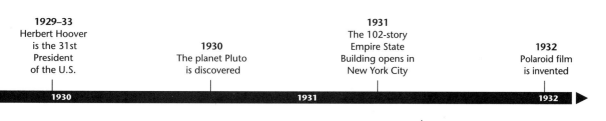

1929–33
Herbert Hoover is the 31st President of the U.S.

1930
The planet Pluto is discovered

1931
The 102-story Empire State Building opens in New York City

1932
Polaroid film is invented

1930   1931   1932

Aspects of Negro Life by Aaron Douglas.
(Schomburg Center for Black Culture. Reproduced by permission.)

1933 A number of Harlem Renaissance writers and artists find employment with the Works Project Administration, a government-sponsored program designed to put Americans back to work.

1934 Wallace Thurman's death in the charity ward of a New York hospital stuns and sobers his Harlem Renaissance friends.

1934 Aaron Douglas is commissioned to create a series of murals, which will be entitled *Aspects of Negro Life*, for the 135th Street (Harlem) branch of the New York Public Library.

1935 Harlem is the scene of a major riot sparked by anger over discrimination by white-owned businesses.

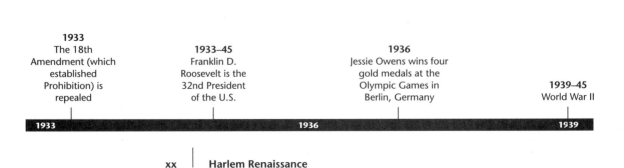

1933
The 18th Amendment (which established Prohibition) is repealed

1933–45
Franklin D. Roosevelt is the 32nd President of the U.S.

1936
Jessie Owens wins four gold medals at the Olympic Games in Berlin, Germany

1939–45
World War II

1933　　　　1936　　　　1939

Words to Know

B

Big Band Sound: A style that originated in the dance music of the Harlem Renaissance. It is created by a jazz orchestra that features more than one player on many instruments (especially horns).

Blues: A musical form rooted in the African American heritage and infused with a special quality of sadness and complaint; the blues were—and still are—sung and played both to express and to conquer sorrow and pain.

C

Civic Club Dinner: An event held on March 21, 1924, to which 110 guests from the worlds of literature and publishing were invited. Supposedly planned to celebrate the publication of Jessie Redmon Fauset's first novel, the dinner brought together young writers and the publishers and editors who could promote their careers.

Crisis: A leading black magazine, published by the National Association for the Advancement of Colored People (NAACP), in which the work of many Harlem Renaissance writers and artists first appeared.

D

The Dark Tower: The nightclub and literary salon opened by wealthy A'lelia Walker in her fancy Striver's Row townhouse as a gathering place for guests to enjoy the music, writing, art, and talk of the Harlem Renaissance.

Discrimination: Treating people differently—and usually worse—simply because they belong to a particular race or group (for example, hiring a white person instead of a better qualified black person).

F

Fire!!: A one-issue literary journal produced by writers Wallace Thurman (who served as editor), Langston Hughes, Zora Neale Hurston, and others to showcase the work of the daring younger generation of Harlem Renaissance artists.

G

Great Depression: The period of economic downturn, widespread unemployment, and general hardship that lasted from 1929, when the stock market crashed, until the beginning of World War II (1939–45), when the demand for war materials put people back to work.

H

Harlemania: The trend that, during the 1920s, made it popular for well-heeled whites to journey uptown from lower Manhattan to the African American community of Harlem to enjoy the lively music, dancing, and other delights to be found there. Also called "Going Uptown."

Harlem Renaissance: Popular name for the blossoming of African American culture—including literature, drama, music, visual arts, and journalism—that took place between the end of World War I and the beginning of the Great Depression. Also called the New Negro movement.

Harmon Foundation: An organization founded by a wealthy white real estate tycoon, William Harmon, who wanted to support, promote and nurture African American art and culture. The Harmon Foundation (which existed until 1967) offered monetary awards and exhibition opportunities, benefitting individual artists and also helping to introduce a much wider audience to black art.

J

Jazz: An original musical form rooted in the African American tradition and including traces of both African and European influences. Jazz features off-beat rhythms and improvisation (solos in which performers take off from the main melody being played but introduce their own stylings or interpretations).

Jim Crow Laws: Unfair laws that, in the southern states from the post-Civil War period to the middle of the twentieth century, were used to keep African Americans from becoming full, equal citizens (an example is the segregation of public facilities, which meant that blacks could not use the same restrooms or drinking fountains as whites).

Jungle Alley: The stretch of Harlem's 133rd Street along which many popular nightclubs and speakeasies (illegal bars or saloons) were located.

K

Ku Klux Klan (KKK): A terrorist organization founded soon after the Civil War (and that still exists today). Spawned by racial hatred, resentment, and resistance to the idea that blacks and other members of minority groups should have equality with whites, the KKK carried out many acts of violence and terror, especially during the first quarter of the twentieth century.

L

Lynching: A crude, cruel form of mob justice in which people (usually blacks) accused of but not formally tried for crimes were hanged; they were sometimes tortured before being killed, and their bodies were often burned during or after the lynching.

M

Migration: The early-twentieth-century movement of African Americans from their rural homes in the south to the northern, industrial cities, where they hoped to find greater opportunities for work and relief from racism and discrimination.

Minstrel shows: An early form of the musical revue dating from the mid-nineteenth century, in which white (and later black) actors sang, danced, and told stories and jokes while wearing "blackface" makeup to create an exaggerated appearance of African features.

N

National Association for the Advancement of Colored People (NAACP): An organization founded in 1910 (and still in existence today) by W.E.B. Du Bois and others to promote the advancement of African Americans to equal status with white citizens.

National Urban League: An organization founded by black and white civil rights advocates to promote the progress of African Americans; led by sociologist Charles S. Johnson, the National Urban League published a popular magazine called *Opportunity* in which many Harlem Renaissance works appeared.

Negrotarians: The name given by writer and folklorist Zora Neale Hurston to the wealthy, influential whites who offered support—in the form of money, advice, encouragement, and introductions to people who could further their careers—to Harlem Renaissance writers, performers, and artists.

New Negro Movement: The contemporary name for the period in which shifting attitudes and self-image among African Americans brought about a blossoming of thought and culture; the *New Negro* anthology, edited by Alain Locke, both showcased and explained this movement.

Niggerati Manor: The name coined by writer Zora Neale Hurston for the boarding house at 267 West 134th Street in Harlem in which many members of the younger generation of the Harlem Renaissance lived, played, and worked together.

O

"O.P.": Old Philadelphia, the common nickname for a member of Philadelpia's old, established, well-to-do African American community; the best known Harlem Renaissance members were Jessie Redmon Fauset and Alain Locke.

Opportunity: The magazine of the National Urban League, in which many Harlem Renaissance writers and artists published their works; *Opportunity* also sponsored an annual contest that offered monetary awards and recognition to winners.

P

Pan-Africanism: The belief that all people of African heritage—whether they live in Africa, the United States, the Caribbean, or elsewhere—share a common heritage and should work together to help each other.

Passing: The practice by which light-skinned African Americans would pretend to be white in order to gain the social and material advantages denied to blacks.

Prejudice: Suspicion, intolerance, or hatred of people of other races, religions, regions, or other perceived differences.

Primitivism: A term referring to the qualities of simplicity, wildness, and purity that were, during the time of the Harlem Renaissance, widely thought to be natural to people of African heritage; many blacks resented the way whites expected them to behave or create in a "primitive" manner, while others embraced the idea as positive.

Prohibition: A ban on the "manufacture, sale, or transportation of intoxicating liquors" that began with the 1918 passage of the 18th Amendment to the Constitution and ended with the repeal of the amendment in 1933 after the government was no longer able to enforce it.

R

Race-building: A term often used during the Harlem Renaissance for activities that promoted the advancement of African Americans or reflected positively on them.

Race Records: Recordings of black singers and musicians, beginning in the early 1920s, that were made by companies like Black Swan Phonograph Company and Okey Records in response to the new, growing interest in blues and jazz music by a wide audience.

Racism: The belief that one's own race is superior to others, and that members of other races should be treated differently.

Realism: An artistic trend that calls for truthful portrayals of human characters and situations.

Red Summer of Hate: The period in 1919 when hatred and resentment of blacks led to 83 lynchings and 200 public meetings of the Ku Klux Klan, a white terrorist group; African Americans reacted with bloody race riots in 26 American cities, including Washington, D.C.; Chicago, Illinois; Omaha, Nebraska; and Knoxville, Tennessee.

Rent Party: An event held by a Harlem resident in his or her home as a way to raise money for rent. Guests would pay a small admission fee to listen and dance to live jazz or blues music, and they could also buy food and drinks.

S

Segregation: The practice, legal until the 1950s, of keeping blacks and whites separated from each other (usually through separate facilities) in neighborhoods, schools, workplaces, and public areas such as restrooms, theatres, and restaurants.

Silent Protest Parade: An event held on July 28, 1917, as a protest against lynchings in Waco, Texas, and Memphis, Tennessee, and a race riot in East St. Louis, Missouri, all of which had occurred a month earlier. Between 10,000 and 15,000 African Americans marched down Fifth Avenue in complete silence.

Spirituals: African American religious songs that combine elements of African and European music.

Stereotype: A fixed idea that all the members of a race or other group have certain characteristics or habits.

Striver's Row: The fanciest neighborhood in Harlem, inhabited by some of its most wealthy and successful residents (such as A'lelia Walker, heir to a hair and skin care product fortune).

T

Talented 10th: The name given by black leader W.E.B. Du Bois to the upper crust of African American society, whose members, it was hoped, would help bring about racial progress through their abilities and achievements.

369th Infantry Regiment: An all-black military unit that earned many honors during World War I and made a triumphant return to Harlem in February 1919.

Tree of Hope: A tree that stood just outside the door of Connie's Inn, a famous Harlem nightclub, that was said to bring good luck to anyone who rubbed its bark.

U

United Negro Improvement Association (UNIA): Organization founded by black nationalist Marcus Garvey to promote the interests of the black race.

W

Works Project Administration (WPA): An agency founded under the administration of President Franklin Roosevelt (1882–1945; served as president from 1933 to 1945) as part of his program to revitalize the U.S. economy and the American people's morale. The WPA provided employment to several Harlem Renaissance figures, including Aaron Douglas and Zora Neale Hurston.

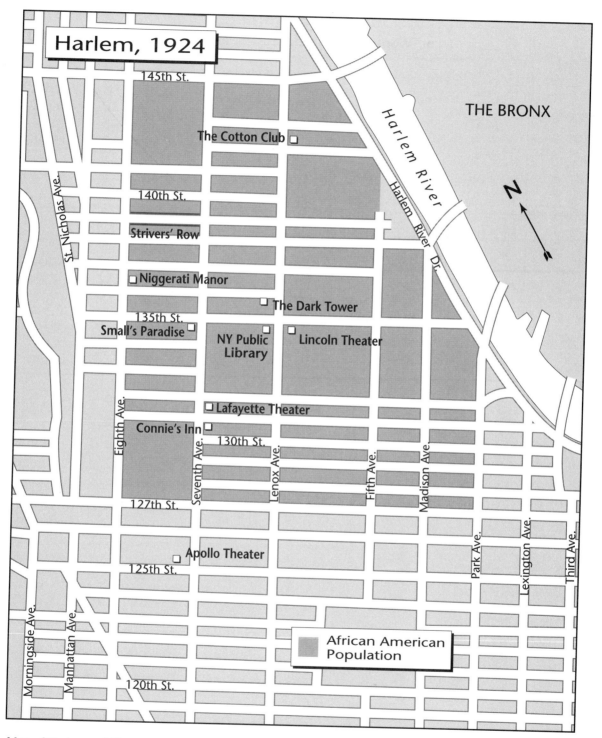

Map of Harlem c. 1924. *(Map by XNR Productions, Inc.)*

Almanac

"If We Must Die": Currents Old and New Combine to Set the Stage

Imagine yourself on Seventh Avenue in New York City in the middle of the 1920s. You are a young African American, and you are in Harlem, a thriving center of African American life and culture and the most exciting place in the world to you. It is Sunday afternoon, and the after-church parade has begun. All around you are people of color. They may be rich or poor or middle class, but they are all dressed in their finest clothes. They stroll along, talking, laughing, debating, and enjoying the sights and sounds of their special part of the world.

If you work as a maid or in a factory, you may have attended a "rent party" last night, where you danced to the thumping music of a solo piano player in a dimly lit apartment and ate hoppin' John (a dish made of black-eyed peas, rice, and pork) and pig's feet (while your small admission fee helped keep your host from being evicted). If you had a little more money in your pocket, you might have joined the fancier crowd at Small's Paradise, the popular jazz nightclub. If you are a writer who has not yet been discovered, you may be planning to attend a literary gathering at the 135th Street branch of the New York Public Library. Once you make your mark in literature, you will proba-

Fifth Avenue and 135th Street in Harlem in 1927.
(UPI/Corbis-Bettmann. Reproduced by permission.)

bly be invited to the "Striver's Row" home of black millionairess A'Lelia Walker, who entertains writers, musicians, and theatrical types in a room with the words to Langston Hughes's poem "The Weary Blues" painted on one wall.

A blossoming of African American culture

If you lived in Harlem during the 1920s, you might have done any or all of these things because you were part of the *Harlem Renaissance.* Although that name suggests an organized movement, it is not so easy to pin down or neatly describe this important era in America's cultural history. It is true that between the end of World War I (1914–18) and the beginning of the period of hard times called the Great Depression (in the early 1930s), African American culture blossomed—some might even say it exploded. Black people had lived in the United States for several hundred years and had already produced art, music, poetry, and novels. But never before had they done so much, at such a fast pace, and with such confidence and enthusiasm. Many African Americans—especially important leaders like W.E.B. Du Bois (surname pronounced doo-BOYCE; 1868–1963; see biographical entry), James Weldon Johnson (1871–1938), and Alain Locke (1886–1954; see biographical entry)—believed that this cultural explosion would show white America what remarkable things blacks could do and thus lead to greater equality.

In literature, poets like Langston Hughes (1902–1967; see biographical entry) and Countee Cullen (1903–1946; see biographical entry) were publishing some of their finest work, and fiction writers like Jean Toomer (1894–1967; see biographical entry) and Zora Neale Hurston (1891–1960; see biographical entry) were using their skills to describe the lives and dreams of a broad spectrum of African Americans. In the field of music, composers, bandleaders, and performers like James Hubert "Eubie" Blake (1883–1983), Duke Ellington (1899–1974; see biographical entry), and Bessie Smith (c. 1894–1937; see biographical entry) were thrilling audiences with the new musical forms of jazz and blues. Visual artists like Aaron Douglas (1899–1979; see biographical entry) and Meta Warrick Fuller (1877–1968) were painting and sculpting in ways that impressed both black and white art lovers, and photographer James Van Der Zee (1886–1983) was documenting Harlem life on film. Meanwhile, dynamic thinkers and leaders like W.E.B. Du Bois, Charles S. Johnson (1893–1956), and Marcus Garvey (1887–1940) were expressing strong opinions about racial progress and politics in the journals and periodicals that catered to African American readers.

All of these writers, artists, and performers were active during the same historical period, but did they have enough in common to make up a "movement"? No, not really. They did not all follow the same creed or the same rules, and they all had different ideas about what they were doing and why they were doing it. When the Harlem Renaissance was over, some critics said that it had not accomplished much, that African Americans were still struggling against prejudice, discrimination, and inequality. But now, more than seventy years later, it is clear that the Harlem Renaissance had a profound impact on American culture. It gave African Americans something to be proud of, to learn from, and to build upon. Before we can understand how that happened, we must look back to the years leading up to the Harlem Renaissance and see how events, ideas, and people came together to bring this cultural blossoming to life.

The Reconstruction era's harsh realities

On September 22, 1862, President Abraham Lincoln signed the Emancipation Proclamation, which declared that after January 1, 1863, slavery would be illegal in the United States. The Civil War (1861–65) ended about two years later, and the North and South once again came together to form one nation. Peace had been restored, and the freedom of African Americans had been won through the efforts and sacrifices of both black and white Americans. But the joy and optimism that African Americans felt was soon dulled by the hard realities of life in the years following the war, especially for those living in the South.

Between 1865 and 1877, during a period called the Reconstruction, the U.S. government tried to help the Southern states recover from wartime devastation and make the transition from slave to paid labor on farms and plantations. The U.S. Army remained on the scene to maintain order, and Freedmen's Bureaus were established to aid newly free blacks as they adjusted to an entirely new way of life. In addition, a small number of Northerners known as "carpetbaggers" (because of the satchels they often brought with them), most of them officials of the Freedmen's Bureaus or the army, got involved in Southern politics. Some of them were honest, but others were corrupt and got involved strictly for their own gain. Many white Southerners resented the presence of the carpetbaggers, but they were even more hostile toward the free blacks. The Old South had been destroyed, and the whites would have to rebuild their lives without the unpaid labor of slaves. They focused their frustration and anger on the African Americans who would now work only for wages.

"Jim Crow" laws enforce segregation

In 1877 the U.S. Army pulled out of the Southern states, leaving them to govern themselves. Soon a system of legalized segregation (separation of the races) was put into place throughout the South. At the root of this segregation was the enforcement of the "Jim Crow" laws, which ensured that whites and blacks would not share the same public facilities or the same privileges. Under these laws, African Americans could not attend the same schools as whites, they were barred from eating in "whites only" restaurants, and they had to sit in separate (always less desirable) sections of movie theaters. By claiming that facilities were "separate but equal," the Southern states were able to get around the Fourteenth Amendment to the U.S. Constitution, which guaranteed full citizenship to former slaves. The Fifteenth Amendment, which gave blacks the right to vote, was also rendered useless: high taxes had to be paid at the polls, and "grandfather clauses" allowed people to vote only if their father or grandfather had the right to vote on January 1, 1867. (African Americans were not actually given the right to vote until March 1, 1867.)

Lynchings terrorize African Americans

As the nineteenth century drew to a close, racial tension in the South worsened when agricultural production went down, due partly to an infestation of insects called "boll weevils" that attacked cotton plants. (Cotton was one of the South's main crops.) At this point, white resentment against blacks began to take a violent turn, and there was a dramatic increase in lynchings. (This was a vile and violent practice in which African Americans accused of various crimes or misdeeds—but rarely legally charged—would be captured by gangs of whites and lynched—hanged without a trial, usually from a tree. The individuals might be killed before or during the lynching.) Law enforcement authorities (most often, white authorities) usually overlooked these cruel and blatant murders of blacks. Between the years 1884 and 1900, around twenty-five hundred lynchings occurred in the South, creating a terrifying atmosphere for African Americans.

Booker T. Washington

Although they were the victims of prejudice and brutality, blacks were also active in trying to improve their position

in society. One of the most dynamic African American leaders of the post-Reconstruction years was Booker T. Washington (1856–1915), who had been born in West Virginia about ten years before the start of the Civil War. In 1881 he founded the Tuskegee Institute in Alabama, a school where blacks could learn how to support themselves and become self-reliant. Washington felt that blacks should learn practical skills rather than become highly educated, and that they should be patient and wait for the whites in power to grant them equality. He assumed that most African Americans would continue to live in rural areas, but by the early twentieth century the course of African American life and culture began to change.

Booker T. Washington, a leader in the African American community during the Reconstruction years. *(Corbis-Bettmann. Reproduced by permission.)*

Blacks migrate to cities in the North

The most important development—one that Washington had not anticipated—was the movement of rural southern blacks to the northern cities. This massive migration occurred as the South's economy declined and violence against African Americans increased. Then, in 1917, the United States entered World War I. The need to produce weapons and equipment for the war effort, as well as the flood of young men joining the armed services, led to a great demand for workers in such northern industrial cities as New York, Philadelphia, and Chicago.

It is estimated that between 1890 and 1920, about two million African Americans left their southern homes for the North. For the first time in U.S. history, blacks were living in tightly packed, segregated urban communities. Their closeness to each other in this new shared life and work led to a growing awareness of themselves as a people who might achieve power through their sheer numbers.

The impact of World War I

In both its aims and its results, the First World War had a great impact on how African Americans felt about themselves and their role in American society. The war was supposed to make the world "safe for democracy." Many blacks supported and served in the war effort not only out of patriotism but out of a desire to show their country that the principles of democracy should be extended to all Americans—including African Americans.

After a heated debate among African Americans regarding their service in the armed forces (some felt they should not sacrifice their lives for a country that treated them as outsiders), several hundred thousand joined the war effort. Due to the segregation and discriminatory practices of the U.S. military, not all African Americans who served saw combat, but some did, including members of the 369th Infantry Regiment, a unit that earned many honors during the war and made a triumphant return to Harlem in February 1919.

"If We Must Die"
by Claude McKay

If we must die, let it not be like hogs

Hunted and penned in an
inglorious spot,

While round us bark the mad and
hungry dogs,

Making their mock at our accursed lot.

If we must die, O let us nobly die,

So that our precious blood may
not be shed

In vain; then even the monsters we defy

Shall be constrained to honor us
though dead!

O kinsmen! we must meet the
common foe!

Though far outnumbered let us
show us brave,

And for their thousand blows deal
one deathblow!

What though before us lies the
open grave?

Like men we'll face the murderous,
cowardly pack,

Pressed to the wall, dying but
fighting back!

From "If We Must Die," in Selected Poems of
Claude McKay *by Claude McKay. Twayne
Publishers, Inc. Copyright 1953.*

Though the African American community was proud of these returning black soldiers, some whites—especially resentful white southerners and workers in the North who feared competition for jobs—felt they posed a threat.

The blacks who served in World War I lived through a horrible bloodbath that made them question the very values for which they had been fighting. But the experience also made them more aware of the world's rich and varied cultures—nonwhite and non-European cultures among them. A period of cultural freedom and experimentation was dawning in the United States, and blacks were becoming more self-aware and less willing to put up with mistreatment and injustice.

The "Red Summer of Hate"

Around the same time, a once-small and obscure white-supremacist organization (a group that believes people of European heritage are superior to those from other racial or cultural backgrounds) called the Ku Klux Klan (KKK) grew into a nationwide organization with membership estimated between five hundred thousand and several million. Members of the KKK carried out terrorist acts against blacks and other hated groups (mainly Jews, Catholics, and immigrants) while concealing their identities beneath white robes and hoods. In mid-1919 the violence culminated in what is now called the "Red Summer of Hate," during which two hundred public Klan meetings were held and eighty-three blacks were lynched. African Americans did not accept the abuse quietly: there were bloody race riots in twenty-six American cities, including Washington, D.C.; Chicago, Illinois; Omaha, Nebraska; and Knoxville, Tennessee.

Harlem: An optimistic place

It was within this atmosphere of mixed emotions—rage and fear as well as faith in the future and a growing pride and self-awareness—that the Harlem Renaissance came into existence. And the place in which it all occurred was Harlem, a corner of New York City, New York, located at the northern tip of Manhattan and taking up less than two square miles. Although Harlem would later be known for its widespread poverty, overcrowding, and crime, in the early 1900s it was a place dominated by (relative) prosperity and optimistic high spirits.

As the twentieth century began, Harlem was an area of broad streets and handsome brick and brownstone buildings built by the German and Dutch people who first settled there. Harlem had few black residents before 1905; most of New York's black people, in fact, lived in a neighborhood called Black Bohemia, which was located farther downtown, around West 53rd Street. But the steady stream of African Americans from the South created an urgent need for more housing in New York City. That need was answered almost accidentally, when the owner of an apartment building at 31 West 133rd Street had trouble finding tenants after a murder occurred there. A black real estate agent helped him fill the building with African Americans who were even willing to pay a little extra for the privilege. Soon other landlords began to follow suit; at the same time, black investors started buying up land and buildings in Harlem. The community's white residents tried to stop this unwelcome invasion of black people, and when they failed to do so many of them moved out, creating room for even more African Americans.

As the population of blacks in Harlem grew, businesses owned and operated by blacks—especially those offering personal services such as barber shops and hair salons, funeral parlors, and shoe repair—began to flourish. Harlem-centered churches, community groups (like the Masons and Elks), and newspapers targeted to black readers also grew. African American doctors, dentists, lawyers, and other professionals found they could make a good living there. Many poor people still

Lenox Avenue in Harlem c. 1927.
(© Underwood & Underwood/CORBIS. Reproduced by permission.)

lived in Harlem, but there was also a solid middle class and even a few millionaires like Madame C.J. Walker (1867–1919), who had made her fortune selling hair and skin care products for African Americans. By the beginning of the 1920s, Harlem had indeed become a center of African American life, where black people—some from areas outside the United States, including parts of the Caribbean, South America, and Africa— lived, worked, and played together.

Artists and intellectuals are drawn to Harlem

Among those who were attracted to the material advantages, community spirit, and exciting atmosphere of Harlem were African American intellectuals, writers, musicians, and artists. Most of the key figures in the Harlem Renaissance were young—many were in their twenties and just trying out their artistic wings. But some older people were on hand to nurture and encourage them. These elders provided a strong foundation for the Harlem Renaissance movement.

W.E.B. Du Bois

Perhaps the most significant of these older figures was William Edward Burghardt Du Bois, who was then (and is now) recognized as the leading black intellectual of the early twentieth century. Born in Great Barrington, Massachusetts, in 1868, Du Bois was educated at Fisk and Harvard universities and spent some time in Europe before beginning a teaching career at colleges in Pennsylvania and Georgia. In his very influential book *The Souls of Black Folk,* a collection of essays about the problems and concerns of African Americans, he presented a viewpoint opposed to that of Booker T. Washington. Du Bois and others who came to be identified as members of the New Negro movement felt that it was too late for the combination of agricultural training and patient waiting recommended by Washington. Black people had to stand up for themselves against violence and discrimination, said Du Bois, and many African Americans agreed.

In May 1910 a group of white social reformers got together with black leaders, including Du Bois, to form the National Association for the Advancement of Colored People (NAACP), an organization devoted to helping blacks achieve equality. As editor of the NAACP's monthly journal, *Crisis,* Du Bois wrote strongly worded articles and editorials about what blacks should fight for and what they could become. He called the most accomplished and high-achieving African Americans the "Talented Tenth" and predicted that, through their example, these individuals would help blacks take their proper place in American society. Du Bois believed that the writers, poets, and other artists in the Talented Tenth should focus not on their own individual views and expressions but on the advancement of blacks as a whole.

One of the "Talented Tenth"

No discussion of the Harlem Renaissance would be complete without mentioning Alain Locke, who would describe the movement's aims and showcase its creativity in *The New Negro* anthology, published in 1925 (see Chapter 2). Before this important work ever came to be, however, Locke was working hard to help and encourage African American writers. He was a shining example of Du Bois's Talented Tenth:

educated at Harvard University, he had been the first black Rhodes Scholar at England's Oxford University (and the last for sixty years); later he became a professor at Washington, D.C.'s Howard University, the leading black college in the United States. Brilliant and energetic, Locke recognized that a new generation of black artists was about to burst upon the cultural scene, and he urged them to study their heritage, find their voices, and express their own personal visions. Locke's position as a mentor to and spokesperson for the younger generation would lead to his appointment as editor of *The New Negro.*

Marcus Garvey gains a huge following

Even as prominent African American intellectuals were starting to discover and express the viewpoint of the "New Negro," a new and very different kind of black leader had emerged. His name was Marcus Garvey, and he won strong support from African Americans, most of them from poor or lower-middle-class backgrounds. Born in Jamaica in 1887, Garvey was a high school dropout but a hard worker and a voracious reader. He became involved in politics after moving to the Jamaican capital of Kingston when he was sixteen. Following a trip to England, he decided to work toward helping black people all over the world and founded the United Negro Improvement Association (UNIA). Inspired by African American leaders like Booker T. Washington and W.E.B. Du Bois, Garvey traveled to the United States in 1916, planning to raise money to start a Jamaican version of the Tuskegee Institute (see subhead above titled "Booker T. Washington").

Garvey soon founded a newspaper, *Negro World,* in which he expressed his ideas on how black people could improve their lives. In his essays, Garvey told African Americans that they should be proud of their blackness, that they were descendants of a mighty race and should no longer tolerate racism. He believed that all people of African descent should join together to reclaim Africa from European control—his most famous political slogan was "Africa for the Africans!"—and he appointed himself "Provisional President" of this hoped-for nation. Usually dressed in a fancy military uniform and plumed hat, Garvey attracted much attention through his magnetic, flamboyant personality, his outspoken

Marcus Garvey founded the United Negro Improvement Association and led the "Africa for Africans" movement. He gained a significant following among blacks in the United States in the early twentieth century. *(The Bettmann Archive. Reproduced by permission.)*

racial pride, and his grand schemes for black advancement. Even though he gained a huge following, he irritated and clashed with other black leaders, especially Du Bois, who felt that his plans were unrealistic and his promises empty. Garvey's downfall came through his attempt to start a black-owned shipping line; after the venture failed, he was jailed for defrauding investors (many of them poor people who had given Garvey all their money). He was finally sent back to

Jamaica, but even those black leaders who were relieved to see him go had to admit that he had tapped into the hopes and dreams of countless African Americans.

Other early leaders

Another prominent older leader was James Weldon Johnson, who became the first black head of the NAACP in 1920. A talented, broad-minded man who was already well into middle age as the Harlem Renaissance began, Johnson had pursued a number of careers before taking his job at the NAACP. He had worked as a high school principal, a lawyer, a playwright, a composer of popular songs, and a consular officer (the overseas representative of the U.S. government) in Central America. He was also the author of *Autobiography of an Ex-Colored Man* (1912), a novel that contained the most psychologically complex black protagonist (hero) of any fiction up to that time. Johnson's friendly, outgoing personality provided a welcome balance to that of the gravely serious Du Bois, who was seldom, if ever, known to laugh. Well educated and well traveled, Johnson could move comfortably in white society but also understood the problems of ordinary black people. He deeply valued such African American folk traditions as storytelling and spirituals (religious songs that combined elements of African and European music), and he believed that black artists could and should call upon their rich cultural heritage in creating new art.

Also important as an encouraging influence on the younger Harlem Renaissance writers was Jessie Redmon Fauset (1882–1961), who served as the literary editor at *Crisis* from 1919 to 1926. She was a member of an old and distinguished, though not particularly wealthy, Philadelphia family (which made her "O.P.," the popular term in African American society for "Old Philadelphia"). Fauset had graduated from Cornell University, studied at the prestigious Sorbonne in France, and worked as a high school French teacher for thirteen years before getting her job at *Crisis*. Originally hired to edit a children's magazine called *Brownies' Book,* Fauset's duties were expanded, and she had the opportunity to review and promote the work of such talented Harlem Renaissance writers as Langston Hughes, Jean Toomer, Countee Cullen, and Claude McKay (1890–1948). Fauset was an accomplished fiction writer as well. She produced some of the period's most renowned novels, including *There Is Confusion* (1924) and *Plum Bun: A Novel without a Moral* (1929).

Publications focus on black concerns

Crisis was just one of many large and small periodicals that catered to black readers by focusing on African American life, issues, and people. Another leading publication was *Opportunity*, established in 1923 by the National Urban League, with the dynamic sociologist Charles S. Johnson as its editor. Johnson's studies had led him to believe that the only way blacks could break through the armor of racism was through the arts, so he set out to give *Opportunity* a cultural focus. In addition to publishing the work of Harlem Renaissance writers and artists, the magazine sponsored an annual literary contest that brought much-needed recognition and rewards to many talented blacks. In addition, Johnson organized a historic gathering at the Civic Club (see Chapter 2) that brought together promising artists and the white publishers and editors who could boost their careers.

During the Harlem Renaissance, the black press had more power and influence over people and events than ever before. The publications that tended to attract the most readers were those that took aggressive, even militant, positions on issues. One of the issues that black journalists felt most strongly about was violence against the African American community, especially in the form of lynchings and attacks by white mobs. Many black newspapers encouraged blacks to fight back, and they reported on and applauded the actions of those who used force to stand up to white attackers.

To fight or not to fight

An important issue for blacks in the pre-Harlem Renaissance years was whether young black men should join their country's armed forces to fight in World War I. Two prominent publications—the *Messenger*, which called itself "The Only Radical Negro Magazine," and the *Challenge*—told readers it was foolish to swear loyalty to a country that did not extend equal rights to black people. The *Messenger*'s editors, A. Philip Ran-

African American soldiers in Europe during World War I. An important issue among blacks early in the twentieth century was whether African Americans should join the U.S. armed forces to fight in World War I. (© *Corbis. Reproduced by permission.*)

dolph and Chandler Owen, gained fame when they were arrested under the Sedition Act (a law intended to root out and punish traitors) for urging blacks not to fight in World War I. W.E.B. Du Bois took a different stance, asserting through *Crisis* that joining the military was a way for blacks to prove their loyalty to the United States, which was *their* country, even if it was seriously flawed. The tension between those who agreed with Du Bois, who were called "integrationists" because they believed that whites and black must learn to live and work together, and the "separatists," who thought blacks should set up their own separate country or state, would continue to dominate black publications in the years following World War I.

The black press grows

The black press grew quickly as African Americans moved in great numbers into the northern cities. The black community looked to the media for news and information, commentary on the social changes and issues that increasingly concerned them, and copies of the essays, poems, short stories, and other literary works that black writers were producing. In 1900 there were about two hundred black newspapers and magazines, but during the 1920s that number more than doubled, reaching five hundred. Some of the best-known periodicals included national publications like Hubert H. Harrison's *Negro Voice* and Cyril V. Biggs's *Crusader,* as well as regional ones like Baltimore's *Afro American,* published by Carl Murphy, and Chicago's *Defender,* published by Robert S. Abbott.

During World War I, these publications stirred black pride with photographs of African American soldiers. After the war, they printed news on the civil rights struggles going on around the country, and they gave activists and organizations (such as trade unions, the NAACP, the National Urban League, the Communist Party, and socialists) the means to promote their ideas. Their defiance and idealism were reflected in their names (*Emancipator, Protest,* the *Harlem Liberator*) and mottoes (*Negro World's* "The Voice of the Awakened Negro" and *Challenge's* "It Fears Only God").

Smaller publications were under the constant threat of running out of money and having to cease publication: it was difficult to attract advertisers, and their readers could not afford to pay much for each issue (the usual rate was five cents per copy). One magazine that folded (ran out of money) was *Fire!!,* the only issue of which was produced by a group of young writers headed by novelist Wallace Thurman (1902–1934; see biographical entry). Hoping to produce a high-quality, glossy magazine that would showcase the work of the new generation of black artists, these friends pooled their own money and also borrowed a thousand dollars to cover publication costs. But they still lacked the money needed to distribute *Fire!!* to a large pool of readers, and they were not able to produce another issue. Faced with similar problems, some black newspapers and magazines resorted to sensationalism (an attempt to arouse the curiosity and emotions of readers through the use of graphic or otherwise shocking details), as did many white publications of the period, to attract more readers. They also published news of the doings of black middle-class society—who had appeared at what party, who was marrying whom, and the like.

Militant publications are popular

The publications with the largest followings were those with the most militant stances. The first to reach a circulation of more than two hundred thousand (during the early 1920s) was Marcus Garvey's *Negro World,* which featured its publisher's fiery editorials, vowing, for example, that blacks would retake Africa from white control "even if all the world is to waste itself in blood." Meanwhile, *Crisis* had about one hundred thousand readers, the *Messenger* had about fifty thousand, the *Crusader* thirty-seven thousand, and *Opportunity* almost fifty thousand. Regional newspapers published in such places as Baltimore, Boston, Chicago, Pittsburgh, Memphis, and cities in Oklahoma and California were also thriving.

A fascinating debate carried on during the Harlem Renaissance took place between W.E.B. Du Bois and Marcus Garvey in the pages of their respective publications and was eagerly followed by readers. Garvey was a separatist and a black nationalist, convinced that African Americans had no future in the United States and that blacks around the world must join together and set up their own nation. Du Bois was a "pan-Africanist," a proponent of empowerment for black Africans. He agreed that all the world's black people were linked by heritage and common concerns and therefore should cooperate with each other. But Du Bois felt that African Americans should first improve conditions in their own country, while Africans worked to solve problems in their own land. The disagreement between the two leaders became more and more personal as Garvey referred to the NAACP as the "National Association for the Advancement of *Certain* People" (meaning Du Bois and his friends, whom, the very dark-skinned Garvey noted, were all light-skinned enough to pass for white) and scorned Du Bois for not being "100% Negro" but a mix of black and European blood. For his part, Du Bois asked *Crisis* readers whether Garvey was a "Lunatic or Traitor?" Journalists with Communist (those who believe in an economic system that promotes the ownership of all property by the community as a whole) sympathies also criticized Garvey, accusing him of having higher-class values despite his appeal to the working class. The debate finally ended with Garvey's imprisonment for mail fraud and departure from the United States.

The Depression hurts the black press

Just as the onset of the Great Depression (a period of economic hardship that lasted from 1929 until about 1941, when the United States entered World War II) signaled the end of the Harlem Renaissance, it killed off many of the black publications that had previously thrived. *Crisis* and *Opportunity* were among the few that survived into the succeeding decades. During the 1930s, the black press turned its attention to documenting key issues and events, among them (1) the campaign to win more jobs for blacks in white-owned businesses operating in black communities and (2) the fight to help Depression-ravaged blacks by stopping evictions (forced removals from homes for nonpayment of rent) and urging higher relief (government assistance) payments.

For More Information

Barbeau, Arthur E. *The Unknown Soldiers: Black American Troops in World War I.* Philadelphia: Temple University Press, 1974.

Bontemps, Arna. *The Harlem Renaissance Remembered.* New York: Dodd, Mead, 1972.

Fax, Elton C. *Garvey: The Story of a Pioneer Black Nationalist.* New York: Dodd, Mead, 1972.

Henri, Florette. *Black Migration: Movement North, 1900–1920.* Garden City, NY: Anchor Press, 1975.

Huggins, Nathan Irvin. *Harlem Renaissance.* New York: Oxford University Press, 1971.

Huggins, Nathan Irvin, ed. *Voices from the Harlem Renaissance.* New York: Oxford University Press, 1976.

Lewis, David Levering. *When Harlem Was in Vogue.* New York: Knopf, 1981.

Logan, Rayford W., and Michael R. Winston, eds. *W.E.B. Du Bois.* New York: Hill & Wang, 1971.

Perry, Margaret. *The Harlem Renaissance: An Annotated Bibliography and Commentary.* New York: Garland, 1982.

Ross, B. Joyce. *J.E. Spingarn and the Rise of the NAACP, 1911–1932.* New York: Atheneum, 1972.

Vincent, Theodore G., ed. *Voices of a Black Nation: Political Journalism in the Harlem Renaissance.* San Francisco: Ramparts Press, 1973.

Wolseley, Roland E. *The Black Press, U.S.A.* Ames, IA: Iowa State University Press, 1971.

"Only we can tell the tale...": The Harlem Renaissance Is Launched

It seems that nobody can agree on the exact moment when the Harlem Renaissance began. Maybe that's because quite a few important things were happening at around the same time. Some historians claim that the return of the 369th Infantry Regiment to Harlem at the end of World War I (1914–18) marked the beginning of the new era. On February 17, 1919, this military unit of more than one thousand black soldiers and eighteen white officers (at that time African Americans were not allowed to command troops) marched up New York City's Fifth Avenue to the jazzy beat of black bandleader James Reese Europe's world-renowned military band. Among the approximately thirty thousand blacks who had fought on the front lines in France (around four hundred thousand had joined the armed forces in other capacities), the men of the 369th served bravely in the 16th and 161st divisions of the French Army. The admiring French had nicknamed them the Hellfighters, and they had been the only American unit awarded France's high military honor, the *Croix de Guerre* medal (name means "war cross").

With the famous black dancer Bill "Bojangles" Robinson (1878–1949) serving as drum major, and surrounded on all

The 369th Infantry Regiment marching up Fifth Avenue in New York City.
(UPI/Corbis-Bettmann. Reproduced by permission.)

sides by cheering bystanders, the unit marched toward "home." When they reached Harlem, the band started playing "Here Comes My Daddy," and their ranks broke up as the delirious crowd surrounded their black heroes. In the May 1919 issue of *Crisis*, American educator, editor, and writer W.E.B. Du Bois (1868–1963) wrote that a new battle would now begin: "We return. / We return from fighting. / We return fighting." (See box on p. 26 for the full text of Du Bois's editorial.)

Pain and protest, joy and poetry

Even before that glorious day, however, African Americans had expressed their growing resolve to overturn racism and reject violence. Some observers point to the Silent Protest Parade, which took place on July 28, 1917, as opening the way toward a new era in African American life. Organized by Du Bois, writer and activist James Weldon Johnson (1871–1938), successful Harlem real estate agent John Nail, and the Reverend Frederick Asbury Cullen, the event was staged as a protest against recent lynchings (when African Americans accused of various crimes or misdeeds—but rarely legally charged—would be captured by gangs of whites and lynched—hanged without a trial, usually from a tree. The individuals might be killed before or during the lynching; see Chapter 1) in Waco, Texas, and in Memphis, Tennessee, and against a race riot that had taken place in East St. Louis, Missouri. Between ten thousand and fifteen thousand African Americans marched down Fifth Avenue (closed to traffic by the order of the mayor of New York City) in complete silence, except for the beating of muffled drums. The parade was led by children dressed in white, followed by women dressed in white and men dressed in black. Holding banners with slogans such as "Mother, Do Lynchers Go to Heaven?," the protesters distributed pamphlets that explained their purpose: "We march because we want our children to live in a better land and enjoy fairer conditions than have been our lot."

Some less profound events have also been linked to the start of the Harlem Renaissance, among them the 1921 opening of the exuberant Broadway show *Shuffle Along*, the most important black-produced theatrical enterprise of its time. With music by Noble Sissle (1889–1975) and Eubie Blake (1883–1983) and lyrics by Flourney Miller (1889–1971) and Aubrey Lyles (1882–1932), the show followed the pattern of many earlier black musicals (including racial stereotypes), but the songs were infectious and the dancing charged with energy. Audiences loved it. Another key event was the 1917 publication of two poems by black poet Claude McKay (1890–1948) in the well-respected but previously all-white literary magazine *Seven Arts*. Some observers felt this heralded the beginning of the literary surge that fueled the Harlem Renaissance.

"We return fighting ..." by W. E. B. Du Bois

We are returning from war! The Crisis and tens of thousands of black men were drafted into a great struggle. For bleeding France and what she means and has meant and will mean to us and humanity and against the threat of German race arrogance, we fought gladly and to the last drop of blood; for America and her highest ideals, we fought in far-off hope; for the dominant southern oligarchy entrenched in Washington, we fought in bitter resignation. For the America that represents and gloats in lynching, disfranchisement, caste, brutality and devilish insult—for this, in the hateful upturning and mixing of things we were forced by vindictive fate to fight, also.

But today we return! We return from the slavery of uniform which the world's madness demanded us to don to the freedom of civil garb. We stand again to look America squarely in the face and call a spade a spade. We sing: This country of ours, despite all its better souls have done and dreamed, is yet a shameful land.

It *lynches.*

And lynching is barbarism of a degree of contemptible nastiness unparalleled in human history. Yet for fifty years we have lynched two Negroes a week, and we have kept this up right through the war.

It *disfranchises* its own citizens.

Disfranchisement is the deliberate theft and robbery of the only protection of poor against rich and black against white. The land that disfranchises its citizens and calls itself a democracy lies and knows it lies.

It encourages *ignorance.*

It has never really tried to educate the Negro. A dominant minority does not want Negroes educated. It wants servants, dogs, whores and monkeys. And when this land allows a reactionary group by its stolen political power to force as many black folk into these categories as it

The "movement" gathers steam

In any case, it is not necessary to pinpoint the start of the Harlem Renaissance, as long as it is understood that by the early 1920s the "movement" (then usually referred to as the New Negro movement) was gathering steam. African American arts and culture were experiencing a period of unprecedented (never-before-seen) intensity and gaining more atten-

possibly can, it cries in contemptible hypocrisy: "They threaten us with degeneracy; they cannot be educated."

It *steals* from us.

It organizes industry to cheat us. It cheats us out of our land; it cheats us out of our labor. It confiscates our savings. It reduces our wages. It raises our rent. It steals our profit. It taxes us without representation. It keeps us consistently and universally poor, and then feeds us on charity and derides our poverty.

It *insults* us.

It has organized a nation-wide and latterly a world-wide propaganda of deliberate and continuous insult and defamation of black blood wherever found. It decrees that it shall not be possible in travel nor residence, work nor play, education nor instruction for a black man to exist without tacit or open acknowledgment of his inferiority to the dirtiest white dog. And it looks upon any attempt to question or even discuss this dogma as arrogance, unwarranted assumption and treason.

This is the country to which we Soldiers of Democracy return. This is the fatherland for which we fought! But it is *our* fatherland. It was right for us to fight. The faults of *our* country are *our* faults. Under similar circumstances, we would fight again. But by the God of Heaven, we are cowards and jackasses if now that war is over, we do not marshal every ounce of our brain and brawn to fight a sterner, longer, more unbending battle against the forces of hell in our own land.

We *return.*
We *return from fighting.*
We *return fighting.*

Make way for Democracy! We saved it in France, and by the Great Jehovah, we will save it in the United States of America, or know the reason why.

From "Opinion of W.E.B. Du Bois." Crisis (May 1919): 13–14.

tion from mainstream American audiences than ever before. Nurtured by senior advisors like Jessie Fauset (1882–1961; see biographical entry) and Alain Locke (1886–1954; see biographical entry), the Harlem Renaissance was sparked and then fully ignited by the younger generation of blacks as they flowed into Harlem in search of inspiration, fame, fortune, and like-minded friends.

In 1920 a talented teen named Langston Hughes (1902–1967; see biographical entry) wrote a beautiful, sophisticated poem called "The Negro Speaks of Rivers"; that same year black actor Charles Gilpin (1878–1930) played the lead role in the Provincetown Players' production of *The Emperor Jones*, by white dramatist Eugene O'Neill (1888–1953). In 1921 blues singer Bessie Smith (1894–1937; see biographical entry) began recording for the Black Swan Phonograph Company, and Connie's Inn, which would become one of Harlem's best-known nightclubs, opened its doors for business.

In 1922 some of the most important writers of the Harlem Renaissance, including Hughes, Jean Toomer (1894–1967; see biographical entry), and Countee Cullen (1903–1946; see biographical entry), gathered for literary talk at the home of Alain Locke. The career of African American classical singer Marian Anderson (1897–1993) was launched with a concert at New York City's Town Hall. On Broadway, *Strut Miss Lizzie* was thrilling audiences, while in another part of town African American artist Meta Warrick Fuller (1877–1968; see biographical entry) was exhibiting her sculpture "Ethiopia Awakening." Bandleader and composer Duke Ellington (1899–1974; see biographical entry) moved from Washington, D.C., to New York City in 1923, eager to try his luck in Harlem. The Cotton Club (soon to be Harlem's most famous nightclub) opened, Toomer's experimental novel *Cane* was published to great acclaim, and "The Chip Woman," written by Willis Richardson, became the first serious black drama to appear on Broadway. During the first few months of 1924, as jazz became more and more popular among white New Yorkers, innovative jazz trumpeter Louis Armstrong (1901–1971) joined Fletcher Henderson's well-known band at the famous Roseland Ballroom. Around the same time, artist Aaron Douglas (1899–1979) arrived in New York and began to develop his trademark style of "geometric symbolism," in which he used geometric forms, patterns, and silhouettes to create distinctive works that linked the burgeoning black scene in Harlem with African Americans' rich ancestral past. National Association for the Advancement of Colored People (NAACP) leader Walter White's novel *The Fire in the Flint* was published, sparking white critic (and photographer) Carl Van Vechten's intense interest in Harlem's cultural scene.

What a cultural scene it was—and what an event-filled few years these had been. In the April 1920 issue of the journal *Crisis,* W.E.B. Du Bois acknowledged this fact and made a prediction: "A renaissance of American Negro literature is due; the material about us in the strange, heart-rending race tangle is rich beyond dream and only we can tell the tale and sing the song from the heart."

The Civic Club dinner

Before going on to discover what other exciting things the 1920s would bring, it's best to pause and consider a significant event that took place on March 21, 1924. Earlier that month, Jessie Fauset's novel *There Is Confusion* had been published, and *Opportunity* editor Charles S. Johnson (1893–1956) decided to use this occasion as a means to accomplish something even bigger. Convinced that African Americans could eventually gain equality through artistic achievements, he planned a gathering—supposedly to celebrate Fauset's accomplishment—that would give promising young black artists a chance to jump-start their careers.

Duke Ellington moved to New York in 1923 to be a part of the jazz scene in Harlem.
(AP/Wide World Photos. Reproduced by permission.)

Johnson chose the Civic Club (a downtown institution close to Fifth Avenue that was known for allowing black and white patrons to intermingle; see Chapter 1) as the site of a dinner to which he invited 110 guests, drawing from both the cream of the Harlem literary crowd (Walter White, Countee Cullen, poets Gwendolyn Bennett and Georgia Douglas Johnson, W.E.B. Du Bois, and James Weldon Johnson) and some of the most influential white writers, editors, and publishers in town. Frederick Lewis Allen, a high-ranking editor at Harper's publishing firm, was there, as were Carl Van Doren, the editor of the magazine *New Century;* Walter Bartlett of Scribner's publishing house; Freda Kimberley of the political periodical *Nation;* and Paul Kellogg of the *Survey Graphic,* a magazine that often focused on social issues.

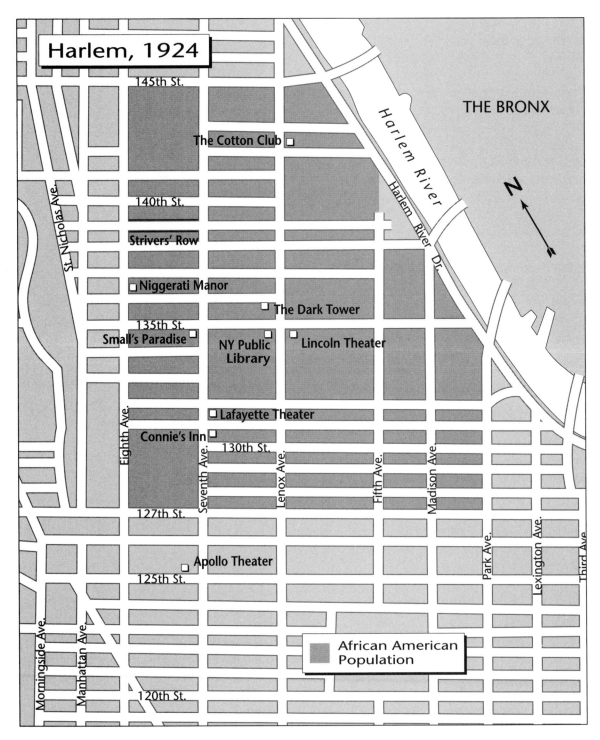

Map of Harlem c. 1924. *(Map by XNR Productions, Inc.)*

In his opening remarks, Charles Johnson paid tribute to Du Bois and Fauset, but the spotlight then shifted to the younger writers. He introduced Alain Locke as the "virtual dean of the [New Negro] movement." (A dean is the leader of something, or the most respected member of a group.) Publisher Horace Liveright praised the recently published novels by Toomer and Fauset, while Van Doren, as related in David Levering Lewis's *When Harlem Was in Vogue,* spoke of his "genuine faith in the imaginative writing among Negroes in the U.S." He claimed that the nation needed "color, music, gusto, the free expression of gay or desperate moods. If the Negroes are not in a position to contribute these items, I don't know what Americans are." The very wealthy Albert Barnes, head of a Philadelphia drug company, spoke about his collection of African art, and Cullen and Bennett read from their works. After the dinner, Johnson wrote to a friend that "a big plug was bitten off" (meaning creativity and recognition could now flow freely for black talent) and added, "Now it's a question of living up to the reputation."

Locke accepts an important assignment

Among the many results of the Civic Club dinner (including the publication of a volume of Cullen's poetry by *Harper's* magazine and the formation of a Writer's Guild to assist African American writers), the most important was probably Paul Kellogg's invitation to Locke to edit a special issue of *Survey Graphic.* The magazine had never before paid attention to African American culture, but Kellogg now envisioned a full issue that would "express the progressive spirit of contemporary Negro life." He knew that Locke was the perfect person to take charge of this task: he had a deep and varied knowledge of African American culture, contacts with many influential and talented people, and a clear sense of confidence in himself.

Locke took on this job with enthusiasm, shaping the *Survey Graphic* issue according to his own ideas about black culture: he wanted to blend the rich material of the African American folk tradition (from stories to songs to a unique way of talking) with modern voices and concerns. He wanted the world to see that Harlem was the thriving capital of black life, bubbling over not only with interesting black people and

Excerpt from Alain Locke's introduction to *The New Negro*

In the last decade something beyond the watch and guard of statistics has happened in the life of the American Negro.... The Sociologist, the Philanthropist, the Race-leader are not unaware of the New Negro, but they are at a loss to account for him.... For the younger generation is vibrant with a new psychology; the new spirit is awake in the masses, and under the very eyes of the professional observers is transforming what has been a perennial problem into the progressive phases of contemporary Negro life.

Could such a metamorphosis have taken place as suddenly as it has appeared to? The answer is no; not because the New Negro is not here, but because the Old Negro had long become more of a myth than a man. The Old Negro, we must remember, was a creature of moral debate and historical controversy.... So for generations in the mind of America, the Negro has been more of a formula than a human being—a something to be argued about, condemned or defended, to be "kept down," or "in his place," or "helped up," to be worried with or worried over, harassed or patronized, a social bogey or a social burden. The thinking Negro even has been induced to share this same general attitude, to focus his attention on controversial issues, to see himself in the distorted perspective of a social problem. His shadow, so to speak, has been more real to him than his personality.... Little true social or self-understanding has or could come from such a situation.

But while the minds of most of us, black and white, have thus burrowed in the trenches of the Civil War and Reconstruction, the actual march of development has simply flanked these positions, necessitating a sudden reorientation of view....

[T]he mind of the Negro seems suddenly to have slipped from under the tyranny of social intimidation and to be shaking off the psychology of imitation and implied inferiority. By shedding the old chrysalis of the Negro problem we are achieving something like a spiritual emancipation....

artists but also with real ideas and real accomplishments. Locke was not much concerned with political issues—like Charles S. Johnson, he believed advancement would come with artistic achievement. He was, however, concerned with overturning racial stereotypes. Many white Americans of the early twentieth century thought of blacks as ignorant rural people who were either totally subservient to whites or violent

With this renewed self-respect and self-dependence, the life of the Negro community is bound to enter a new dynamic phase....The migrant masses, shifting from countryside to city, hurdle several generations of experience at a leap, but more important, the same thing happens spiritually in the life-attitudes and self-expression of the Young Negro, in his poetry, his art, his education and his new outlook, with the additional advantage, of course, of the poise and greater certainty of knowing what it is all about....

The tide of Negro migration, northward and city-ward, is not to be fully explained as a blind flood started by the demands of war industry coupled with the shutting off of foreign migration, or by the pressure of poor crops coupled with increased social terrorism in certain sections of the South and Southwest. Neither labor demand, the boll weevil nor the Ku Klux Klan is a basic factor, however contributory any or all of them may have been. The wash and rush of this human tide on the beach line of the northern city centers is to be explained primarily in terms of a new vision of opportunity, of social and economic freedom, of a spirit to seize, even in the face of an extortionate and heavy toll, a chance for the improvement of conditions. With each successive wave of it, the movement of the Negro becomes more and more a mass movement toward the larger and the more democratic chance—in the Negro's case a deliberate flight not only from countryside to city, but from medieval America to modern.

Take Harlem as an instance of this. Here in Manhattan is not merely the largest Negro community in the world, but the first concentration in history of so many diverse elements of Negro life.... In Harlem, Negro life is seizing upon its first chances for group expression and self-determination. It is—or promises at least to be—a race capital....

From *"The New Negro."* Voices of the Harlem Renaissance, *edited by Nathan Irvin Huggins. Oxford University Press, 1995. © 1995 by Brenda Smith Huggins. Reproduced by permission.*

and animalistic. Locke also wanted to provide a balance to what he saw as the rather straitlaced properness of the middle and upper classes of African American society—the world represented in the person and work of Jessie Fauset. He was more interested in what he termed "realism," meaning that black artists should portray ordinary black people authentically, showing how they actually lived and spoke.

Announcing the "New Negro"

Locke chose the work of thirty-four African American contributors and four whites, including almost all of those whose names would forever after be linked to the Harlem Renaissance. There were poems by Hughes, Cullen, and others, short stories, a play, and many essays. There were drawings by white artist Winold Reiss, who was commissioned to provide sketches of all the important "New Negro" leaders, and by Aaron Douglas, an African American who by this time had become the official artist of the Harlem Renaissance. Locke himself contributed four essays on various aspects of African American culture. In his introduction, he announced the arrival of a new generation of African Americans—blacks who had come to terms with their past and were ready to prove themselves to the world. He called Harlem the "laboratory of a great race-welding" where black people from all over the world were gathered and noted that whites were becoming increasingly interested in the rich cultural history of black Americans. Locke made the rather lofty claim that the writers, thinkers, and artists whose work he had collected would act as the "advance guard [leaders; pioneers; pacesetters] of the African peoples in their contact with twentieth century civilization." Later critics would say that Locke had been naive in expecting so much and believing that a small and very loosely organized cultural movement could change the course of history, but his faith and enthusiasm are proof of the optimistic spirit of the time and place in which he lived.

The special issue of the *Survey Graphic* appeared in March 1925 and quickly sold out two printings; it was the most popular issue in the magazine's history, with an estimated total readership of forty-two thousand. Some influential white supporters helped boost the circulation by purchasing one thousand copies each and distributing them to friends and acquaintances. Toward the end of the year, publishers Albert and Charles Boni issued *The New Negro: An Interpretation*, a book version of the magazine issue that also included new works by the winners of *Opportunity*'s first literary contest. One of these winners was Zora Neale Hurston (1891–1960; see biographical entry), a folklorist and short-story writer with a sparkling personality who made a jubilant appearance at the magazine's awards dinner in May.

Harlem Renaissance themes and aims

Poet Sterling Brown (1901–1989), who began his career during the Harlem Renaissance and continued to write for many decades after it was over, identified five major themes that occupied the artists of the period: (1) the expression of racial pride, which was closely tied to an awareness of African history and culture, (2) the celebration of African American achievers and heroes—the portrayal of black people as capable of great things, (3) the advancement of the black race, (4) the use of elements from the African American folk tradition, and (5) the exploration of self or individual identity. (Note that the last three themes include the use of art as political propaganda—materials intended to persuade people to adopt a certain viewpoint or opinion. Examining the very different works, personalities, and ideas of those who made up the Harlem Renaissance reveals that these themes were often intertwined.)

In an essay published in the June 1926 issue of *The Nation*, Langston Hughes gave voice to the proud spirit of his generation:

> *We younger artists who create now intend to express our individual dark-skinned selves without fear or shame. If white people are pleased we are glad. If they are not, it doesn't matter. We know we are beautiful. And ugly too. The tom-tom cries and the tom-tom laughs. If colored people are pleased we are glad. If they are not, their displeasure doesn't matter either. We build our temples for tomorrow, strong as we know how, and we stand on top of the mountain, free within ourselves.*

A debate: The role of art and artists

Hughes's words are confident, full of the joy and certainty with which so many Harlem Renaissance writers, musicians, and visual artists approached their work. But these black talents also experienced some doubts and uncertainty, especially regarding their role in the black community. In fact, this question created considerable controversy and became one of the central issues of the Harlem Renaissance.

W.E.B. Du Bois had long made it clear that he had no use for art that did not help to promote equality for black people. He felt that African Americans should be portrayed in the best possible light, as people who were just as law-abiding, industrious, and "respectable" as the most law-abiding, industrious, and respectable white people. Many black leaders and artists shared this opinion, including poet Countee Cullen, who claimed that "every phase of Negro life should not be for the white man's concern" (in other words, white people did not need to know *everything* about blacks and their culture). At the heart of this viewpoint was the strong belief that if whites could be made to see blacks as "worthy" of equality, white society would take it upon itself to end discrimination based on race.

How should black people be portrayed?

Those who held this view of art as propaganda, as a tool in "race-building" (helping to improve the image and position of blacks) tended to be members of the older generation and representatives of Du Bois's Talented Tenth (see Chapter 1). On the other side of the fence were the younger writers and artists, especially those who lived in a funky Harlem boarding house that Zora Neale Hurston—who was part of their crowd—called "Niggerati Manor." Writers like Wallace Thurman (1902–1934) and Langston Hughes and artists like Richard Bruce Nugent (1906–1987) led the charge, insisting that their job was to portray the whole spectrum of African American people, situations, and communities, just as they really were. In their fiction and poetry they used the latest Harlem slang as well as rural dialect and (in Hughes's case) rhythms taken from jazz and blues music. They created a portrait of Harlem that included prostitutes, homosexuals, rent parties, and poverty—in other words, the real world they saw around them. Older leaders like Du Bois considered this raw and honest approach to be needlessly vulgar. They argued that white people already viewed blacks as poor, base, criminal, and loose-moraled, so why encourage the stereotype?

The issue of "primitivism"

Central to Du Bois's argument was the idea of blacks as "primitive." The horrors of World War II (1939–45) had caused many people to turn away from European values in search of cultures that were considered simpler and more pure, and African Americans seemed to embody this purity. Some artists embraced the concept of primitivism because it connected them with their African heritage and countered the conservatism (safe traditions) of mainstream America. But others claimed that accepting the image of blacks as "primitive"—honest, open, emotional people who loved to dance and laugh, who were both sexually free and deeply religious—reinforced a negative stereotype and denied black people the right to be treated as individual human beings.

These were complicated issues, and they were hotly debated among the intellectuals of the Harlem Renaissance. Alain Locke tried to maintain a middle ground. An educator, critic, and leader of the Harlem Renaissance, Locke was both sophisticated and well traveled. He cherished European high culture and had little in common with the lower classes of Harlem. Nevertheless, he deeply valued his African American heritage and wished to encourage the younger artists whose work he found so exciting. In the end, he advised them to follow their own hearts and visions, to use the rich material they found in both the past and the present to create the best works they could.

Zora Neale Hurston was among the Harlem Renaissance writers who believed that African American art should reflect the whole spectrum of the African American experience. *(The Estate of Carl Van Vechten. Reproduced by permission.)*

White America takes notice

And so they did, working in a wide variety of styles and forms, from carefully crafted sonnets to free verse that imitated jazz, from novels depicting the conventional lives of the black middle class to those revealing Harlem's seamier side, from documentary folklore to modernist prose. Black artists carved out lifelike sculptures and splashed canvases with bold, abstract images (those that do not represent objects realistically); black singers sang classical music, spirituals, and blues songs with equal devotion and skill.

By the mid-1920s the Harlem Renaissance was under way, and white America was taking notice. At the forefront of this wave of enthusiasm were some wealthy, influential whites who offered considerable support to the black writers, per-

Caspar Holstein: The Bolito King

New York's African American community had mixed feelings about Caspar Holstein, a wealthy businessman who'd brought big-time gambling to Harlem but who also provided material, much-needed support to charities and to Harlem Renaissance artists.

Born in the Virgin Islands, Holstein had been working in a low-paying job in New York when he came up with a successful gambling scheme called "bolito" (leading to his nickname "the Bolito King") or "numbers." It involved betting on three-digit numbers drawn from daily stock market reports, and the 600 to 1 odds made it very profitable for winners as well as for Holstein. At the height of his success, he owned three apartment buildings, a Long Island house, Virginia farm property, a fleet of cars, and a Harlem cabaret called the Turf Club.

Despite his reputation as a mobster (someone involved in organized crime), Holstein was an upright citizen in many ways, especially in Harlem's West Indian community. He gave large sums of money to charities and wrote conscientious articles for *Negro World* and *Opportunity* magazines about the mistreatment of blacks in the Virgin Islands. And in 1925, proclaiming his interest and pride in African American artistic achievements, Holstein announced that he would donate prize money for the *Opportunity*'s literary contest, allowing it to become a yearly rather than one-time event (in 1926, for instance, he gave one thousand dollars).

In the 1930s, Holstein served three years in prison for committing minor crimes linked to his gambling operation.

formers, and artists who interested them. Called "Negrotarians" by Zora Neale Hurston (who was known for her ability to coin memorable phrases), these supporters dispensed money, advice, encouragement, and introductions (to publishers, gallery owners, theatrical directors, and the like); their influence allowed talented young blacks the freedom to pursue their careers with fewer financial worries.

The "Negrotarians" lend their support

Although they came from different backgrounds, the Negrotarians were all people who had broadminded, positive attitudes toward blacks. They also had different reasons for getting involved in the Harlem Renaissance: some of them wanted to help make up for the injustices African Americans had faced since their arrival in the New World; others held a positive image of blacks as more sensuous and "primitive," more spiritual, and in general more "authentic" than whites. Among the earliest supporters of Harlem Renaissance artists were wealthy Jews who sensed a connection between the plights of their own people and that of blacks; these included Julius Rosenwald (1862–1932; the heir to the Sears-Roebuck Company fortune) and brothers Joel and Arthur Spingarn, along with Joel's wife, Amy. Later in the decade, well-established leaders of the white literary and art worlds began to lend their support in various ways, such as by putting black characters and actors into their novels and plays (Sherwood Anderson and Eugene O'Neill) or by incorporating elements of blues and jazz into their music (George Gershwin and Paul Whiteman).

Carl Van Vechten and Charlotte Mason

Perhaps the two most important white patrons of the Harlem Renaissance, critic and photographer Carl Van Vechten (1880–1964) and wealthy widow Charlotte Mason (1854–1946), were also the most controversial: some observers felt they were motivated by self-interest.

Van Vechten had been interested in African American culture since his boyhood and had written about black music, drama, and literature for several years before reading Walter White's novel *The Fire in the Flint.* This story of a black physician who fails to rise above the rabid racism of the South stirred Van Vechten's soul, and he began traveling to Harlem to meet black writers and to listen to jazz and blues in clubs and at rent parties. He brought other whites with him, including famous people like novelist Somerset Maugham, literary critic Edmund Wilson, and publisher Alfred Knopf. Van Vechten helped to spark the wave of "Harlemania" caught by so many white New Yorkers. He also hosted mixed-race parties in his downtown apartment, where African Americans rubbed elbows with "Nordics" (a popular term for white people at the time).

But Van Vechten undermined his ties to the black community by writing a novel about Harlem called *Nigger Heaven* (1926)—the title refers to the common term for the segregated theater balconies in which blacks were forced to sit. The book offended many African Americans, who accused the author of exploiting black culture for his own gain. Some blacks defended Van Vechten, though, because he had helped many black writers get their work published and had promoted African American literature, music, and art through his articles in such big-name magazines as *Vanity Fair*.

Charlotte Van der Veer Quick Mason also caused a controversy, but for a different reason. A very rich widow in her seventies as the Harlem Renaissance began, Mason had long been on a quest to attain the pure spirituality she sensed in "primitive" people. After having pursued an interest in Native American life, she attended a lecture by Alain Locke and developed a fascination with African Americans. Locke introduced Mason to several of the era's most promising young black writers and artists, including Hughes, Hurston, Douglas, and sculptor Richmond Barthé (1901–1989), and she was soon offering financial support to several of them. A warm and encouraging figure who asked to be called "Godmother," Mason wanted no public recognition for her generosity. (She spent about seventy-five thousand dollars—which by today's standards would be worth about a half-million dollars—on these artists.) But several of Mason's "godchildren" (most notably Hughes) bristled against her desire to control the content of their work and ended up breaking off their relationships with her.

For More Information

Bontemps, Arna. *The Harlem Renaissance Remembered.* New York: Dodd, Mead, 1972.

Du Bois, W.E.B. "The Opinion of W.E.B. Du Bois: Returning Soldiers." *Crisis* (May 1919): 13–14.

Huggins, Nathan Irvin. *Harlem Renaissance.* New York: Oxford University Press, 1971.

Huggins, Nathan Irvin, ed. *Voices from the Harlem Renaissance.* New York: Oxford University Press, 1976.

Leuders, Edward. *Carl Van Vechten.* New York: Twayne, 1965.

Lewis, David Levering. *When Harlem Was in Vogue.* New York: Knopf, 1981.

Perry, Margaret. *The Harlem Renaissance: An Annotated Bibliography and Commentary.* New York: Garland, 1982.

"In a deep song voice...": Fiction and Poetry

Although many different kinds of artistic expression flourished during the Harlem Renaissance, the period is probably most famous for its literature. For many people, the first names that come to mind when considering the Harlem Renaissance are those of writers like Langston Hughes (1902–1967; see biographical entry) and Zora Neale Hurston (1891–1960; see biographical entry). Indeed, the novels, short stories, and poems that these and other writers produced are among the most interesting and valuable products of a fascinating cultural period. But African American literary history as a whole extends far back into the eighteenth century.

Early African American writing

Even when most of America's black population was held fast within the brutal bonds of slavery, the storytellers and writers among them were carrying on their craft. In 1771 Phillis Wheatley (c. 1753–1784) became the first African American to have her poems published. Other blacks produced slave narratives—real-life stories about their lives as slaves—that were printed and distributed with the help of abolitionists (people who opposed and worked to end slavery). In 1847 the great African American leader Frederick Douglass (1818–1895) published a newspaper called *North Star,* and over the following decade the first novels by black American authors appeared in print.

In 1853 William Wells Brown's (c. 1816–1884)*Clotel; or, The President's Daughter: A Narrative of Slave Life in the United States* was published outside the United States. (Brown could find no American publisher willing to publish his work.) An abolitionist lecturer, historian, and essayist, Brown wrote this story of a young slave girl—who is supposedly the daughter of U.S. president Thomas Jefferson and one of the women slaves on his plantation—more as an antislavery document than as a work of literature. Much more carefully crafted prose fills the pages of Harriet E. Wilson's (c. 1828–c. 1863) *Our Nig* (1859), the first novel published in the United States by a black writer and the first published anywhere in the world by a black woman. The story centers on the experiences of a plucky biracial girl (her father is a wealthy white man, her mother a black servant) in the northern United States and reveals how some whites who claim to be Christians nevertheless treat black people unjustly. Other African American novels of the nineteenth century include *The Garies and Their Friends* (1857) by Frank J. Webb, which anticipates a major concern of Harlem Renaissance fiction with its emphasis on the inner conflicts of light-skinned black people who are able to "pass" as white; and *Blake; or, The Huts of America* (1859), a radical work about black revolt written by the energetic and accomplished Martin Delany (1812–1885) who was a journalist, physician, Civil War officer, and justice of the peace (though, according to some critics, not much of a novelist).

After the Civil War, before the Harlem Renaissance

More significant works by African American novelists appeared at the end of the nineteenth century and the beginning of the twentieth. After a long career as a poet, essayist, and lecturer, sixty-seven-year-old Frances Ellen Watkins Harper (c. 1825–c. 1911) wrote *Iola Leroy; or, Shadows Uplifted* (1892), a work motivated by the author's deep desire to help her fellow blacks.

The novel follows the adventures of the title character before, during, and after the Civil War. The biracial daughter of a plantation owner, Iola Leroy is initially sold into slavery; after the war, she opens a school for freed blacks and eventually moves to the North with her reunited family members.

Charles Waddell Chesnutt's (1858–1932) *Conjure Woman* (1899) is a critically acclaimed collection of short stories set on a North Carolina plantation just after the Civil War. Chesnutt is considered one of the first American writers to create a vivid and honest portrait of Southern plantation life. During the Harlem Renaissance, the still-active Chesnutt encouraged the period's young writers to create authentic, lasting works that were true to their own experiences and creative visions.

In 1912 a writer who would later become a friend and guide to Harlem Renaissance artists produced a highly influential novel. James Weldon Johnson's *Autobiography of an Ex-Coloured Man* concerns a very light-skinned narrator who grows up in the South and actually believes he is white until he moves to the North. There, he learns that, as the son of a black mother and a rich white father, he is indeed black (at that time—and to some extent to this day—any amount of black blood determined black identity), and he begins to explore his racial heritage. The narrator lives for a time in Florida, then becomes a gambler in New York City. He travels to Europe but still feels drawn to African American life, so he returns to the United States and lives in various northern and southern cities as well as in rural Georgia. After witnessing the lynching (a vile and violent practice in which African Americans accused of various crimes or misdeeds—but rarely legally charged—would be captured by gangs of whites and lynched— hanged without a trial, usually from a tree; see Chapter 1) of a black man, the narrator decides he can no longer bear to be black, so he begins to live life as a white person. *Autobiography*

Charles Waddell Chesnutt.
(Fisk University Library. Reproduced by permission.)

of an Ex-Coloured Man was an important work of African American literature because it portrayed so many different kinds of black life and tackled many vital issues, including biracial identity, color snobbery within black society, Jim Crow laws (see Chapter 1), and violence against blacks.

Fiction of the Harlem Renaissance

Toomer's masterpiece

Among the writers, artists, performers, and intellectuals flocking to Harlem in the early 1920s was a young man from Washington, D.C., named Jean Toomer (1894–1967; see biographical entry). He had spent his young adulthood as a wanderer, moving around from university to university and from odd job to odd job, trying to decide what to do with his life. At the same time, he was honing his own literary skills and talking to other writers about their craft. After spending a year as the temporary principal of a small black agricultural and industrial school in Georgia, Toomer traveled to New York and began to publish his short stories in literary journals. He was soon recognized as a talented writer, and in 1923 his novel *Cane* was published. Although only about five hundred people bought the book, it was hailed as an African American masterpiece.

Cane is composed of three sections that are connected by the thoughts and words of a sensitive, modest narrator (based on Toomer himself) who is exploring his own racial identity. This unusual novel includes fifteen poems, six vignettes or character sketches, seven stories, and a play. It is written in colorful, musical language with a strong undercurrent of spiritual feeling. The novel's themes include miscegenation (the mixing of black and white people in sexual relationships or marriage), the strengths and richness of African American culture, and the difficulties of finding one's own racial identity. While some critics faulted *Cane* as merely a collection of fragments with little to bind them together, most called it a highly successful experimental novel. Not long after *Cane*'s publication, Toomer became involved in a group that followed the teachings of Russian mystic Georgi Ivanovitch Gurdjieff (c. 1866–1949), who advocated achieving a balance of mind, body, and soul in order to reach a higher consciousness. Consequently, Toomer published little else during the remaining years of his life.

Walter White: Exposing southern racism through fiction

Another important early work of the Harlem Renaissance is the 1924 novel *The Fire in the Flint* by Walter White (1893–1955), who would later become one of the most dedicated and active African American leaders in the country. Raised in Atlanta, Georgia, White had blonde hair and blue eyes and could easily have "passed" for a white person, but he fully embraced his black heritage and identity. When he was only twenty-six years old, he became assistant secretary of the National Association for the Advancement of Colored People (NAACP; he became its head in 1930), and he stayed with the organization until his death in 1955. *The Fire in the Flint* exposes the true horrors of southern racism through the experiences of its main character, black physician Kenneth B. Harper, who returns to his Georgia hometown after attending medical school in the North. Eager to prove his skills and help the townspeople, Harper is greeted with hostility and fear. The town's two leading doctors—one white and one black—are suspicious of his modern methods, and the Ku Klux Klan (KKK; a white-supremacist organization; see Chapter 1) opposes his plan to help black farmers. The novel ends in violence and chaos, as Harper's sister is raped by a gang of whites, his brother dies in an attempt to avenge the attack, and Harper himself is finally lynched. Among the readers most impressed by *The Fire in the Flint* was white critic, photographer, and supporter of black culture Carl Van Vechten, who immediately sought out and befriended White.

Walter White.
(Courtesy of the Library of Congress)

Jessie Fauset's middle-class world

One of the most momentous events of the Harlem Renaissance was the famed Civic Club dinner (see Chapter 2), which was organized by *Opportunity* editor Charles S. Johnson (1893–1956) in 1924. This gathering enabled many young black writers to meet influential figures from the white literary and publishing establishment, although it was initially planned to celebrate the publication of *There Is Confusion* by *Crisis* literary editor Jessie Redmon Fauset (1882–1961; see biographical entry). The very proper and well-mannered daughter of a respected black Philadelphia family, Fauset played a key role in nurturing the careers of many Harlem Renaissance writers. She also left her own mark on literature, writing four novels, as well as poetry and essays. *There Is Confusion* reflects Fauset's own background in that it takes place in Philadelphia's black middle-class society in the 1920s. Central character Joanna Marshall, the daughter of wealthy parents, must triumph over racial prejudice and relationship problems before achieving success and happiness.

Fauset's other novels also focus on racial identity. In *Plum Bun* (1929), she explores the issue of "passing" through the well-drawn character of light-skinned Angela Murray, who resents the limitations imposed on her by her black heritage. Not until the end of the novel does Angela truly embrace her blackness. *The Chinaberry Tree* (1931) concerns another search for identity—this one conducted by Laurentine Strange, the daughter of a white man and his black servant; *Comedy: American Style* (1933) tells the story of Olivia Cary, whose three children suffer the consequences of her obsession with color and her determination to pass as white.

Zora Neale Hurston: Folklorist and fiction writer

Although she did not produce a full-length novel until after the Harlem Renaissance was over, black writer Zora Neale Hurston (1891–1960; see biographical entry) attracted a lot of attention during the 1920s with her short fiction. These stories feature colorful descriptions of black life and the authentically rendered dialect the author had absorbed while exploring her deep interest in African American folklore. Born in Eatonville, Florida, Hurston met educator, critic, and leader of the Harlem Renaissance Alain Locke (1886–1954) while attending Howard University in Washington, D.C. She published her first short story, "John Redding Goes to Sea," in Howard's literary magazine, *Stylus,* in 1921. The story came to the attention of literary editor Charles S. Johnson (1893–1956) , who later accepted

Hurston's stories "Drenched in Light" and "Spunk" and her play *Color Struck* for publication in *Opportunity.*

"Drenched in Light" centers on Isis ("Isie") Watts, a clearly autobiographical character who lives in a small Florida town. An intelligent, lively, joyful eleven-year-old, Isie is considered "different" and odd by her neighbors, but she finds acceptance during an encounter with a white couple. Hurston's story has been praised for its sensitive portrayal of the exuberant Isie, but some critics found the author too eager for white approval (a criticism often leveled at Hurston herself). "Spunk" features an all-black cast of characters and traces the gradual breakdown of a strong, much-admired man who feels tortured by the ghost of his lover's husband.

In 1925 Hurston won second prize in *Opportunity*'s literary contest for "Spunk." That same year she moved to Harlem, where her outgoing personality and bold sense of humor soon made her one of the most memorable figures of the Harlem Renaissance. Hurston traveled to the South in 1928 to collect African American songs, tales, jokes, dances, games, customs, and other folklore. Encouraged and monetarily supported by "Godmother" Charlotte Mason (see Chapter 2), she made another trip South the next year, accompanied for part of the time by Langston Hughes, with whom she planned to collaborate on a play called *Mule Bone.* Hurston's friendship with Hughes ended over a dispute about the play (see biographical entries on Hughes and Hurston).

During the 1930s Hurston's extensive research on African American folklore and her apprenticeship in short story writing came to fruition in three novels. She is probably best remembered for *Their Eyes Were Watching God* (1937), which is now viewed as a masterpiece of African American literature. The novel earned praise for its warm, rich portrayal of southern black people and life, and particularly for its central character, Janie Woods, a strong, passionate, independent woman. More than thirty years after its initial publication, *Their Eyes Were Watching God* would be championed by contemporary African American author Alice Walker, who credited Hurston as a source of literary inspiration.

Hurston's other novels of the 1930s include *The Jonas Gourd* (1934) and *Moses, Man of the Mountain* (1939), neither of which has received as much critical attention or acclaim as

Their Eyes Were Watching God. She published two other significant works before her death: her autobiography, *Dust Tracks on a Road* (1942), and a final novel, *Seraph on the Suwanee* (1948), which features a white protagonist.

Van Vechten's controversial work

In the Spring 1926 issue of *Crisis,* white critic Carl Van Vechten called attention to the rich culture of Harlem, asking, "Are Negro writers going to write about this exotic material while it is still fresh, or will they continue to make a free gift of it to white authors who will exploit it until not a drop of vitality remains?" Only three months later, it appeared that Van Vechten had himself made "a free gift of it" when his novel *Nigger Heaven* was published (see Chapter 2). The book immediately caused a big controversy, for many readers and critics were offended by Van Vechten's use of the derogatory term "nigger" and by the book's content. It features a very thin plot about a troubled romance between a prim and proper librarian, Mary Love, and a university graduate and aspiring writer named Byron Kasson. There are vivid descriptions of Harlem nightspots and racy love scenes as well as parts devoted to the lives and concerns of African American intellectuals; in fact, many of its characters are based on real Harlem Renaissance figures. Those blacks who defended Van Vechten (including Charles Johnson, James Weldon Johnson, and Langston Hughes) praised him for his realistic re-creation of Harlem scenes and people and for portraying not only the "low life" but the world of educated, middle-class blacks.

Claude McKay's *Home to Harlem*

Among those who disapproved of *Nigger Heaven* most strongly was black leader W.E.B. Du Bois (others included Locke and Countee Cullen). So it is not surprising that in a review in *Crisis* his reaction to Claude McKay's similarly earthy, grittily realistic *Home to Harlem* (1928) was to say that it "nauseates me." Many other critics and readers disagreed, however, and the novel went on to become the first bestselling book by an African American author and the winner of the Harmon Foundation's gold medal for literature. (The Harmon Foundation was an organization that gave annual awards in recognition of African American achievement.)

Born in Jamaica, McKay arrived in Harlem in 1914 and began gaining fame three years later with the publication of several of his poems in the white literary journal *Seven Arts*. Although he spent most of the Harlem Renaissance living outside the United States, he is considered one of the period's most talented poets—and a skilled novelist, as well. His novel *Home to Harlem* concerns two central characters: honest, loyal, streetwise Jake, who has deserted the army (while serving in France during World War I) to return to the pleasures of life in Harlem; and his friend Ray, a serious, pessimistic intellectual of West Indian heritage. Critics and readers admired the novel's realistic dialogue and descriptions, although some complained that McKay had pandered to white stereotypes about blacks through his characters' loose sexual morals.

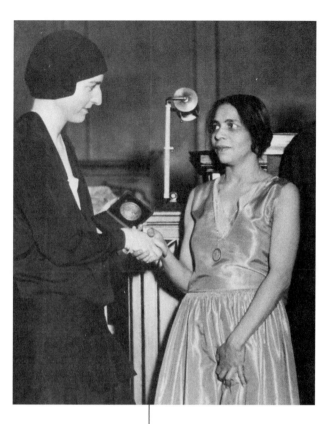

Nella Larsen (right) receiving the Harmon Foundation's bronze medal for her novel *Passing*. (UPI/Corbis-Bettmann. Reproduced by permission.)

Nella Larsen: Exploring a black woman's psyche

A year after McKay had received his Harmon Foundation award for *Home to Harlem,* Nella Larsen (1893–1963) won the organization's bronze medal. Her novel *Quicksand* had been published in 1928, and it was hailed as the first in-depth exploration of a black woman's psyche (her soul, self, spirit, mind, or being). The daughter of a white Danish mother and a black West Indian father, Larsen no doubt incorporated some of her own experiences and struggles into *Quicksand,* which tells the story of Helga Crane, who bounces back and forth between the white and black sides of her heritage, trying to determine where she belongs. Larsen was praised for skillfully rendering Helga's feelings of rejection, loneliness, and alienation in her confused search for her own identity. Larson's second novel, *Passing* (1929), contrasts the results of the choices made by two light-skinned black women. Like the work of Jessie Fauset, this story takes place within the sheltered "respectable" world of the black middle class and centers on the issue of "passing" and the risks of abandoning one's true heritage. *Passing* sensitively conveys the unique predicament of the black middle class and the special pain of those who choose to deny their blackness.

Rudoph Fisher: A talented doctor and writer

In 1925 a young medical student and short story writer named Rudolph Fisher (1897–1926) won first prize in a literary contest sponsored by Amy Spingarn, one of several important white supporters of African American art (see Chapter 2). Three years later, Fisher's first novel, *Walls of Jericho,* was published. Written in response to Fisher's feeling of shock and dismay at the "invasion" of Harlem by curious white New Yorkers, the novel concerns a black piano mover named Joshua "Shine" Jones and the innocent but ambitious maid he loves, Linda Young. Linda works for Agatha Cramp, an elderly, unmarried white woman who is constantly trying to "improve" other peoples' lives. In telling the story of how, after a series of misunderstandings, Shine and Linda are united, Fisher portrays some famous Harlem sites (such as the Savoy Ballroom) and people (including Charlotte Mason and Carl Van Vechten) and explores the theme of class distinctions within African American society.

Fisher also wrote the first detective novel by a black author, *The Conjure Man Dies* (1932). Set in Harlem, the story overturns the stereotypical portrayals of black characters found in the white-authored mystery novels of the period. In 1934, at the age of 38, Fisher died of cancer that was thought to be related to his work as an x-ray specialist.

The brilliant but insecure Wallace Thurman

Another important Harlem Renaissance novelist who died before reaching middle age was Wallace Thurman. He grew up in California and wrote his first novel when he was only ten years old. Thurman moved to Harlem in 1924, and within two years he was working as a critic and editor for various black publications, including the *Messenger* and the *World Tomorrow;* he also served as an editor (the first black in such a position) at the Macauley publishing company and as a ghost-writer (someone who writes without credit for someone else) for *True Story* magazine. The brilliant, slender, fast-talking Thurman—he was known for his high-pitched laugh and heavy drinking—worked hard to promote black culture and was a leader of the younger Harlem Renaissance crowd. He lived in a boarding house at 267 West 134th Street, an address that became famous as a gathering place for avant-garde (experimental) writers and artists. In the summer of 1926— with the help of such friends as Langston Hughes, Zora Neale Hurston, artist Aaron Douglas, and poet Gwendolyn Bennett— he founded a literary journal called *Fire!!* (see Chapter 1), which ceased publication after only one issue. Thurman died of tuberculosis—made worse by excessive drinking—in 1934, when he was thirty-two years old.

Thurman's insecurities about his own very dark skin and his obsession with the issue of color prejudice within black society were evident in his first novel. Its title, *The Blacker the Berry* (1929), refers to the African American folk saying, "The blacker the berry, the sweeter the juice." The novel concerns a dark-skinned girl, Emma Lou, who is the victim of discrimination by other, lighter-skinned black people. After attempting to go along with the values expressed by those around her through an unsuccessful, dangerous attempt to bleach her skin, Emma Lou finally accepts her blackness and experiences a new sense of freedom.

Soon after the Harlem Renaissance had ended, Thurman wrote a novel that was sharply critical of the period and the people who took part in it. The central character of *Infants of the Spring* (1932) is Raymond Taylor, a young writer who lives at "Niggerati Manor" (Zora Neale Hurston's actual name for the boarding house on 136th Street) with a number of other artist characters, all of them based on real people. Critics found *Infants of the Spring* a little too bitter in tone, as well as rather heavy on dialogue and light on action, but it serves as insightful commentary on the disappointment experienced by Harlem Renaissance writers after the period of promise came to an end.

Other notable Harlem Renaissance fiction

The authors already discussed in this chapter are considered the most talented and accomplished fiction writers of the Harlem Renaissance. But several other works by writers of this period are also worth noting. These include W.E.B. Du

Novelist and poet Arna Bontemps.
(Harold Ober Associates. Reproduced by permission.)

Bois's *Dark Princess* (1928), a heavily moralistic novel (written in response to what Du Bois considered "vulgar" and "irresponsible" works by younger writers) about a group of African American and Asian revolutionaries who plan a revolt; and Langston Hughes's *Not without Laughter* (1930), the story of a deeply religious woman and her three daughters, who choose vastly different paths in life.

Other notable fiction writers of the Harlem Renaissance include Arna Bontemps (1902–1973) (also a poet; see page 64), author of *God Sends Sunday* (1930), which depicts the colorful world of southern racetracks during the 1890s, and *Black Thunder* (1936), a historical novel about a failed slave revolt; Eric Walrond (1898–1966), whose well-written, very avant-garde short stories—collected in *Tropic Death* (1926)—focus on the cultural dislocation experienced by blacks moving from rural to urban settings; and George Schuyler (1895–1977), whose novel *Black No More* (1931), the first full-length satire written by an African American, tells the story of a doctor who invents a potion that lightens skin color and finds—after the entire black population turns white—that black skin becomes more desirable.

Poetry of the Harlem Renaissance

Phillis Wheatley: A slave and a talented poet

African Americans were producing poetry as early as the eighteenth century. The most famous early black poet was Phillis Wheatley, who was born around 1753 in West Africa and taken to Boston as a slave when she was seven or eight years old. Her owner's daughter taught her to read and write. By the time Wheatley was twelve years old, she had gained a reputation in Boston as a talented writer of "occasional" poems (which were written to mark important events, especially deaths). In 1773 a London-based publishing company agreed to publish some of her poems. (No American publisher would do so.) Wheatley spent five weeks in England, where she was treated as a celebrity and visited by many famous people. The resulting volume, *Poems on Various Subjects, Religious and Moral* (1773), was the first book of any kind published by an African American. Wheatley's poems feature traditional verse forms and very formal vocabulary and tone; they reflect her thorough knowledge of classical literature and the Bible. In her poetry, Wheatley makes little or no mention of her own status as a black person in America, of other slaves, or of Africa itself, focusing instead on the mostly white environment in which she lived and worked and the interests of those who were reading her work.

Black poets of the nineteenth and early twentieth centuries

George Moses Horton (c. 1797–1883) was the first black southern poet to have a volume of poetry published in the United States, the first black poet to protest slavery, and the first black author who earned money from his writing. His first book, *The Hope of Liberty,* was published in 1829. Other early African American poets include Jupiter Hammon, James Madison Bell, and Albery A. Whitman. But the best-known black poet of the nineteenth century was probably Frances Ellen Harper Watkins (already discussed as the author of the novel *Iola Leroy*), whose *Poems on Miscellaneous Subjects* (1857) sold ten thousand copies in the first five years after it was published. Her other works include *Sketches of Southern Life* (1872) and *Moses: A Story of the Nile* (1869).

The twentieth-century blossoming of African American poetry began with the works of Paul Laurence Dunbar (1872–1906), who was regarded as one of the first truly accomplished African American poets and who was widely imitated by the poets who followed him. Although two-thirds of Dunbar's poetry was written in standard English, he is most remembered for his "dialect" poems, which were meant to re-create the rhythms and speaking style of rural blacks. The poems collected in *Lyrics of Lowly Life* (1896) and other volumes told funny, dramatic, or touching stories about very human, likable black characters, and they were popular with both black and white readers. In later years, however, critics

Poet and novelist James
Weldon Johnson.
*(© CORBIS. Reproduced by
permission.)*

faulted Dunbar for painting an idealized picture of African American life in the South; at a time when blacks were experiencing harsh discrimination, voting rights violations, and even lynchings, Dunbar portrayed his characters dancing, singing, and being grateful and devoted to their white masters. But in a few poems—and especially in those written in standard English—Dunbar did include some softly worded protests, and he expressed an awareness of how black people used "masks" to hide their pain (in other words, they pretended to be happy and carefree to make white society think that prejudice didn't hurt them). Dunbar is said to have regretted that most readers were familiar only with his dialect poems.

James Weldon Johnson: A leader and a poet

One of the most important leaders and guides of the Harlem Renaissance was a skilled and popular poet during the first two decades of the twentieth century. James Weldon Johnson started writing poetry when he was in college (when he met and befriended young Dunbar) and had his first poem—"Sence You Went Away," a love lyric written in black dialect—published in *Century* magazine in 1900. He then put his writing career on hold for a few years, teaming up with his brother John Rosamond Johnson (1873–1954) and their friend Bob Cole to write songs for black musical revues produced on Broadway. The three men wrote many hit numbers, including "Under the Bamboo Tree," "The Congo Love Song," and "The Maiden with the Dreamy Eyes." Although he was pleased with the money he earned from these songs, Johnson knew that they were helping to keep alive white stereotypes about black life, and he decided to turn back to more serious work.

While serving as U.S. consul (the official representative of the U.S. government) in Venezuela, Johnson worked on his poetry and also wrote his masterwork, the novel *Autobiography of an Ex-Coloured Man*. It was published in 1912 while Johnson was assigned to a U.S. consulate in Nicaragua. On January 1, 1913, the *New York Times* published his long poem "Fifty Years," which traced African American history and progress since the first blacks arrived in the United States. Johnson soon returned to New York City, took a job as an editor at the black newspaper *New Age,* and continued to write poetry. His collection *Fifty Years and Other Poems,* which appeared in 1917, contains sixty-five poems in both dialect and standard English.

A tribute to African American spirituality Johnson had earlier expressed his deep admiration for composers of black spirituals (religious songs that included elements of both African and European music) in one of his most famous poems, "O Black and Unknown Bards," but his respect for black spirituality—despite his own agnosticism (neither believing nor disbelieving in God)—is most evident in *God's Trombones: Seven Negro Sermons in Verse* (1927). Johnson used the real speech patterns of the most skilled and inspirational black preachers he had heard, as well as the language and structure of Biblical stories, to create a colorful, deeply moving work that is easy to read but also reflects the dignity and depth of the African American religious experience. *God's Trombones* continues to be hailed as Johnson's finest literary work.

An important anthology Johnson made another major contribution to African American literature by compiling the works of thirty-one poets in *The Book of American Negro Poetry* (1922), one of three anthologies (the other two collect black spirituals) he produced during the 1920s. In the volume's detailed preface, Johnson traces the development of African American poetry and discusses some of the poems included in the book. He focuses especially on the great contributions made by blacks to American culture (citing especially folktales, spirituals, dance, and ragtime music, an early form of jazz) and the important role he felt art would play in the advancement of blacks. Although *The Book of American Negro Poetry* appeared before the careers of most of the younger Harlem Renaissance poets had taken off, it fostered a climate of respect for African American writing that no doubt benefited them; a revised edition of the anthology (1931) included works by many of these younger writers.

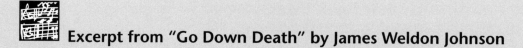

Excerpt from "Go Down Death" by James Weldon Johnson

A Funeral Sermon

Weep not, weep not,
She is not dead;
She's resting in the bosom of Jesus.
Heart-broken husband—weep no more;
Grief-stricken son—weep no more;
Left-lonesome daughter—weep no more;
She's only just gone home.

Day before yesterday morning,
God was looking down from his
    great, high heaven,
Looking down on all his children,
And his eye fell on Sister Caroline,
Tossing on her bed of pain.
And God's big heart was touched
    with pity,
With the everlasting pity.

And God sat back on his throne,
And he commanded that tall, bright angel
    standing at his right hand:
Call me Death!
And that tall, bright angel cried
    in a voice
That broke like a clap of thunder:
Call Death!—Call Death!

And the echo sounded down the streets
    of heaven
Till it reached away back to that
    shadowy place,
Where Death waits with his pale,
    white horses.

And Death heard the summons,
And he leaped on his fastest horse,
Pale as a sheet in the moonlight.
Up the golden street Death galloped,
And the hoofs of his horse struck fire
    from the gold,
But they didn't make no sound.
Up Death rode to the Great White Throne,
And waited for God's command.

And God said: Go down, Death, go down,
Go down to Savannah, Georgia,
Down in Yamacraw,
And find Sister Caroline.
She's borne the burden and heat
    of the day,
She's labored long in my vineyard,
And she's tired—
She's weary—
Go down, Death, and bring her to me.

Langston Hughes: A star of the Harlem Renaissance

Langston Hughes is generally considered the brightest and most-recognized star of the Harlem Renaissance. Although he produced poems, two novels, plays, short stories, essays, an autobiography, and seven children's books during his long career, he was primarily a poet, and most of his best poems were written at the height of the Harlem Renaissance. Hughes was born in Joplin, Missouri, and raised mainly by his mother; his

And Death didn't say a word,
But he loosed the reins on his pale,
   white horse,
And he clamped the spurs to his
   bloodless sides,
And out and down he rode,
Through heaven's pearly gates,
Past suns and moons and stars;
On Death rode,
And the foam from his horse was like
   a comet in the sky;
On Death rode,
Leaving the lightning's flash behind;
Straight on down he came.

While we were watching round
   her bed,
She turned her eyes and looked away,
She saw what we couldn't see;
She saw Old Death. She saw Old Death
Coming like a falling star.
But death didn't frighten Sister Caroline;
He looked to her like a welcome friend.
And she whispered to us: I'm
   going home,
And she smiled and closed her eyes.

And Death took her up like a baby,
And she lay in his icy arms,
But she didn't feel no chill.
And Death began to ride again—
Up beyond the evening star,
Out beyond the morning star,
Into the glittering light of glory,
On to the Great White Throne.
And there he laid Sister Caroline
On the loving breast of Jesus.

And Jesus took his own hand and
   wiped away her tears,
And he smoothed the furrows from
   her face,
And the angels sang a little song,
And Jesus rocked her in his arms,
And kept a-saying: Take your rest,
Take your rest, take your rest.

Weep not—weep not,
She is not dead;
She's resting in the bosom of Jesus.

From "Go Down Death," in God's Trombones, *by James Weldon Johnson. Viking Press, 1927. Copyright 1927 by the Viking Press, Inc., copyright © renewed 1955 by Grace Nail Johnson. Reproduced by permission of Viking Penguin, a division of Penguin Putnam Inc.*

father lived in Mexico City. Soon after graduating from high school in 1920, Hughes traveled by train to visit his father. As the train crossed the Mississippi River into the city of St. Louis, the young writer penned "The Negro Speaks of Rivers." This poem features a narrator who speaks in plain but musical language of the various rivers near which black people have lived. The speaker—who seems to identify with all black people everywhere—concludes, "My soul has grown deep like rivers."

"The Weary Blues" by Langston Hughes

Droning a drowsy syncopated tune,
Rocking back and forth to a mellow croon,
  I heard a Negro play.
Down on Lenox Avenue the other night
By the pale dull pallor of an old gas light
  He did a lazy sway ...
  He did a lazy sway ...
To the tune o' those Weary Blues.
With his ebony hands on each ivory key
He made that poor piano moan
   with melody.
  O Blues!
Swaying to and fro on his rickety stool
He played that sad raggy tune like a
   musical fool.
  Sweet Blues!
Coming from a black man's soul.
  O Blues!

In a deep song voice with a melancholy
   tone
I heard that Negro sing, that old piano
   moan—
  "Ain't got nobody in all this world,
  Ain't got nobody but ma self.

I's gwine [I'm going] to quit ma frownin'
  And put my troubles on the shelf."
Thump, thump, thump, went his foot on
   the floor.
He played a few chords then he sang
   some more—
  "I got the Weary Blues
  And I can't be satisfied.
  Got the Weary Blues
  And can't be satisfied—
  I ain't happy no mo' [no more]
  And I wish that I had died."
And far into the night he crooned
   that tune.
The stars went out and so did the moon.
The singer stopped playing and went
   to bed
While the Weary Blues echoed through
   his head.
He slept like a rock or a man that's dead.

From Selected Poems of Langston Hughes. *Vintage Books, 1990. Copyright © 1994 by the Estate of Langston Hughes. Reproduced by permission of Alfred A. Knopf, a Division of Random House, Inc. In the British Commonwealth by Harold Ober Associates Incorporated.*

In the fall of 1921 Hughes arrived in New York City and enrolled at Columbia University, but he was more interested in the exciting cultural happenings in Harlem than in his studies. Soon he became part of a group of young artists who were in the midst of producing some of the finest works of the Harlem Renaissance. "The Negro Speaks of Rivers" was published in *Crisis* in June 1921, and over the next year and a half about a dozen more poems by Hughes would appear in various publications. In 1923—thanks partly to the encouragement and assistance of Carl Van Vechten, who introduced Hughes to publisher Alfred Knopf—Hughes's book *The Weary Blues* was published. The poems collected in this volume include some of the author's most famous, and they highlight his main concerns. Hughes wanted to write in an authentic, personal voice that also spoke for other African Americans, in whose varied lives he was intensely interested. He wanted to use modern forms (especially free verse, in which the poet does not follow any particular pattern or rhyme scheme) without making his poetry too hard to understand, and he sought to portray the lives of black people with both realism and dignity.

Most readers and critics felt that Hughes had achieved these aims in *The Weary Blues,* although a few (especially members of Du Bois's Talented Tenth, who always wanted blacks to be portrayed in a flattering light) complained that Hughes's writing only reinforced white stereotypes about African American life. The volume's title poem, which is written in black dialect, focuses on a piano player in a Harlem nightclub who sings a blues song full of despair, but finally goes home and sleeps "like a rock," suggesting that his music has helped him shoulder the burdens of his life. In "Mother to Son," a weary but unbeaten middle-aged woman encourages her son to keep going, to keep climbing the staircase of life despite its hardships. "Negro," a poem of racial pride, reviews some of the roles blacks have played in American history (such as slave, worker, and singer) and concludes: "I am a Negro: / Black as the night is black, / Black like the depths of my Africa."

Hughes's next volume, *Fine Clothes to the Jew* (1927), was even more controversial because it included many more details of life among Harlem's poor and working-class residents: here are people working in low-paying jobs, going to nightclubs, getting in fights. Here are prostitutes, gamblers, and heavy drinkers. Here is Harlem at its best and worst. Like the poems in *The Weary Blues,* these reveal Hughes's special interest in jazz; he wove the rhythms of that new musical form into his writing. Those who disapproved of Hughes's poetry claimed that it was too simple and too rooted in the "low life" to be real poetry, while his defenders argued that he wrote with honesty, compassion, and the technical skill to make it all seem easy.

The poems that Hughes wrote during the 1930s, after the Great Depression and other factors had brought an end to the Harlem Renaissance, reflect the more militant social protest in which Hughes was becoming involved. But his poetry returned to Harlem in the 1940s, with the publication of *Shakespeare in Harlem* (1942) and *One Way Ticket* (1949). The poems in these volumes convey the bitterness and despair that had overtaken once-exuberant Harlem in the wake of the Depression, which hit poor blacks even harder than it did other Americans. Hughes's portrayal of the African American community's frustration and anger continued in *Montage of a Dream Deferred*, which contains one of his strongest and most-quoted poems, "Harlem." The speaker asks "What happens to a dream deferred?" What happens when a people's desire for advancement and equality is continually denied—does it "dry up like a raisin in the sun" or "fester like a sore," or sag "like a heavy load?" Or, intones the poem's dramatic last line, "... does it explode?" Here Hughes suggests that the result of centuries of racism and discrimination could lead to a violent revolt.

Countee Cullen: The darling of the Talented Tenth

Perhaps no poet of the Harlem Renaissance represents as dramatic a contrast to Hughes as Countee Cullen does. His name is often put alongside that of Hughes as one of the most important and popular poets of the period, but the two took very different approaches to their craft. Cullen is considered the darling of the Talented Tenth, for he supported the notion that artists should portray blacks in a favorable light, rather than exposing the steamy, gritty underside of Harlem life. He also differed with Hughes in his conception of black identity. Whereas Hughes embraced and celebrated his African American identity, Cullen wanted very much to be known simply as a poet, not a black poet. His works reflect this concern, along with his great regard for the British poets of the romantic period (which took place during the late eighteenth to early nineteenth centuries) such as William Wordsworth, John Keats, and Percy Bysshe Shelley. These writers followed traditional forms but used more emotional and imaginative language than earlier poets.

Cullen lived with a woman who was probably his maternal grandmother until he was fifteen years old, when he was unofficially adopted by a prominent black religious leader, the Reverend Frederick A. Cullen, and his wife. The Reverend Cullen was involved in the race-building activities of the early 1900s (he was an organizer, for instance, of the Silent Protest Parade; see Chapter 2) and helped his adoptive son develop a strong sense of racial pride and consciousness. Some of the poems in Countee Cullen's first collection, *Color* (1925), focus on racial topics; others are about love, friendship, and nature. They conform to traditional poetic forms and are often spoken in a very formal voice. A prominent theme in his work is the tension between his Christian upbringing and the paganism (a popular name for a belief system that honors no single God or any traditional religious rules) connected with African heritage.

In "Yet Do I Marvel," which may be Cullen's best-known poem, the speaker wonders why God would make a poet black and yet "bid him sing"; in other words, it is not fair, because the world is too racist to appreciate a black poet.

One well-known poem from *Color*—titled "Heritage"—expresses the speaker's feelings about Africa; he feels drawn to the distant continent even though his life is far removed from the world of his ancestors: "One three centuries removed / From the scenes his fathers loved, / Spicy grove, cinnamon tree, / What is Africa to me?" In the poem "Incident," the speaker recalls his first encounter with racism: on a trip to Baltimore, a white boy called him "nigger"; the psychologically damaging effects of racist hatred become crystal clear when the speaker admits that this unfortunate incident is now all he can recall about the trip.

Cullen's second collection, *Copper Sun* (1927), was less successful than his first, but it did include the notable poem

 ### "Yet Do I Marvel" by Countee Cullen

I doubt not God is good, well-meaning,
  kind,
And did He stoop to quibble could
  tell why
The little buried mole continues blind,
Why flesh that mirrors him must
  someday die,
Make plain the reason tortured Tantalus
Is baited by the fickle fruit, declare
If merely brute caprice dooms Sisyphus
To struggle up a never-ending stair.
Inscrutable His ways are, and immune
To catechism by a mind too strewn
With petty cares to slightly understand
What awful brain compels His awful
  hand.
Yet do I marvel at this curious thing:
To make a poet black, and bid him sing!

From On These I Stand. *Amistead Research Center, Tulane University, New Orleans, Louisiana. Administered by JJKR Associates. Reproduced by permission.*

"From the Dark Tower." (Cullen would later use this title as the name for his literary column in *Crisis*.) A sonnet (a fourteen-line poem that follows specific rhythm and rhyme pattern) about the African American experience, "From the Dark Tower" acknowledges the pain caused by racial discrimination but encourages blacks to move beyond their suffering. Some of the same themes are evident in the title poem of *The Ballad of the Brown Girl: An Old Ballad Retold* (1927), which retells an earlier European ballad with an African American setting and characters.

Of the verse collected in Cullen's *Black Christ and Other Poems* (1929), only the title poem, about a rebellious black man who undergoes a crisis of faith, has earned acclaim. Cullen's last volume, *The Medea and Some Poems* (1935), features a retelling of the story of Medea, a tragic character created by the ancient Greek dramatist Euripedes (pronounced you-RIP-uh-deez). The volume also includes the notable poem "Scottsboro, Too, Is Worth Its Song," which recounts the true story of nine black men who were charged, based on very flimsy evidence, of raping two white women; public outcry led to the release of five of the accused, while the remaining four served long jail sentences. The poem denounces the American justice system for treating members of ethnic and minority groups differently than whites.

The passionate poems of Claude McKay

A decade before he became one of the best-known writers of the Harlem Renaissance, Claude McKay was already a celebrated poet in Jamaica, the land of his birth. In 1912 he received a medal from the Jamaica Institute of Arts and Sciences for two poetry collections, *Songs of Jamaica* (published in Kingston, Jamaica's capital) and *Constab Ballads* (published in London). Written in black Jamaican dialect, the poems center on such themes as love, family, nature, and the wanderer's longing for home, and they make clear McKay's early and passionate belief in black self-respect and racial equality.

McKay arrived in Harlem in 1914. Three years later came the historic publication of two of his poems, "Harlem Shadows" and "Invocation" (which appeared under the pen name Eli Edwards) in the white literary journal *Seven Arts*. Some regard this event—the first time a black poet's work had appeared in a white publication since the days of Paul Laurence Dunbar—as marking the start of the Harlem Renaissance. "Harlem Shadows" evokes a "stern harsh world, that in the wretched way / Of poverty, dishonor and disgrace" has forced a black girl to become a prostitute.

Vivid portraits of Harlem life McKay's first volume of poems written in standard English rather than black dialect, titled *Spring in New Hampshire and Other Poems,* was published in London in 1920; two years later a collection entitled *Harlem Shadows* was published in the United States. Through its vivid portraits of life in Harlem, *Harlem Shadows* helped establish McKay as a major poet of the Harlem Renaissance, even though he lived outside the United States from 1922 to 1934 and often disagreed with the central figures of the period.

These poems reflect the anger and alienation that African Americans were feeling in the years when racism showed no sign of dying and blacks were being lynched by the thousands. "If We Must Die" (see Chapter 1), which has become McKay's most famous poem, was written in response to the bloody "Red Summer of Hate" that occurred in 1919. It begins with the lines: "If we must die, let it not be like hogs / Hunted and penned in an inglorious spot, / While round us bark the mad and hungry dogs, / Making their mock at our accursed lot." The speaker encourages blacks to resist oppression and behave "like men ... / Pressed to the wall, dying but fighting back!" Other poems in this volume include "The Harlem Dancer," the central character of which is a beautiful, graceful dancer, ogled by drunken men; and "The Tropics in New York," a poem of memory and longing for the speaker's tropical home.

In the remaining years of his life McKay published no more poetry. Instead, he wrote novels, including *Home to*

 "The Tropics in New York" by Claude McKay

Bananas ripe and green, and ginger-root,
  Cocoas in pods and alligator pears,
And tangerines and mangoes and
      grape fruit,
  Fit for the highest prize at parish fairs,

Set in the window, bringing memories
  Of fruit-trees laden by low-singing rills,
And dewy dawns, and mystical blue skies
  In benediction over nun-like hills.
My eyes grew dim, and I could no
      more gaze;
  A wave of longing through my
      body swept,
And, hungry for the old, familiar ways,
  I turned aside and bowed my head
      and wept.

From "The Tropics in New York," in Selected Poems of Claude McKay, *by Claude McKay. Twayne Publishers, Inc. Copyright ©1953.*

"A Black Man Talks of Reaping" by Arna Bontemps

I have sown beside all waters in my day.
I planted deep within my heart the fear
That wind or fowl would take the
    grain away.
I planted safe against this stark, lean year.

I scattered seed enough to plant the land
In rows from Canada to Mexico.
But for my reaping only what the hand
Can hold at once is all that I can show.

Yet what I sowed and what the
    orchard yields
My brother's sons are gathering stalk
    and root,
Small wonder then my children glean
    in fields
They have not sown, and feed on
    bitter fruit.

From Personals © *1963 by Arna Bontemps.*
Reproduced by permission of Harold Ober
Associates Inc.

Harlem, Banjo, and *Banana Bottom,* and short stories collected in *Gingertown.* After his death, however, some previously unpublished poems were included in *Selected Poems* (1953).

Arna Bontemps

Though later known primarily as a novelist, Arna Bontemps began his career—and established his Harlem Renaissance reputation—as a poet. His poem "Golgotha Is a Mountain," which expresses the speaker's longing for Africa and praises African Americans for enduring and rising above racial hardship, won *Opportunity* magazine's Alexander Pushkin Award for poetry in 1926. The next year Bontemps's poem "The Return"—which blends the personal theme of a returning lover with images drawn from the speaker's African heritage—won the same prize. The poet's "Nocturne at Bethesda" also earned the top award in a literary contest sponsored by *Crisis.* "Nocturne at Bethesda" centers on a black man's need for spiritual healing—difficult to achieve because of the loss of faith that has come with modern times. These and other poems were collected in *Personals* (1963), a volume published much later in Bontemps's life. The collection includes the well-known "A Black Man Talks of Reaping," a poem that focuses on how African Americans have performed so much labor and received little reward, while others have benefited from their efforts.

Sterling Brown

Sterling Brown did not live in Harlem during the 1920s, and his first book, *Southern Roads,* was not published until 1932. But Brown was an active participant in the Harlem Renaissance, especially as the author of a monthly literary column in *Opportunity*. Born and raised in Washington, D.C., in the 1920s he spent three years teaching in Lynchburg, Virginia, where he absorbed the details of a vibrant African American culture and tapped into the strength and humor of the black people he met. He put some of those real people into his *Southern Roads* poems, among them the tough, religious Miss Bibby of "Virginia Portrait" and the wandering guitar player Calvin "Big Boy" Davis of "Odyssey of Big Boy" and "Long Gone." In addition to his literary pursuits, Brown taught at Howard University for forty years.

Gwendolyn Bennett

Graphic artist and art teacher Gwendolyn Bennett drew several cover illustrations for noted Harlem Renaissance magazines, but she also contributed many poems to these same publications. She was considered one of the period's most promising young writers. Born in Texas, Bennett studied in Washington, D.C., New York , and Paris before becoming an assistant editor at *Opportunity,* where she wrote "Ebony Flute," a column of news and information about the literary world. Bennett's poems include "To a Dark Girl," which projects a positive image of black womanhood and pride in black beauty; "Hatred," a poem of personal emotion rather than racially motivated rage; and "To Usward," a celebration of the diverse visions of the young generation of black writers. Bennett read "To Usward" aloud at the Civic Club dinner that introduced those young writers to the white literary establishment (see Chapter 2).

Georgia Douglas Johnson

Georgia Douglas Johnson was famous as both a Harlem Renaissance poet and for hosting parties where prominent writers of the time gathered. In fact, her Washington, D.C., home was a gathering place for black writers for several decades. Johnson's very conventional poetic style featured regular meter (repeating rhythms) and rhyme and formal language. Her poems centered on such themes as love, religion, and motherhood. Johnson did not want to be considered a "Negro poet" exclusively, but some of the verses collected in her three volumes—*The Heart of a Woman* (1918), *Bronze: A Book of Verse* (1922), and *An Autumn Love Cycle* (1928)—have

"Sonnett to a Negro in Harlem" by Helene Johnson

You are disdainful and magnificent—
Your perfect body and your
    pompous gait,
Your dark eyes flashing solemnly
    with hate,
Small wonder that you are incompetent
To imitate those whom you so despise—
Your shoulders towering high above the
    throng,
Your head thrown back in rich,
    barbaric song,
Palm trees and mangoes stretched
    before your eyes.
Let others toil and sweat for labor's sake
And wring from grasping hands their
    meed of gold.
Why urge ahead your supercilious feet?
Scorn will efface each footprint that
    you make.
I love your laughter arrogant and bold.
You are too splendid for this city street.

From The Book of American Negro Poetry, *2nd edition, edited by James Weldon Johnson.*

racial themes, including one that describes a black mother's awareness of the hateful racism her children will have to face.

Helene Johnson

The only female Harlem Renaissance poet to use the street language common in the work of several male poets (especially Langston Hughes) was Helene Johnson. She was one of the period's most promising literary figures, but she faded from view in the 1930s. Johnson's first published poem, "Trees at Night," won an honorable mention in *Opportunity*'s first literary contest, and the magazine's July 1925 issue included her poem "My Race," which laments the unrealized potential of black people. Among Johnson's other poems are the much-praised "Sonnett to a Negro in Harlem," which celebrates the beauty and boldness of a "jazz prince" of Harlem (it won fourth prize in *Opportunity*'s third contest), and "The Road," which affirms racial identity by comparing the speaker's color with that of natural images, especially the brown dirt road on which he or she stands. Johnson gained fame in 1927, when her poem "Bottled" appeared in the May issue of the mainstream magazine *Vanity Fair.* "Bottled" compares a fancily dressed black man to a bottle of sand from the Sahara Desert and suggests that both have been "bottled" or trapped by Western civilization. After the Harlem Renaissance ended, Johnson moved back to her native Boston and published little else.

African American poet Anne Spencer, a librarian who lived in Lynchburg, Virginia, wrote poems from the time she was a young girl. None were published, however, until they came to the attention of writer, activist, and NAACP head James

Weldon Johnson (1871–1938). A member of the NAACP herself, Spencer allowed Johnson to stay at her home when he was in town on association-related business. Johnson encouraged Spencer to publish her works, and in February 1920 "Before the Feast of Shushan" appeared in *Crisis*. Johnson included five of Spencer's poems—many of which focus on the position of women both in society and in private relationships—in his *Book of American Negro Poetry;* ten also appeared in Countee Cullen's anthology *Caroling Dusk* (1927). Spencer's writing features rich imagery, as illustrated in her best-known poem "At the Carnival," in which the speaker describes the ugly sights and unpleasant smells of a street fair, where unexpected beauty appears in the form of a girl seated at a diving tank.

Evident in nearly all the poetry of the Harlem Renaissance is the poets' delight in feeling free to describe and celebrate aspects of African Americans' lives and culture that had never been so described and celebrated before. In language elegant or plain and in formats traditional or new, they set an example for the African American poets of later decades.

For More Information

Adoff, Arnold, ed. *The Poetry of Black America: An Anthology of the 20th Century.* New York: Harper & Row, 1973.

Barton, Rebecca C. *Black Voices in American Fiction: 1900–1930.* Oakdale, NY: Dowling College Press, 1976.

Benson, Brian J., and Mabel Mayle Dillard. *Jean Toomer.* New York: Twayne, 1980.

Berry, Faith. *Langston Hughes.* Westport, CT: Lawrence Hill, 1983.

Bone, Robert A. *The Negro Novel in America.* New Haven, CT: Yale University Press, 1958. Reprinted 1970.

Brown, Sterling. *Negro Poetry and Drama.* Washington, DC: Association of Negro Folk Education, 1937.

Christian, Barbara. *Black Women Novelists: The Development of a Tradition, 1892–1976.* Westport, CT: Greenwood Press, 1980.

Cooper, Wayne F. *The Passion of Claude McKay.* New York: Shocken Books, 1973.

Davis, Arthur P. *From the Dark Tower: Afro-American Writers, 1900 to 1960.* Washington, DC: Howard University Press, 1974.

Emmanuel, James A. *Langston Hughes.* New York: Twayne, 1967.

Ferguson, Blanche E. *Countee Cullen and the Negro Renaissance*. New York: Dodd, Mead, 1966.

Giles, James R. *Claude McKay*. New York: Twayne, 1976.

Hemenway, Robert E. *Zora Neale Hurston: A Literary Biography*. Urbana: University of Illinois Press, 1977.

Howard, Lillie P. *Zora Neale Hurston*. New York: Twayne, 1980.

Huggins, Nathan Irvin. *Harlem Renaissance*. New York: Oxford University Press, 1976.

Kellner, Bruce, ed. *The Harlem Renaissance: A Historical Dictionary of the Era*. Westport, CT: Greenwood Press, 1984.

Lewis, David Levering. *When Harlem Was in Vogue*. New York: Alfred Knopf, 1981.

Lewis, David Levering. *The Portable Harlem Renaissance Reader*. New York: Viking, 1994.

Perry, Margaret. *The Harlem Renaissance: An Annotated Bibliography and Commentary*. New York: Garland, 1982.

Singh, Amritjit. *Novels of the Harlem Renaissance: Twelve Black Writers, 1923–1933*. University Park: Pennsylvania State University Press, 1975.

Sylvander, Carolyn Wedin. *Jessie Redmon Fauset, Black American Writer*. Troy, NY: Whitson, 1981.

Wagner, Jean. *Black Poets of the United States from Paul Laurence Dunbar to Langston Hughes*. Urbana: University of Illinois Press, 1973.

Watson, Steven. *The Harlem Renaissance: Hub of African-American Culture, 1920–1930*. New York: Pantheon Books, 1995.

"Yes! It captured them ....": The Performing Arts

In the early part of the twentieth century, the United States was a country dominated by racism and racial segregation; for the most part, white and black people lived separate lives. Harlem was the center of New York's (and perhaps the whole nation's) African American community, but during the Harlem Renaissance white people flocked there by the hundreds. They were eager to experience the art and culture and maybe eat the fried chicken and sweet potato pie that they knew they would find there. This trend (which some blacks resented because they felt that Harlem had been invaded by whites) was called "Harlemania" or "Going Uptown." How did it start—how did white New Yorkers get so interested in Harlem?

For many whites, one major window into African American culture was the musical theater. Theatergoers had seen exuberant dancers with seemingly boundless talent and energy accompany the great black actress Florence Mills (1895–1927) as she sang "Love Will Find a Way" in the Broadway show *Shuffle Along*. Audiences were eager to experience more of the same. Aspects of African American culture were

Poster advertising William H. West's minstrel show. Minstrel shows were a popular form of entertainment in the nineteenth century. White performers would paint their faces black and act out disparaging stereotypes of southern blacks.
(Courtesy of the Library of Congress.)

also being explored in serious dramas by both black and white playwrights, on Broadway as well as in the theaters of Harlem. And music lovers were excited by the jazz and blues they could hear in Harlem nightclubs.

The blackface minstrel tradition

Slavery came to an end in the United States in 1863, but in the years that followed, African Americans began to realize that they were still not totally free. One of the few arenas of American life in which blacks were allowed to participate—and even attain fame and fortune—was in the performing arts, particularly the theater. Some African Americans tried to produce drama that reflected the black experience accurately, but most playwrights and actors continued to give audiences (at the time mostly white audiences who could afford expensive theater tickets) the formats and characters they expected to see. These stereotypes (based on the idea that all the members of a group have certain fixed characteristics or habits) came out of the blackface minstrel tradition, which kept a strong hold on the American imagination well into the twentieth century.

Sometime during the early nineteenth century, white circus performers began putting on "blackface" makeup (they used facial makeup that was tinted black with burnt cork) to portray stereotypes of rural southern black people. The standard blackface characters included Jim Crow, a rough, coarse, country dweller, and Jim Dandy, a city man who always appeared decked out in the most flamboyant, stylish clothes; both spoke in black dialect and were oafish characters who were easily fooled. A typical blackface minstrel show featured singing, dancing, and an exchange of jokes and conundrums (a riddle whose answer contains a pun or play on words).

African Americans form minstrel troupes

Eventually African Americans themselves became involved in this form of theater, first as actors and eventually as managers of their own troupes. The first such troupe, called the Georgia Minstrels, was founded by Charles Hicks. Black minstrels played the character of the "stage Negro," who was childlike, vulgar, lazy, slow-moving (unless running away from work or ghosts), self-indulgent, irresponsible, and always eager for music, food, and sex. Sometimes black minstrels even put on blackface, so they could present the exaggerated faces that white audiences expected to see.

Why did blacks go along with these absurd stereotypes? One major reason is that they were paid well to do so and earned the kind of praise and acclaim that every performer craves. Critics and historians have also suggested that they would not have been acceptable to white audiences in any other form: as Jim Crow and Jim Dandy, black people were less than real human beings and therefore not threatening. So African Americans hid their true selves beneath the masks of the minstrel tradition, while yearning for richer, more authentic, ways to express themselves.

The musical revue develops

In the years just before the turn of the century, black performers managed to bring some minor changes to the minstrel shows. In 1890 Sam T. Jack included dancing girls (all of them very light-skinned blacks) in his *Creole Show*. Dance numbers were also emphasized in John W. Isham's *Octoroons* (1895). *In Oriental America* (1896) featured black singers per-

Black musical revues were produced on Broadway, for mostly white audiences, but black theatergoers were enjoying the same kinds of shows at the Apollo Theater in Harlem.
(© Lee Snider/CORBIS. Reproduced by permission.)

forming solos and choruses from famous operas like *Faust* and *Carmen*. The talented black opera singer Sissieretta Jones—who was called the "Black Patti" because she reminded people of a renowned white opera singer named Adeline Patti—was showcased in *Black Patti's Troubadours* (1896). All of these productions moved the black theater closer toward the musical revues that would dominate the Harlem Renaissance period.

A major turning point came with Bob Cole's show *A Trip to Coontown* (1898), the first musical organized, written, produced, and managed entirely by blacks. It followed an actual story line (using the usual stereotypical characters) and proved a great commercial success. This and other shows increased the popularity of what came to be known as "coon songs" (coon was a derogatory name for black people), which featured ragtime tunes and lyrics in black dialect. (Ragtime is an American musical form that was popular from the 1890s through the 1920s, when it gave way to jazz. Ragtime music features syncopated rhythms, which are formed by shortening beats or stressing a weak beat.)

Perhaps the most famous team of black actors in the late 1800s was that of Bert Williams and George Walker, who got together in 1893 and billed themselves as "Two Real Coons" (as compared to white actors in blackface who merely pretended to be "coons"). After Walker's death, Williams struck out on his own and performed with the otherwise all-white *Ziegfield Follies* show from 1910 to 1920. Famous for his wonderful, loose-limbed dancing, sad-voiced singing, and expressive face, Walker is said to have brought a little more depth and dignity to the black theatrical tradition.

In 1906 and 1908, respectively, the team of Bob Cole and brothers John Rosamond Johnson and James Weldon Johnson (1871–1938; see biographical entry)—James would later gain fame as an older-generation Harlem Renaissance leader—produced *The Shoofly Regiment* and *Red Moon*. These shows improved on the minstrel-based tradition with their well-written stories, catchy song lyrics, and a brand of humor that did not make black people look ignorant or foolish. Within a few years, some fledgling theater companies—including the Pekin Theatre in Chicago, Illinois; the Karamu Theatre in Cleveland, Ohio; and the Anita Bush Players in Harlem—were presenting black actors in plays by white authors. The

stage was literally being set for the boom in black musical productions and dramas that the Harlem Renaissance would bring.

James Weldon Johnson (center) with John Rosamond Johnson (right) and Bob Cole (left).

Shuffle Along is a sensation

When the young poet Langston Hughes (1902–1967; see biographical entry)—who would later become the most famous figure of the Harlem Renaissance—arrived in Harlem in 1921, he was immediately swept up in the excitement surrounding the Broadway show *Shuffle Along*. Hughes was just one of many, many theatergoers of both races who loved *Shuffle Along,* which has been called the most important black theatrical production of the 1920s. It came after a long dry spell in theater caused by World War I (1914–18) and proved just the thing for audiences in dire need of cheering up.

With story and lyrics by Flournoy Miller and Aubrey Lyles and music by Eubie Blake and Noble Sissle (all of them African Americans), *Shuffle Along* centers on an election in the

Florence Mills, one of the stars of the hit Broadway musical *Shuffle Along*, in a publicity shot for the show. *(UPI/Corbis-Bettmann. Reproduced by permission.)*

all-black town of Jimtown, Mississippi. Two grocery owners, Jenkins and Peck, run for mayor against Harry Walton, who is trying to clean up the town. The real strength of *Shuffle Along*, by all accounts, was in its music and dancing. The cast sang songs such as "Love Will Find a Way" and "I'm Just Wild about Harry" (which presidential candidate Harry Truman would later use as a campaign song), and they danced with skill and gusto. The *New York Times* gave the show a lukewarm review, but the *New York Sun* praised the chorus for their "dash and ginger," and the *New York Herald* said that *Shuffle Along* made the world seem "a brighter place to live in."

Theatergoers flocked to *Shuffle Along,* which had been produced on a small budget (using borrowed, already sweat-stained costumes) in a dilapidated theater on 63rd Street. Later, the show had a long run on Broadway. Several of the actors in *Shuffle Along* went on to become the African American community's best-known entertainers, among them Florence Mills (c. 1896–1927; who got her big break when she replaced the original star, Gertrude Saunders), Josephine Baker (1906–1975; who would make her name a few years later as an entertainer in Paris), and the talented actor and classical singer Paul Robeson (1898–1976), who appeared briefly as one of the Four Harmony Kings. When its Broadway run was finished, the show toured other cities for two years.

In addition to providing weary Americans with some much-needed entertainment and jump-starting the careers of some talented black singers and actors, *Shuffle Along* ushered in an era of black musical revue that lasted as long as the Harlem Renaissance did; in fact, some regard the show as the spark that lit the period's fuse.

Shuffle Along was followed by a long string of similar black musical revues, beginning with *Strut Miss Lizzie* (1922), *Seven Eleven* (1922), and *Liza* (1923). Florence Mills starred in *Dixie to Broadway* in 1924, and that same year the show *Runnin' Wild* introduced audiences to the Charleston, a lively dance that became wildly popular and has continued to be associated with the 1920s. *Chocolate Dandies* opened in 1925 and enjoyed a long run; Mills appeared in *Blackbirds* in 1926; and *Africana* (1927) marked the Broadway debut of Ethel Waters (1896–1977), who had already made a name for herself as a blues singer. In the second version of *Blackbirds,* which opened in 1928, renowned dancer Bill "Bojangles" Robinson (1878–1949) completed an unbroken string of 518 performances. The team of Miller, Lyles, Blake, and Sissle united again in 1928 with *Keep Shufflin',* which wasn't quite as successful as their first effort, and *Hot Chocolates* (1929) made pianist Fats Waller's (1904–1943) song "Ain't Misbehavin'" a hit.

Florence Mills: "A Little Blackbird"

One of Harlem's most beloved stage performers, actress Florence Mills (c. 1896–1927) charmed audiences with her appearances in *Shuffle Along* and other popular shows. She created a dainty, pixyish impression onstage, and her theme song was "I'm a Little Blackbird Looking for a Blackbird."

Mills began her career at age five, when she won several dance contests. At age eight she appeared as Baby Florence Mills in a show called *Sons of Ham* in Washington, D.C., singing "Miss Hannah from Savannah." Mills toured with a number of vaudeville companies and formed the Panama Trio with Ada "Bricktop" Smith (who would later make a name for herself in Paris) and Cora Green.

Mills's rise to stardom began in 1921, when she replaced Gertrude Saunders in the lead female role in *Shuffle Along*. Audiences loved Mills. The next year she joined the cast of another popular show, the *Plantation Revue,* for a London tour; the show returned to Broadway in 1924 as *Dixie to Broadway*. It was the first musical revue to showcase a female star rather than a comedy team.

Florence Mills in 1927. *(UPI/Corbis-Bettmann. Reproduced by permission.)*

Mills starred in *Blackbirds of 1926,* traveling with the show to Paris and London and gaining international fame. She had returned to New York when, in November of 1927, she died suddenly of appendicitis. Her fans were stunned and heartbroken. At her funeral, a six-hundred-person choir performed, a flock of blackbirds was released from an airplane overhead, and as many as fifty-seven thousand mourners viewed her body.

Small theater groups present serious drama

The black musical revues were all produced on Broadway, which is located in midtown Manhattan, and were enjoyed by mostly white audiences. But uptown in Harlem, black theatergoers were enjoying the same kinds of shows at the Apollo and Lafayette theaters, where the performance of a musical revue doubled as a social event for the noisy, happy crowd in attendance. Although these theaters provided people of all economic levels in Harlem with a source of entertainment, they were owned by whites, and some black intellectuals felt that the time was right for the development of dramas that would both reflect and benefit African Americans. Such a movement never really took root during the Harlem Renaissance, but some small serious theater groups were formed, and a few plays by black writers gained attention.

In a 1926 essay about African American theatre, W.E.B. Du Bois (1868–1963; see biographical entry) wrote in *Crisis* that black people needed plays that were "about us .... by us .... [and] near us"; in other words, plays that had been written by African American authors for African American audiences and that were presented in black communities. This was the idea behind the Krigwa Players Little Negro Theatre, which had its start in 1925 in the basement of the Harlem branch of the New York Public Library. For two years the Krigwa Players put on short plays that were written, directed, and acted by African Americans for African American audiences. Other Harlem Renaissance theater groups included the Negro Experimental Theatre, founded in 1929 by some young intellectuals interested in serious drama. Their first production was a one-act play called *Plumes* by poet Georgia Douglas Johnson (see Chapter 3). Also in 1929 the short-lived Negro Art Theatre was established at the Abyssinian Baptist Church in Harlem, with Adam Clayton Powell, Jr. (1908–1972)—son of the church's famous pastor—starring in *Wade in the Water*. Small black theaters were set up in other American cities as well: Chicago was the home of the Ethiopian Art Players, founded in 1923; and in Cleveland actor Charles Gilpin (1878–1930) helped two white social workers start the Karamu Theatre back in 1916.

Black playwrights produce their work

Perhaps the best-known black playwright of the Harlem Renaissance was Willis Richardson, who wrote forty-two plays during his long career. A graduate of Washington, D.C.'s prestigious Howard University, Richardson was encouraged by Du Bois to submit his work to the Ethiopian Art Players in Chicago. In the spring of 1923 the company brought

African American audiences enjoyed musical revues at the Lafayette Theatre in Harlem.
(© Bettmann/CORBIS. Reproduced by permission.)

three plays to Harlem, one of which was Richardson's critically acclaimed drama *The Chip Woman's Fortune*. (The others were William Shakespeare's *Comedy of Errors* and Oscar Wilde's *Salome*.) *The Chip Woman's Fortune* is a one-act play about a black man named Silas who has just lost his job. Faced with the prospect of losing his beloved record player because he cannot continue to make his loan payments, Silas plots to murder Aunt Nancy, an old woman who pays for her room in

Silas's home by selling coal chips. Aunt Nancy has been saving her money to give to her son, who has recently been released from prison. The son appears at the end of the play and divides the money his mother has saved with Silas's family. *The Chip Woman's Fortune* opened on Broadway in May, becoming the first serious drama by a black playwright to reach the Broadway stage.

Two years after *The Chip Woman's Fortune* opened on Broadway, another African American playwright, San Francisco native Garland Anderson, made his mark there with *Appearances* (1925), an unusual play that featured a mixed-race cast and nonstereotypical characters. *Appearances* is about a black bellhop falsely accused of rape. It ends optimistically, with the main character's faith finally overcoming the malice of his enemies. Anderson had sent the play to white singer and actor Al Jolson (who often performed in blackface), and Jolson financed the young playwright's trip to New York to raise money for its production. *Appearances* had a short Broadway run, then toured the Midwest, the West Coast, and London.

Thurman's *Harlem* is a success on Broadway

Toward the end of the Harlem Renaissance, novelist Wallace Thurman (1902–1934; see biographical entry) collaborated with a white freelance writer named William Jourdan Rapp. Together, they wrote a play called *Harlem* (1929) that was based on Thurman's short story "Cordelia the Crude." Presented on Broadway with a cast of sixty actors, most of them inexperienced, the play ran for ninety-three performances. *Harlem* shows the effects of migration on a black family, focusing on the conflict between hardworking Ma and Pa Williams and their daughter Cordelia, who gets involved with gangsters and prostitution. With its frank portrayal of Harlem's lower classes, the play was considered vulgar by some critics and truthful by others.

White dramatists take up black subjects

Just as black playwrights strove to create works that reflected African Americans more authentically, white dramatists were moving away from the melodramas (dramas with exaggerated conflicts and emotions and stereotypical charac-

Paul Robeson as Emperor Jones in Eugene O'Neill's *Emperor Jones.*
(Corbis-Bettmann. Reproduced by permission.)

ters) of the early twentieth century. The trend was toward realism, which called for truthful portrayals of human characters and situations. Blacks became rich subject matter for prominent white playwrights, who, in turn, gave some of the period's most talented African American actors opportunities to appear in serious, respectable works.

White playwright Ridgely Torrence (1875–1950) brought three plays about African Americans to the Garden Theatre in 1917: *Granny Maumee,* which focuses on the power of religious faith; *The Rider of Dreams,* a play about black folklife; and *Simon the Cyrenian,* which centers on the idea that the man who helped Jesus Christ bear his cross was black (also see section on Roland Hayes below). These plays were regarded as a big step forward because they avoided stereotypical portrayals of black people.

Perhaps the most famous white playwright to use black subject matter in his plays was Eugene O'Neill (1888–1953), who was just starting his career as the Harlem Renaissance flourished. *The Emperor Jones* (1921) featured the great black actor Charles Gilpin (and in a later production, Paul Robeson) as a former Pullman (passenger train) porter named Brutus Jones, who sets himself up as the emperor of a West Indian island community. Jones becomes a victim of his own fears and desires, and the people he has tried to rule finally kill him. In O'Neill's *All God's Chillun Got Wings* (1924), a struggling black law student played by Robeson marries a white woman who, without even realizing it herself, holds hidden racist beliefs.

Paul Green's (1894–1981) *In Abraham's Bosom,* which won the Pulitzer Prize for drama in 1927, tells the tragic story of the black son of a white plantation owner who makes two unsuccessful attempts to establish a school for black children. Produced by a famous, cutting-edge white theater group called the Provincetown Players, the drama featured a number of black actors, including Rose McLendon, Julius Bledsoe, and Abbie Mitchell, all of whom won praise for their performances. A more sentimental and hugely popular play, *Porgy*, was written by husband and wife team Dubose and Dorothy Heyward in 1927. *Porgy* was later made into the opera *Porgy and Bess* by white composer George Gershwin. The story makes use of the stereotypically "simple Negro" character in relating the story of the morally strong but physically crippled Porgy and his virtuous but vulnerable lover, Bess, who live in the all-black community of Catfish Row. The original production featured a big cast of Harlem actors, including some inexperienced ones (like writers Wallace Thurman and Richard Bruce Nugent) in small parts.

Another commercially successful work was Marc Connolly's (1890–1980) *Green Pastures* (1930), an allegory (symbolic representation) featuring a black Sunday school class being taught lessons through parables (short, simple stories from which moral or religious messages may be drawn). Biblical stories about the Creation, Noah and the great flood, and the birth, death, and resurrection of Jesus Christ were simply but vividly rendered through childlike images and southern black dialect. Critics claimed the play lacked any meaningful social content because it created a peaceful southern plantation world that had never really existed. White audiences warmed to the religious theme and cozily stereotypical characters in *Green Pastures*.

Music in the Harlem Renaissance—important but controversial

By the time the novels, poetry, and dramas of the Harlem Renaissance were being recognized, African American music had already gained fame worldwide. Jazz and blues provided the background, the spirit, and the style for the achievements of the period's literary and visual artists as well as for the white onlookers who flocked to Harlem to soak up some of its excitement. But music was actually a source of controversy in the 1920s. W.E.B. Du Bois and his Talented Tenth (that elite segment of the African American community who would forge recognition and thus reconciliation with whites through their abilities and achievements) disapproved of the new forms of

Josephine Baker: A Paris Sensation

Josephine Baker appeared in several black musical revues in New York during the Harlem Renaissance, but always as a part of the chorus line, not as a headlining performer. That changed after her 1925 move to Paris, where she became the queen of "Le Jazz Hot," the popular French term for the music and style of entertainment that had overtaken the nightclubs of Paris.

Born into poverty in Kansas City, Missouri, Baker left home at thirteen to join blues singer Clara Smith's traveling show. Hired as a dresser, she was sometimes allowed to dance in the chorus or to play small comic roles. Baker auditioned for the popular show *Shuffle Along* in Philadelphia in 1921, but she was considered too young, too skinny, and too dark-skinned and was turned down. Nevertheless, she followed the show to New York and finally got a job as a dresser for the second touring company. While on tour she substituted for a chorus girl, and her funny performance made her so popular that she was promoted to the first touring company.

Baker's career received another boost when producers Noble Sissle and Eubie Blake of *Shuffle Along* fame wrote in a special part for her in their new show, *In Bamville*. When the show arrived on Broadway in 1924 it was renamed *Chocolate Dandies,* and Baker appeared as a clowning, clumsy, bug-eyed chorus girl who was always out of step. Billed as "that comedy chorus girl," she delighted audiences. The next year, Baker was part of the chorus for *Plantation Revue*, which starred the famous Ethel Waters; Baker replaced Waters for one performance, with such success that Waters made sure it never happened again.

In 1925, a wealthy white American woman named Caroline Dudley decided to bring a little bit of Harlem to Paris, where she was living with her diplomat husband.

black music, which they considered expressions of the "low" life and just another way of fulfilling white people's negative expectations about blacks. Du Bois and the Talented Tenth preferred spirituals because they were religious in nature and came out of the black folk tradition. Jazz and blues were viewed as uncivilized and vulgar. Nevertheless, many Harlem Renaissance writers—most notably Langston Hughes—found inspiration in the music they heard at Harlem's nightclubs and rent parties.

Josephine Baker. *(AP/Wide World Photos, Inc. Reproduced by permission.)*

She started the *Revue Negre,* an all-black musical revue, and hired Baker to star in it. Baker made her first appearance wearing a girdle made of bananas. Parisians saw her as the embodiment of the "primitive" energy and passion of the black race, and they adored her. She was soon starring in the *Folies Bergere*—the hottest show in Paris—and in nightclubs all over Europe, creating a sensation and performing such songs as "Yes, We Have No Bananas" and "Two Loves Have I."

Baker did not return to the United States until 1936, when her appearance in the *Ziegfield Follies* (an almost all-white musical company) was only coolly received. She went back to Europe, and during World War II she served with the French Resistance (that movement that carried out underground activities to undermine France's German occupiers). Baker later received three medals from the French government, including the prestigious Legion of Honor.

During the 1970s, Baker performed again in New York, giving concerts at Carnegie Hall and in Harlem. She died in 1975, only four days after opening a new revue in Paris to celebrate her 50 years in show business.

The roots of African American music

Jazz and blues are two musical forms that have their roots far back in the history of black America—perhaps even farther back, in the rhythms and instruments that the slaves and their ancestors had played in Africa. But the distinctive music that blacks developed in the United States was not just African: it also included elements of European music, like the folk music that settlers from the British Isles had brought with them to the New World. (Musicologists have detected, for example, traces of Scottish dance tunes in early jazz.) This blended music was played on instruments brought from Africa by the slaves (the banjo and makeshift rhythm instruments) and on the fiddles used by white musicians; it was spread and popularized through the minstrel shows of the late nineteenth century. Meanwhile, spirituals—the deeply emotional songs sung by African American Christians—were being sung around the United States and Europe by the Fisk Jubilee Singers, a choir founded at Fisk University (in Nashville, Tennessee; one of the earliest primarily black colleges in the United States) in 1871.

During the 1890s, a musical style called ragtime emerged. It was based on the popular music being written then by white composers like Stephen Foster (1826–1864) and John Philip Sousa (1854–1932), but it added strong rhythms and syncopated melodies, which are formed by shortening beats or stressing a weak beat. Serious composers—especially the famous Scott Joplin (1868–1917)—wrote formal piano pieces called "rags" in this style. Gradually, the popular ragtime songs were taken over by Tin Pan Alley (the name given to the white publishers of popular music, most of whom were based on New York City's 28th Street), while the piano playing became part of an even newer style called jazz. This word is thought to have been taken from a black slang term, "jass," that had a sexual meaning but was used to refer to anything that caused excitement.

Jazz: New Orleans and beyond

The city often identified as the birthplace of jazz was New Orleans, Louisiana, situated where the Mississippi River empties into the Gulf of Mexico. This city was the site of a busy international port where blacks from the Caribbean and from Africa mixed with African Americans as well as "Creoles," people of mixed (African, European, and Native American) heritage who populate southern Louisiana. There, musicians began to take up instruments that had been discarded by the Civil War military bands (especially trumpets, trombones, and clarinets). They created a style that blended the sounds of a typical white marching band with off-beat rhythms and improvisation (solos in which performers take off from the main melody being played, introducing their own stylings or interpretations).

The first group to benefit financially from the new jazz style was the all-white Original Dixieland Jazz Band, which had started playing in New Orleans around 1905 and made the first jazz recordings in 1917. But black bands and musicians were also playing this music and gaining prominence. One of the earliest was the forward-thinking Ferdinand "Jelly Roll" Morton (1885–1941), who started his career playing ragtime piano for minstrel shows and vaudeville (stage shows featuring specialty acts, such as singing, dancing, and comedy routines). Morton helped take the New Orleans style to Chicago, the thriving midwestern city that would emerge as the next great jazz center. By the late 1920s Morton would fade into the background as jazz artists moved farther away from the New Orleans style he had championed.

Other influential figures in pre-Harlem Renaissance music included Ford Dabney, who came up with the concept of the black dance orchestra that would become so wildly popular on Broadway; James Reese Europe, who brought the black dance orchestra to Europe, where it created a sensation (he also led a top-notch military band during World War I); and Will Marion Cook, who wrote the first serious syncopated orchestral arrangements.

Two early jazz leaders: Oliver and Armstrong

Among the New Orleans musicians who moved on to Chicago and then to New York, the two best known are Joe "King" Oliver (1885–1938) and Louis "Satchmo" Armstrong (1900–1971). Oliver started playing the cornet professionally in 1908. Nine years later he won a musical competition in New Orleans's fabled Storyville district and earned his lifelong nickname. He moved to Chicago in 1919 and played for a while in trombonist Kid Ory's band, then founded his own group, the Creole Jazz Band, which in 1922 would became the first black band to make jazz records. Working with fellow cornet player Louis Armstrong, Oliver developed a two-cornet lead that listeners found original and exciting. Oliver's next group, the Dixie Syncopators, played at New York's Plantation Café from 1925 to 1927 and then at the Savoy Ballroom, making famous such songs as "Canal Street Blues," "New Orleans Stomp," and "Mournful Serenade." Unfortunately, Oliver's career went into a slump in the late 1920s and 1930s.

Louis Armstrong's career continued well beyond the end of the Harlem Renaissance. Here, he is marching in a parade in Germany in 1952.
(AP/Wide World Photos, Inc. Reproduced by permission)

Louis Armstrong was an extremely talented musician who made a permanent impact on jazz, partly by serving as an example of a soloist whose playing could be showcased within the bounds of a jazz tune performed by a band. Born in Louisiana in 1900, Armstrong learned to play the cornet (he later switched to trumpet) during a stay at the Colored Waifs Home, where he had been sent as punishment for firing a gun during a street celebration. Armstrong went on to perform in clubs in Storyville and on riverboats that floated along the Mississippi River, and he replaced Joe "King" Oliver in Kid Ory's band in 1919. Three years later Oliver asked him to join his Creole Jazz Band in Chicago. There, Armstrong continued to perfect what would become his distinctive solo style, featuring a broad tone, a smooth vibrato (a slightly pulsating effect), and great skill in managing high notes.

It was with Oliver's group that Armstrong made his first jazz recordings, including "Chimes Blues" and "Dippermouth Blues" (both in 1923). Armstrong went to New York to play with Fletcher Henderson's band at the Roseland Ballroom in 1924, but he returned to Chicago a year later to join his new wife's group, Lil Hardin's Dreamland Syncopators. By 1927 he was leading his own band, the Stompers, at the Sunset Café and recording such songs as "Willie the Weaper" and "Weary Blues." Two years later Armstrong took his band to New York and began an engagement at Connie's Inn, one of Harlem's most famous nightclubs. At the same time, he was performing on Broadway in the show *Hot Chocolates,* delighting audiences with his scat-singing (in which the singer makes up meaningless syllables, sometimes in imitation of the sound of a musical instrument) on the popular song "Ain't Misbehavin'."

Armstrong's career continued well beyond the end of the Harlem Renaissance. He made the first of several European tours in 1932 and began a string of numerous movie, radio, and television appearances. In later decades some critics accused Armstrong of demeaning African Americans by playing up to white stereotypes and using black dialect humor. His defenders claim that he had been trained not just as a musician but as an entertainer and was simply performing in the tradition of his times. In any case, his accomplishments in jazz are recognized universally.

Fletcher Henderson and Duke Ellington create the "Big Band" sound

Perhaps the most famous figures of the Harlem jazz scene were two bandleaders, Fletcher Henderson (1898–1952) and Duke Ellington (1899–1974; see biographical entry), who helped originate the "Big Band" sound (created by a jazz or dance orchestra and including more than one player on each instrument) that would remain popular for several decades.

Fletcher Henderson with
his orchestra in 1927.
*(Bettmann. Reproduced
by permission.)*

Henderson was a Georgia native and a college graduate who
went to New York in 1921 to work as a chemist. But he had also
studied piano for many years and was an avid jazz fan, so he
was able to land a job as a song demonstrator with the music
publishing company owned by Harry Pace and W.C. Handy
(1873–1958; also see subhead titled "W.C. Handy: 'Father of
the Blues'?"). When Pace founded Black Swan Records, he
hired Henderson as a recording manager and accompanist.

In 1924 Henderson formed his own sixteen-member
band, which performed first at the Club Alabam and then at
the Roseland Ballroom. Known for his original, ambitious
arrangements and excellent piano playing, Henderson
employed many of jazz's greatest names over the years, including Louis Armstrong, Coleman Hawkins, Don Redman, and
Benny Carter. Duke Ellington would later call Henderson's
group "the greatest dance band anyone ever heard." Like
Ellington, Henderson was tolerated by the Talented Tenth
leaders because he was cultured, educated, and strait-laced,

thus countering the prevailing image of the hard-living jazzman. After the end of the Harlem Renaissance, Henderson worked with white jazz greats Tommy and Jimmie Dorsey and Benny Goodman.

Edward Kennedy Ellington earned the nickname "Duke" early in his life because of his love of fine clothing. The always well-dressed young man—who was to become the best-known and possibly most influential figure in American jazz—grew up in Washington, D.C., and formed his first band, Duke's Washingtonians, in 1920. He soon moved his band to New York and started performing at the Kentucky Club. In 1927 Ellington began a long engagement at Harlem's famous Cotton Club, where he always appeared in a white tuxedo, with his band members dressed in satin-trimmed beige tails. During this period Ellington and his band came up with their trademark "jungle" sound, featuring the use of mutes (plugs placed in horns to change their sound) and growl techniques.

Although his most respected achievements came later, Ellington wrote more than fifty songs in the 1920s, including "Black and Tan Fantasy," "Creole Love Call," and "Mood Indigo." Other tunes, among them "Rent Party Blues" and "Dicty Glide," were direct reflections of Harlem Renaissance life. (Dicty was the slang term for a person who put on airs.) His "Creole Rhapsody," composed in 1931, was an extended work that impressed both American and European listeners. Even though Ellington was the creator of the "jungle style," which smacks of the notion of black people as "primitive," the Talented Tenth leaders liked him for his elegance, dignity, and devotion to the advancement of African Americans. He was successful, for instance, in getting the famed Cotton Club to loosen its policy against admitting black patrons.

The piano players

Among the key figures on the Harlem Renaissance music scene were the talented and innovative musicians who played piano in the big bands, in musical revues, at nightclubs, and at rent parties. Unlike the sophisticated Henderson and Ellington, these pianists were "show" people, part of a rowdy, hard-living crowd of entertainers; they weren't concerned about what W.E.B. Du Bois and his friends thought of them. Early "show" pianists included Charles Luckeyth "Lucky"

The Real "Mr. Bojangles"

Fondly remembered as someone who brought tap-dancing to a new level, Bill "Bojangles" Robinson was one of the most popular performers of the Harlem Renaissance period.

Born Luther Robinson in Richmond, Virginia, in 1876, he was raised by his grandmother after his parents died. When he was eight he moved to Washington, D.C., where he worked in a racetrack stable (and where one of his co-workers gave him the nickname "Bojangles") and also earned money by dancing in bars. Robinson began to appear on stage as a "pickaninny" (the term for black children who performed in minstrel shows and musical revues). He made his first New York appearance in 1891, when he was twelve, in a show called *The South Before the War.*

After being wounded in the Spanish American War (in which he was not officially a soldier but an interested hanger-on), Robinson formed a vaudeville team with George Cooper. After five years he became a solo act, delighting audiences not only with his excellent dancing but with his expressive face, singing ability, and the comic patter he kept up while he danced. Billed as "The Dark Cloud of Joy," Robinson was soon earning as much as two thousand dollars a week.

Nevertheless, he didn't begin his New York theatrical career until 1927, when he was over fifty years old. He first appeared there in the *Pepper Pot Revue,* in which he performed his famous "stair dance" and began to be widely proclaimed as the greatest tap dancer of all time. Robinson was also a big hit in *Blackbirds of 1928,* which hadn't been doing well before he joined the cast. Other shows in which Robinson appeared included *Brown Buddies* (1930), *Hot from*

Roberts and James P. Johnson, who got their start playing ragtime piano. Johnson was the creator of the "stride" style, which added strong left-hand playing to the basic ragtime method. Willie "The Lion" Smith, who earned his nickname through his bravery as a soldier in World War I, was known for his unusual rhythms and harmonies and a personal style that combined power with delicacy.

The most famous of the Harlem Renaissance piano players, however, was probably Thomas "Fats" Waller (1904–1943), a large, extravagant, and generous man. Raised in

Tap dancer Bill "Bojangles" Robinson (right), shown with actress Shirley Temple (left), was one of the most popular performers of the Harlem Renaissance. *(AP/Wide World Photos. Reproduced by permission.)*

Harlem (1931) and *The Hot Mikado* (1939). Meanwhile, he was also a headline act at many New York clubs, and his income rose as high as sixty-five hundred dollars per week.

During the 1930s Robinson had a successful film career, appearing with the popular child actress Shirley Temple in *The Little Colonel* (1935), *The Littlest Rebel* (1936), and *Rebecca of Sunnybrook Farm* (1938). Although he was much beloved by the whites who saw these movies, some blacks criticized Robinson for playing the stereotypical role of the meek, always grinning, faithful black servant. But even his detractors admitted that he was a great dancer and a generous person who shared much of his income with charities and gave many benefit performances.

At the time of Robinson's death in 1949, most of the nearly three million dollars he had made over his sixty-three-year career was gone. He ended his life as he had begun it, in poverty.

New York City, Waller had learned to play the piano and organ from his musician mother, and at age fifteen he won a contest by playing Johnson's stride composition "Carolina Shout." Johnson recognized Waller's talent and took the younger musician under his wing. Waller soon became part of the group of piano players who were much in demand around Harlem. He started publishing songs—including "Bloody Razor Blues," "Bullet Wound Blues," and "Squeeze Me"—in the early 1920s, and by the middle of the decade he was working with lyricist Andy Razaf. The pair wrote many songs together, including memorable tunes for Broadway shows like *Keep Shufflin'* (1928) and *Hot Chocolates* (1929). Waller's song "Ain't Misbehavin'" became famous when the great trumpet player Louis Armstrong sang it in the Broadway play *Hot Chocolates.*

Waller wrote four hundred songs during his career (some of them, such as "Your Feet's Too Big," reflecting his great sense of humor), made many recordings, toured Europe and the United States, appeared in films, and played often in New York both with a band and as a solo act. Some of his most famous compositions include "Honeysuckle Rose," "The Joint Is Jumpin'," and "Keepin' Out of Mischief Now."

Just as a white jazz band was the first to make money from recordings (even though African Americans had created the music), a white musician who was talented but not as influential as Ellington, Henderson, or other black jazz greats was given the title "King of Jazz." Paul Whiteman was a very popular bandleader and composer who did play an important role in symphonic jazz, though most critics agree that he did not deserve his nickname. His band's performance of George Gershwin's extended work *Rhapsody in Blue* at New York's Aeolian Hall in February 1924 was considered the first true jazz concert.

The evolution of the blues

The young musical form of jazz went through some major growth spurts during the Harlem Renaissance. Meanwhile, a closely related kind of music called the blues was also evolving. Like jazz, blues music is rooted in the African heritage of the black people who created it, as well as in the spirituals sung well before the dawn of the twentieth century. Blue is the color of emotional pain, and the earliest blues songs served as both expressions of sadness and ways to conquer sorrow. The blues of the Harlem Renaissance period exerted a profound influence on modern-day blues and rock compositions.

W.C. Handy: "Father of the Blues"?

There is no critical consensus on when, where, and how the blues began, and most music experts feel that no single person could have invented it. Nevertheless, W.C. (William Christopher) Handy has been dubbed the "Father of the Blues" because he was the first person to collect and write down blues melodies, and he was a major influence on the blues artists who followed him. Handy's Alabama minister-father did not approve of his son's budding interest in music. In spite of the opposition, though, young Handy became a professional cornet player around the turn of the century. He played with the Bessemer Brass Band and then led the Mahara Minstrels. While touring the South, he heard local musicians playing the blues, and he started writing blues pieces for his own band, establishing a standard twelve-bar musical structure with lyrics written in a three-line rhymed pattern. In 1907 Handy teamed with Harry Pace to start a music publishing business, and five years later he published his own song "Memphis Blues," which was a big success. Handy's strong influence led to a shift in popular music—away from the ragtime songs to ballads tinged with the blues. He continued working as a bandleader and composer in the 1920s, producing such famous songs as "Joe Turner Blues," "Beale Street Blues," and "Harlem Blues." Handy also arranged folk songs and ballads and edited a number of anthologies, including *Blues: An Anthology* (1926).

The influential Ma Rainey

If blues had a "father," it follows that some female musician would be called its "mother." Gertrude "Ma" Rainey (1886–1939), one of the first women to perform the blues on stage, was known as the "Mother of the Blues." The daughter of minstrel troupers, Rainey started performing when she was only fourteen. She gradually developed a singing style all her own, combining the roughness of the early rural blues songs with a newer, more sophisticated, urban flavor. Beginning in 1917 Rainey toured with her own bands and shows: first Madame Gertrude Rainey and her Georgia Smart Sets, then the Georgia Wild Cats Band, and, in 1927, the *Louisiana Blackbirds* revue. She made her first recording in 1923, singing with Lovie Austin and Her Blues Serenaders, and she cut about ninety more records over the next five years, including some with famous jazz musicians like Louis Armstrong and Coleman Hawkins. Although Rainey probably never performed in New York, her songs and style were well known in Harlem, and she exerted a strong influence on younger blues singers, especially Bessie Smith (c. 1894–1937; see biographical entry).

Race records become popular

The growing demand by African Americans for recognition in the arts also applied to music, especially in the form of so-called "race records." In 1916 the Chicago *Defender,* a black newspaper, started a campaign to put African American compositions and voices on vinyl. The call was answered by Okeh Records, which released a song written by black composer Perry Bradford and sung by Mamie Smith. Called "Crazy Blues," it became a bestseller and propelled Smith into the forefront of the blues music scene.

Mamie Smith achieves success

Born in 1883, Smith began working as a dancer while she was still a child, and by 1913 she was singing in New York City nightclubs. In 1918 she starred in the musical revue *Maid in Harlem,* and it was that show's lyricist, Perry Bradford, who helped her get a record contract with Okeh. In February 1920, working with an all-white orchestra, she first recorded "That Thing Called Love" and "You Can't Keep a Good Man Down." These songs were so successful that Okeh called Smith back a few months later to record "Crazy Blues" (the name was changed from "Harlem Blues" to make it sound less black) and "It's Right Here for You (If You Don't Get It, T'ain't No Fault of Mine)." These were the first solo recordings by an African American artist.

"Crazy Blues" was a huge hit, selling seventy-five thousand copies the first month after its release and more than one million copies in six months; the song's success showed the earning potential of race records. Over the next two years, Smith made twenty-three more recordings for Okeh and toured with her own group, the Jazz Hounds. In 1923 she starred in a West Coast revue called *Struttin' Along.* Throughout the 1930s Smith appeared in a number of shows at Harlem's Lafayette and Lincoln theaters, as well as in some films.

"Nobody messed with Bessie"

Mamie Smith was one of a group of dynamic female blues singers whose careers took off during the Harlem Renaissance. Another was Bessie Smith (no relation to Mamie), who performed with and learned from Ma Rainey and went on to

Bessie Smith's career took off during the Harlem Renaissance.
(Courtesy of the New York Public Library.)

even greater fame. Smith started performing in various shows in 1912, and she started her own group, the Liberty Belles, in 1918. By 1920 she was a well-known blues singer in the South. Her first attempts to enter the race record industry failed when she was rejected by both the Black Swan and Okeh record companies, but in 1923 she signed a contract with Columbia Records, earning $125 for each song she recorded. Her first record—with "Downhearted Blues" on one side and "Gulf

Coast Blues" on the other—was a big hit, selling 780,000 copies in six months. Billed as the "Empress of the Blues" by Columbia, Smith became the company's best-selling artist. Despite this fact, she had no agreement to collect royalties (a percentage of profits made from sales of records), and during her career she made only $28,575 from all of her recordings.

Smith was very busy throughout the 1920s and 1930s, making appearances in black theaters (along with an occasional special appearance for a white audience) throughout the South; she rarely appeared in New York; her fame there was based solely on her recordings. A rough, tough, 200-pound woman with a hot temper, she inspired the phrase: "Nobody messed with Bessie." Smith reportedly chased off a gang of Ku Klux Klan (KKK) members who tried to stop her show, and she once performed on stage after receiving a stab wound in a fight the day before. She ran her show herself, traveling with her own well-equipped railroad car. Smith's popularity declined somewhat during the early 1930s, and she was just starting to make a comeback when, in 1937, she died of injuries sustained in a car accident.

Ethel Waters and other great blues singers

Unlike Bessie Smith, Ethel Waters (1896–1977; see biographical entry) had a career that stretched well beyond the Harlem Renaissance. Born in 1896, she grew up in poverty and was married at thirteen. In 1917 she sang "St. Louis Blues" on a Baltimore stage, and thereafter she toured the South as Sweet Mama Stringbean with a group called the Hill Sisters. After a one-week engagement at the Lincoln Theatre in Harlem, Waters started performing at Edmond's Cellar, a very seedy nightclub frequented by prostitutes, gamblers, and others from Harlem's underside. But Waters's polished, smooth style of blues singing soon attracted notice, and she was able to make a record—featuring the songs "New York Glide" and "At the New Jump Steady Ball"—for Cardinal Records in 1919. After moving to Black Swan Records, Waters scored hits with "Down Home Blues," "Oh Daddy," "There'll Be Some Changes Made," and "One Man Nan."

Following a tour of the South to promote her records, Waters went back to New York to appear in various revues in black theaters. In 1924 she starred in the *Plantation Revue* in

Chicago to critical acclaim, then returned to New York for a singing engagement at the Plantation Club. Waters's first appearance on Broadway, in *Africana* in 1927, made her even more famous, and she was in demand in London and Paris and on Broadway. In 1929 she became the first black singer to work with white bands, appearing with Benny Goodman and Tommy and Jimmie Dorsey. During the 1930s, through stints at the Cotton Club, on Broadway, and at Carnegie Hall, she had hits like "Stormy Weather," "Heat Wave," and "Am I Blue?" For the next several decades Smith worked as a straight dramatic actress on Broadway and in the movies.

The third famous blues singer with the name Smith (again, no relation) was Clara Smith (1894–1935), who got her start on the southern vaudeville circuit in 1910. She toured the South with black musical revues until 1923, when she settled in New York and began singing in Harlem clubs. Smith made her first recording in 1923, the same year as Bessie Smith, but she was not considered a threat by the stronger-voiced and better-paid Bessie. The two had a friendly rivalry until they got into a fistfight in 1925 and never spoke to each other again. Clara Smith was the second-bestselling blues artist of the 1920s (Bessie Smith was the first) and was praised by critic Carl Van Vechten for expressing a "mystic kind of grief" in her singing.

Other renowned women blues singers of the Harlem Renaissance included piano player Victoria Spivey and entertainer Gladys Bentley. Spivey's first recording—of "Black Snake Blues," a song she'd written herself—sold 150,000 copies within a year of its release. Bentley's engagements at the Clam House, Connie's Inn, and other Harlem hot spots were real attention-getters. Famous for her loud, hoarse voice and her masculine style of dress (she often appeared in a tuxedo), she was open about her homosexuality and well known for adding her own, racier lyrics to popular songs.

African Americans create and perform classical music

Those Harlem Renaissance leaders who hoped that African Americans would express their unique experience through classical music (which they considered a "high" art form superior to jazz and blues) were gratified with the work of several black composers and performers. These musicians called on black folk music, especially the tradition of spirituals, for their inspiration. Prominent black classical pieces include Harry T. Burleigh's *Plantation Melodies for Violin and Piano* (1916), Clarence Cameron White's violin piece *From the Cotton Fields* (1925), and the symphonic music—*Darker America* (1924) and *Africa* (1930)—and ballets—*La Guiablesse* (1927) and *Sahdji* (1930)—of William Grant Still. Among the black operas of the period were Robert Nathaniel Dett's *Chariot Jubilee* (1921), which was based on the spiritual "Swing Low, Sweet Chariot"; Harry Lawrence Freeman's *Vendetta* (1923) and *Voodoo* (1928); and Clarence Cameron White's *Oanga* (1930–1931). Dett also composed a number of piano suites (*Enchantment* and *The Cinnamon Grove*) that incorporated elements of African American heritage.

The Harlem Renaissance years brought milestone events in literature, theater, popular music—and classical music. The National Association of Negro Musicians (meant to promote the interests and progress of African American composers and performers) was formed in 1919. In December 1923 singer Roland Hayes performed in concert at New York's Town Hall. (The concert featured the accompaniment of the Negro String Quartet, a dynamic group of four, conservatory-trained musicians that played many concerts in the 1920s and 1930s in New York and Philadelphia and showcased the works of both white and black composers.) The acclaimed Hall Johnson Choir was formed in 1924. And the "First American Jazz Concert" (see discussion of Paul Whiteman) took place that February. Also active during this period were Jules Bledsoe, a classical baritone singer who acted on the Broadway stage, concert pianist Hazel Harrison (one of the first African Americans to have a successful career in this field), and opera singers Caterina Jarboro and Lillian Evanti.

Another exciting event was the 1928 premiere of *Yamekraw,* an extended piece for symphony orchestra and piano, at Carnegie Hall. *Yamekraw* was the collaborative effort of four renowned black musicians: James P. Johnson, who composed it; William Grant Still, who had orchestrated the piece; W.C. Handy, who conducted the orchestra; and Fats Waller, who performed the piano solo. *Yamekraw* made use of the rich store of black spirituals as well as blues songs, and it was played by an all-black orchestra.

Hayes and Robeson: World-renowned singers

Two Harlem Renaissance performers who made a significant impact on the world of classical music were Roland Hayes and Paul Robeson. Hayes had been born on a Georgia farm to a very poor family, but he learned to sing in a church choir and was later able to study voice at Fisk University. In 1911 Hayes joined the Fisk Jubilee Singers. His fine tenor voice attracted large audiences in Boston, and he made his New York debut at the Aeolian Music Hall in 1917, returning for later performances in 1919 and 1920. Hayes then studied for two years in Europe, perfecting his ability to sing in Italian, German, and French. He returned to the States, and in December of 1923 gave a solo recital at New York's Town Hall, performing a program of "Lieder [a type of German song] and Spirituals." This marked a turning point in his career: the concert was so highly praised by critics that a second Town Hall concert and a recital at Carnegie Hall were quickly sold out. Later, Hayes toured the United States, presenting programs that were very formal but always ending with spirituals. He is now credited with opening doors for the black singers who followed him.

Paul Robeson was a minister's son who first gained fame when he overcame prejudice and discrimination to become an outstanding student-athlete at Princeton University. He earned a law degree and opened a law practice, but his interest in acting and singing propelled him into a performing career. While still in law school, Robeson appeared briefly in the Broadway show *Shuffle Along* and starred in Ridgely Torrence's play *Simon the Cyrenian*. In 1924 he landed the lead role in *All God's Chillun Got Wings,* which Eugene O'Neill had written with Robeson in mind. The play caused a controversy due to its mixed-race cast and theme.

Robeson also appeared in O'Neill's *Emperor Jones* (1925), *Black Boy* (1926), *Porgy* (1928), and the London version of *Showboat* (1928). He played the title role in Shakespeare's *Othello* at London's Savoy Theatre to great acclaim in May 1930 and then reprised the role in New York from 1943 to 1945. (This *Othello* would be the longest-running Shakespeare play in Broadway history, with 296 performances.)

A skilled actor, Robeson was even more praised for his magnificent bass voice. He sang in several plays in the early 1920s, but in April 1925 he made his true singing debut with a concert of spirituals and songs by black composers. By 1929 he was such a popular singer that he was able to sell out Carnegie Hall as well as several European concert halls. During the course of his career, Robeson made three hundred widely varied recordings (blues, spirituals, folk, classical, popular songs, and songs from Broadway musicals). Surprisingly, he received little formal training and claimed that he was not interested in perfecting his voice, as he considered himself "essentially a folk singer." Robeson was also a committed fighter for civil rights for African Americans.

Marian Anderson and the Daughters of the American Revolution

Another famous black singer of classical music was Marian Anderson (1902–1993), whose career began during the

Harlem Renaissance. Born in 1902 in Philadelphia, she studied music from an early age and as a teenager began giving recitals at churches, schools, and other venues; she even sang with Roland Hayes (see earlier section on Hayes). In 1925 Anderson won a vocal competition sponsored by the New York Philharmonic Symphony. She performed at Town Hall in 1929 and soon thereafter went to Europe to study voice. Her 1932 European debut (in Berlin) was well received, and she went on to complete a successful tour of other European cities. Anderson then returned to the United States and toured extensively.

In 1939 Anderson grabbed the news headlines when the Daughters of the American Revolution (DAR) denied her permission to sing at Constitution Hall in Washington, D.C. The incident was fueled by racial politics: Anderson could not use the hall because she was an African American. Outraged by the DAR's policies, Eleanor Roosevelt (1884–1962), wife of then-president Franklin D. Roosevelt, resigned from the organization and came to Anderson's defense, arranging for her to sing before an adoring crowd of seventy-five thousand people at the Lincoln Memorial on Easter Sunday of 1939. Anderson's long, productive career stretched across the next several decades, and she became one of the most famous and beloved singers in the world.

In 1939, classical singer Marian Anderson was denied permission to perform at Constitution Hall in Washington, D.C., by the Daughters of the American Revolution because of her race. *(UPI/Corbis-Bettmann. Reproduced by permission.)*

White and black musicians interact

The decade of the 1920s was full of growth and changes in the field of music. White composers such as Aaron Copland (1900–1990), Frances Poulenc (1899–1963), Erik Satie (1866–1925), Igor Stravinsky (1882–1971), and Maurice Ravel (1875–1937) began to incorporate elements of jazz and blues into their work as they searched for ways to break away from the traditions of Western classical music. In addition, the

Harlem Renaissance sparked much interaction between black and white musicians. George Gershwin, composer of *Rhapsody in Blue* and other works, went to Harlem often and was frequently seen at rent parties, where he focused his attention on the lively or soulful music of highly skilled pianists and other musicians. Irving Berlin (1888–1989), Paul Whiteman (1890–1967), Benny Goodman (1909–1986), Artie Shaw, and other big names of the white popular and big band jazz scenes were frequent patrons of Harlem nightclubs. All of this mutual interest and intermingling insured that African American music would make its way to the ears of white listeners across the United States and in other parts of the world.

For More Information

Abdul, Raoul. *Blacks in Classical Music.* New York: Dodd, Mead, 1977.

Albertson, Chris. *Bessie.* New York: Stein & Day, 1972.

Arata, Esther S. *Black American Playwrights: 1800 to Present.* Metuchen, NJ: Scarecrow Press, 1976.

Case, Brian, and Stan Britt. *The Illustrated Encyclopedia of Jazz.* New York: Harmony Books, 1978.

Charters, Ann. *Nobody: The Story of Bert Williams.* New York: Macmillan, 1970.

Charters, Samuel B. *Jazz: A History of the New York Scene.* Garden City, NY: Doubleday, 1962.

Chilton, John. *Who's Who in Jazz: Storyville to Swing Street.* Philadelphia: Chilton, 1978.

Dance, Stanley. *The World of Duke Ellington.* New York: Scribner's, 1970.

Feather, Leonard, ed. *The Encyclopedia of Jazz.* New York: DeCapo Press, 1984.

Floyd, Samuel A., Jr., ed. *Black Music in the Harlem Renaissance: A Collection of Essays.* Knoxville: University of Tennessee Press, 1993.

Fox, Charles. *Fats Waller.* New York: A.S. Barnes, 1961.

Green, Stanley, ed. *Encyclopedia of the Musical Theatre.* New York: Dodd, Mead, 1980.

Handy, D. Antoinette. *Black Women in American Bands and Orchestras.* Westport, CT: Greenwood Press, 1981.

Harris, Sheldon. *Blues Who's Who: A Biographical Dictionary of Blues Singers.* New Rochelle, NY: Arlington House, 1979.

Haskins, James. *Black Theatre in America*. New York: Crowell, 1982.

Hentoff, Nat. *Jazz: New Perspectives on the History of Jazz by Twelve of the World's Foremost Jazz Critics and Scholars*. New York: Rinehart, 1959.

Kirkeby, Ed. *Ain't Misbehavin': The Story of Fats Waller*. New York: Dodd, Mead, 1966.

Lieb, Sandra. *Mother of the Blues: A Study of Ma Rainey*. Amherst: University of Massachusetts Press, 1981.

Mapp, Edward. *Dictionary of Blacks in the Performing Arts*. Metuchen, NJ: Scarecrow Press, 1978.

McCarthy, Albert J. *Louis Armstrong*. New York: Barnes, 1961.

Mitchell, Loften. *Black Drama: The Story of the American Negro in the Theatre*. New York: Hawthorn Books, 1967.

Oakley, Giles. *The Devil's Music: A History of the Blues*. New York: Harcourt Brace Jovanovich, 1978.

Rose, Al. *Eubie Blake*. New York: Schirmer, 1979.

Southern, Eileen. *Biographical Dictionary of Afro-American and African Musicians*. Westport, CT: Greenwood Press, 1982.

Stewart-Baxter, Derrick. *Ma Rainey and the Classic Blues Singers*. New York: Stein & Day, 1970.

"The beauty of the African and the Afro-American": The Visual Arts

S ome of the most colorful and memorable visual images we have of the Harlem Renaissance were created by the painters, sculptors, and photographers who were active during the 1920s. While African American writers, dramatists, and musicians were exploring their black identity, tapping into their rich cultural heritage, and forging new paths of their own, visual artists were doing the same thing. But before reaching the exciting years of the Harlem Renaissance, they had to overcome many obstacles to even practice their art forms.

Early African American artists faced obstacles

During the long period of slavery in the United States, African Americans with talent in the visual arts were not considered "artists." They could not pursue art as a career, nor could they obtain the training and education necessary to hone their skills. In the years before and after the Civil War (1861–65), the talent of African American visual artists was poured into practical skills and crafts such as ironwork, cabinetmaking, quilting, and silversmithing. Black artisans produced useful objects for the homes of white people (and, in some instances, their own homes) and often gained some status or recognition for their abilities. A few black painters—examples include Scipio Moorehead of Boston, Massachusetts, and Joshua E. Johnston of Baltimore, Maryland—even managed to earn money by painting portraits of whites and free black subjects.

As the twentieth century began, however, African American artists gained more recognition as actual painters and sculptors. They had gained greater access to education so that they could learn about the historical traditions that had dominated the world of art for many centuries. But they still had to overcome prejudice. So while white European and American artists were beginning to explore new artistic styles (such as impressionism, in which the artist tries to capture a momentary glimpse of a subject, using short strokes of paint) and expand their creative horizons, most African Americans still had to fight just to prove their ability and gain acceptance. As a result, their work at this time took rather conventional forms: realistic paintings of landscapes, historical scenes, and portraits of famous people and prominent or wealthy families. Some black artists managed to travel to European cities, especially Paris, where there was less discrimination against them and where they felt freer to learn, experiment, and generally practice their art.

Tanner achieves international recognition

The first African American artist to gain international prominence was Henry Ossawa Tanner (1859–1937). His career was nearing its end by the time of the Harlem Renaissance, but he influenced many younger artists. Born in 1859 to a Baptist minister and his wife, Tanner grew up in Pennsylvania. He decided to become an artist after attending the 1876 Centennial Art Exhibition in Philadelphia, where he saw the works of many important European and American painters. Tanner studied at the Pennsylvania Academy of Fine Arts and was particularly influenced by one of his teachers, the eminent painter Thomas Eakins (1844–1916). Eakins impressed Tanner with his ability to portray African Americans in natural, dignified ways rather than as exaggerated, stereotypical figures.

Tanner began his career as a magazine and book illustrator, and in 1889 he opened a photography studio in Atlanta. He went on to become an art instructor at Atlanta's Clark University, then spent a year studying art and painting in Paris. It was during this sojourn in France that Tanner painted one of his best-known works, *The Thankful Poor* (1894); with money from the sale of this painting, Tanner could afford another year in Paris. In 1895 he painted *Daniel in the Lion's Den,* and the next year his *Resurrection of Lazarus* won a gold medal from the Salon du Societe des Artistes Francais.

These successes built Tanner's reputation and helped him attract financial backing from art patrons (people who give artists money to encourage and support their work). He continued to win many prizes and honors and exhibited his paintings widely. Some were shown at the London Exhibition of 1914, which featured the works of such famous artists as Gilbert Stuart (1755–1828), James Whistler (1834–1903), and Winslow Homer (1836–1910). Tanner's paintings usually depicted religious scenes and rarely contained black subjects or references to African American history or culture; nevertheless, his career served to demonstrate the potential for greatness among black artists. He was considered a classic example of W.E.B. Du Bois's (1868–1963; see biographical entry) Talented Tenth (that elite segment of the African American community who, through their abilities and achievements, would forge recognition and thus reconciliation with whites). During the Harlem Renaissance, Tanner's works were exhibited at the New York Public Library (1921) and in Washington, D.C. (1922). Many young artists visited his Paris home to obtain advice and encouragement from the older, much lauded, and very influential artist.

Meta Warrick Fuller uses African American themes

Like Henry Tanner, sculptor Meta Warrick Fuller (1877–1968) is considered a transitional figure between the conventional artists of the early twentieth century and the slightly more daring ones of the Harlem Renaissance. Trained at the Pennsylvania Museum and School for Industrial Arts, Fuller went to Paris in 1899 and studied with the famous French sculptor Auguste Rodin (1840–1917). After returning to the United States, she married a Liberian (Liberia is a country in West Africa) physician and settled in Framingham, Massa-

Ethiopia Awakening. (Art Resource/Reproduced by permission.)

chusetts, where she worked from a studio she had built with her own hands.

Fuller was one of the first artists to consciously incorporate elements of the African American experience into her work. This effort began with a sculpture of a black boy and girl that she created at the request of W.E.B. Du Bois for a special work commemorating the fiftieth anniversary of the signing of the Emancipation Proclamation (the document guaranteeing freedom for slaves in the United States; see Chapter 1).

Like Du Bois, Fuller believed in "pan-Africanism" (the idea that all people of African heritage share a common heritage and should work together to help each other), and she looked toward her African ancestry for inspiration. This is especially evident in her most famous sculpture, *Ethiopia Awakening*, which uses the simplified form of much African sculpture in depicting a woman who seems to be emerging from a deep sleep. The bottom half of the figure is covered in the traditional wrappings of Egyptian mummies, while the upper half is uncovered and the figure's face is upraised. Critics have seen in this sculpture a theme of rebirth and self-discovery that refers specifically to African Americans as they migrated from the South to the North, forging new identities while continuing to explore their past in both Africa and the United States.

Another of Fuller's well-known works, *Mary Turner (A Silent Protest against Mob Violence)* (1919), was inspired by the 1917 Silent Protest

Parade (see Chapter 1), which was staged in response to a series of violent and racist acts against blacks. One such incident was the hideous lynching (a vile and violent practice in which African Americans accused of various crimes or misdeeds—but rarely legally charged—would be captured by gangs of whites and lynched—hanged without a trial; see Chapter 1) of a black woman named Mary Turner, who had been accused along with her husband and two other black men of plotting to murder a white person. Fuller's sculpture is fairly classical and conventional in form, but it is infused with a sensitivity to the hardships endured by African Americans.

More appreciation for African and African American art

Like African American writers and performers, visual artists of the Harlem Renaissance were exploring their own identities and their connections with black history and culture, celebrating the beauty of black people, and sharing African American folk traditions. They found wider appreciation for their work than ever before, in part because of the relatively new interest that well-known white artists—including Paul Gauguin (1848–1903) of France, Pablo Picasso (1881–1973) of Spain, and Henri Matisse (1869–1954) of France—had taken in African art. These artists were experimenting with and incorporating distinctly African elements into their own paintings and sculptures. The surging popularity of African art, in fact, encouraged black artists to try new methods (such as including images based on African masks) and popularize different standards of beauty in the art world.

Two important elements in the evolution of visual arts in the Harlem Renaissance were the 1925 publication of the *New Negro* anthology (see Chapter 3), which featured numerous illustrations by African American artists, and the establishment of the Harmon Foundation in 1926. This organization was founded by a wealthy white real-estate tycoon, William Harmon, who believed that the problems and obstacles faced by blacks were "a national problem, not simply a burden on blacks alone." Harmon sought to support, promote, and nurture African American art and culture; the Harmon Foundation (which existed until 1967) would prove a very important force in achieving these goals. Through the financial awards and exhibition opportunities it offered, it not only benefited individual artists but helped introduce a much wider audience to black art.

Every year, the Harmon Foundation recognized African American achievement with awards in seven categories—literature, fine arts, science, education, industry, religion, and music—and gave a special prize to the person, black or white, who had done the most to help improve race relations. In January 1928 at the International House in New York City, the organization sponsored the first all-black art exhibition in the United States. By 1933 the Harmon Foundation had sponsored five more such exhibitions, and some 150,000 viewers in fifty cities had seen a traveling exhibit of works by 150 artists. Although some artists complained that the organization sponsored too much mediocre art and that it favored works that imitated those of white artists, most agreed that the Harmon Foundation had a positive impact on Harlem Renaissance art.

Aaron Douglas: "Official artist" of the Harlem Renaissance

Often called the "official artist" of the Harlem Renaissance, painter Aaron Douglas (1899–1979) created many of the period's most dramatic and distinctive images. Born in Topeka, Kansas, he received a bachelor's degree from the University of Nebraska in 1922 and taught in Kansas City high schools for two years. In 1925 he moved to New York City, hoping to pursue a career in art. Douglas soon began studying with German artist Winold Reiss (1887-1953), who was famous for using folk themes and characters in his work. Reiss was very interested in African American culture and artists. He encouraged Douglas to look back to his African American roots for artistic ideas.

Douglas went even further back into the past, calling on African traditions for inspiration. He started fashioning a style that imitated African art in its simplicity and its emphasis on design over representation (he didn't try to make his images look exactly like objects in real life). He was also influenced by such modern art trends as cubism, in which objects are represented as geometric shapes. His paintings were done in flat, understated colors—often black and white, but also green, brown, and mauve—and frequently featured two-dimensional faceless silhouettes. The figures in his work are meant as symbols, not as imitations of actual individuals, yet they convey emotion and meaning through their postures, gestures, and surroundings.

Douglas's talent was recognized with a fellowship from the Barnes Foundation in 1928, followed by an exhibition of his work at the Harmon Foundation building the same year. He became widely recognized for the magazine covers he created for such publications as *Vanity Fair, Theatre Arts Monthly, Crisis, Opportunity,* and even the one-issue literary journals *Fire!!* and *Harlem.* Douglas also painted illustrations and dust jackets (paper covers) for a number of books by the most famous authors of the Harlem Renaissance, including Langston Hughes (1902–1967; see biographical entry), Countee Cullen (1903–1946; see biographical entry), James Weldon Johnson (1871–1938), Alain Locke (1886–1954; see biographical entry), and Carl Van Vechten (1880–1964; see biographical entry).

Douglas's most famous work was completed just after the Harlem Renaissance ended. Funded by the Work Projects Administration (WPA; a U.S. government agency founded in 1935 to lower Depression-era unemployment; called the Works Progress Administration until 1939), *Aspects of Negro Life* is a series of murals that charts the African American experience by blending elements and images from history, religion, myth, politics, and social studies. The piece was unveiled in 1934 and consists of four parts: "The Negro in an African Setting," which shows Africans dancing amidst spears, drums, and ancestral symbols; "From Slavery through Reconstruction," which includes images of backbreaking field work, the Emancipation Proclamation, and the threat of the Ku Klux Klan (KKK; a violent white-supremacist organization); "The Idyll of the Deep South," which shows African Americans working, singing, and grieving over a lynching; and "Song of the Towers," which brings black people into an urban, industrial setting with representations of machinery and smokestacks, as well as the music that provides a creative outlet for city dwellers.

Other Harlem Renaissance painters

Other important Harlem Renaissance painters include
Palmer Hayden (1893–1973), Archibald Motley (1891–1981),
Hale Woodruff (1900–1980), and William H. Johnson (1901–
1970). Hayden was a veteran of World War I who worked low-
paying jobs throughout the 1920s to finance his artwork. His
colorful, vibrant paintings of Harlem street scenes and other

subjects caused some controversy: critics said he portrayed black people in stereotypical ways (for example, with exaggeratedly large lips), but Hayden's defenders claim he used these images intentionally, as a form of satire (a spoof or parody that exposes evils). Archibald Motley's paintings veered away from realism while still conveying truths about their subjects; one of his best paintings, *Blues* (1929), shows a densely packed, lively nightclub scene complete with musicians, dancers, and patrons enjoying themselves. Hale Woodruff is best known for his dramatic murals illustrating the *Amistad* mutiny (an actual event in which a group of Africans who took over their slave ship were eventually allowed to return to Africa).

William H. Johnson was trained at the National Academy of Design in New York and began his career as a conventional painter. Later, he turned away from realism toward a kind of primitive style, featuring bright colors and simplified, even childlike, forms. His paintings were often of black people or scenes from black life, and he portrayed the inner

Ezekiel Saw the Wheel by William H. Johnson. *(Courtesy of the Library of Congress.)*

strength of the people and the richness of their culture through his use of color and telling details. Notable paintings by Johnson include his *Self-Portrait* (1929), which calls to mind the work of the pioneering Dutch artist Vincent van Gogh (1853–1890); *Jesus and the Three Marys* (1935), which portrays these biblical figures as African Americans; and *Minnie,* which reveals its subject's strong personality and unconventional beauty.

Sculptors depict African and African American beauty

Several important Harlem Renaissance-era sculptors followed Meta Warrick Fuller's lead in creating works that portrayed African and African American subjects. The best known of these was probably Richmond Barthé (1901–1989), who—after a childhood and early adulthood spent in Mississippi, Louisiana, and Chicago, Illinois—gained fame as the recipient of a Harmon Foundation award in 1926. Devoted to an ideal kind of African beauty, Barthé created graceful sculptures infused with an African spirit. His most-praised works include *Flute Boy* (1928), which earned him his award; *African Dancer* (1933), the figure of a nude girl with sensually raised arms and an upturned face; and *Feral Benga* (1935), a male figure raising a machete (pronounced muh-SHETT-ee; a long, curved knife) above his head, with the rest of his body forming the bottom half of a graceful "S" curve.

Sargent Johnson (1888–1967), another recipient of Harmon Foundation awards (in 1928 and 1929), was born in Boston and educated at that city's School of Fine Arts. He worked in terra cotta, porcelain, and enameled wood and frequently created sculptures depicting the heads of children. So plain, simple, and expressionless that they resemble African masks, these heads feature full lips, broad noses, and large, almond-shaped eyes. Augusta Savage (1882–1962), a Florida native who traveled to New York City in 1921 to attend the Cooper Union art school, did many portrait sculptures (including the heads of W.E.B. Du Bois, Marcus Garvey (1887–1940), Frederick Douglass (1818–1895), and James Weldon Johnson. Her works were shown at the Philadelphia Sesquicentennial Exposition in 1926 and the Harmon Foundation exhibits of

1928, 1930, and 1931. Savage's sculpture *Gamin,* a realistic yet tender depiction of a Harlem street boy, earned her a scholarship to study art in Rome in 1929. After three years of further study in Paris, Savage founded the Savage Studio of Arts and Crafts in New York. For the rest of her life she worked hard to encourage and support black artists—especially disadvantaged children with artistic talent.

Photographers chronicle the Harlem Renaissance

James Van Der Zee

In addition to the paintings and sculptures of the Harlem Renaissance, some vivid and revealing photographs help to bring the period alive for us today. Many of these were taken by Harlem's most popular and famous photographer,

James Van Der Zee (1886–1983). After opening a studio in Harlem in 1916, Van Der Zee gradually built a reputation as the African American community's photographer of choice. Much in demand for photographs commemorating special occasions, Van Der Zee used carefully crafted background sets of various scenes, among them the garden of a villa or a cozy drawing room with a fireplace. His subjects were always neatly, sharply dressed, and he was known to correct any flaws in clothing or complexion. Thus the people in his photographs were seen in their best light.

Van Der Zee's photographs provide a fascinating and varied chronicle of life in Harlem in the 1920s: they portray famous scenes like A'lelia Walker's "Dark Tower" literary salon and the ceremonies of Marcus Garvey's United Negro Improvement Association, more ordinary events like weddings and funerals, and group photos of bridge clubs, fraternities, and church organizations. Van Der Zee managed to capture the true spirit of the Harlem Renaissance—the self-esteem, confidence, and optimism that people felt and the special style they created—as they forged their identities as "New Negroes."

Carl Van Vechten

In addition to his important role as a white supporter and encourager of Harlem Renaissance writers and as a literary critic and novelist, Carl Van Vechten was a skilled photographer who took many portraits of famous figures of the period, including writers, actors, and musicians. For his portraits of individuals such as Langston Hughes, Zora Neale Hurston (1891–1960; see biographical entry), Countee Cullen, W.E.B. Du Bois, Paul Robeson (1898–1976), and Bessie Smith (c. 1894–1937; see biographical entry), Van Vechten used formal poses and artfully patterned backgrounds. He always portrayed his subjects with dignity, but often made them look somewhat exotic and mysterious. (Some critics claimed that was the way white people expected African Americans to look.)

African American art after the Harlem Renaissance

With the onset of the Great Depression in 1929 came a drying up of funds for the arts. By 1933 the Harmon Foundation had stopped giving monetary awards. But throughout the decade a new breed of African American artists flourished, among them Selma Burke, Romare Bearden, Lois Mailou Jones, and Jacob Lawrence. Their works, like others supported by the Work Projects Administration (WPA; a U.S. government agency founded in 1935 to lower Depression-era unem-

Oscar Micheaux: An Early African American Filmmaker

Among the entertainment choices available to black audiences during the 1920s was viewing the films made by director Oscar Micheaux, who is considered a pioneer of the black film industry. He was born in Illinois (the son of former slaves) and worked as a Pullman (passenger train) porter before settling on a ranch in South Dakota.

Micheaux began his artistic career not as a director but as a writer, penning three pulp fiction novels aimed at black audiences: *Conquest* (1913), *The Forged Note* (1915), and *The Homesteader* (1917). He founded the Micheaux Film Corporation and made a film of *The Homesteader* in 1919 after another film company had expressed interest in the novel but wouldn't let him direct the movie version. Micheaux made the film—a lurid melodrama involving interracial marriage, murder, and a happy ending— for fifteen thousand dollars, shooting no retakes of any scenes.

In the next few years, Micheaux made more than two dozen films, which were shown to segregated black audiences in both the northern and southern states.

Despite bad acting, crude sets, and more action (including Harlem nightclub scenes complete with chorus girls) than solid story lines, the films were very popular. Micheaux was a flashy character and an expert self-promoter who strutted around in big hats and fur coats. He went bankrupt in 1928 but was able to reorganize in 1929, thanks to backing from investors.

In later years, Micheaux was criticized for using only light-skinned performers in his films and for creating stereotypical portraits of black people. Still, he did make a few films with some substance. These included *Within Our Gates* (1920), a lynching story with characters from many different levels of black society; *Birthright* (1924), about a black graduate of Harvard University whose attempt to found a black college in a southern town is thwarted by both white and black opponents; *Body and Soul* (1924), featuring the great African American actor and singer Paul Robeson; and *The House Behind the Cedars*, based on a novel by Charles Waddell Chesnutt and the first film version of a book by a black author.

ployment; called the Works Progress Administration until 1939), tended to depict political and social themes. This was a time of great growth for African American artists. They were given space and an atmosphere of acceptance in which to develop their skills and try new techniques and styles such as mixed media (in which elements of painting, sculpture, and other art forms are combined into one work), abstract art, and social realism.

The WPA came to an end in 1943, setting off a long period of hardship and lack of recognition for black artists. Not until the 1960s would their works be widely seen and appreciated in museums and galleries.

Some early artists and critics considered the visual art of the Harlem Renaissance to be rather uninspired and unadventurous; they claimed that the black artists of the 1920s were too eager for white approval to create original art. Yet, with the passage of time, it has been generally agreed that the artists of the period faced a difficult task: they were trying to gain acceptance in the white-dominated art world while exploring their own unique heritage, identities, and artistic visions. Despite the obstacles, the painters, sculptors, and photographers of the Harlem Renaissance still managed to create many arresting, unforgettable images of African American life in the 1920s.

For More Information

Chederholm, Theresa Dickason. *Afro-American Artists: A Bio-Bibliographical Dictionary.* Boston: Boston Public Library, 1973.

Covarubbias, Miguel. *Negro Drawings.* New York: Knopf, 1927.

Huggins, Nathan Irvin. *Harlem Renaissance.* London: Oxford University Press, 1971.

Kaplan, Margaret, and others, eds. *Harlem Renaissance: Art of Black America.* New York: Harry N. Abrams, 1994.

Kellner, Bruce. *The Harlem Renaissance: A Historical Dictionary for the Era.* Westport, CT: Greenwood Press, 1984.

Mathews, Marcia M. *Henry Ossawa Tanner, American Artist.* Chicago: University of Chicago Press, 1969.

McGhee, Reginald. *The World of James Van Der Zee.* Dobbs Ferry, NY: Morgan & Morgan, 1973.

Powell, Richard J., and others, eds. *Rhapsodies in Black: Art of the Harlem Renaissance.* Berkeley: University of California Press, 1997.

"Oh, play it, Mr. Man!": Harlem Nightlife Is Hot

The 1920s were interesting and unusual years in America's history. World War I (1914–18) had ended and the economy was strong. A Republican government was in power, and mainstream society was dominated by conservatism (the tendency to oppose changes, especially those that lead to greater individual freedom). The majority of Americans wanted to be known as upright, clean-living citizens, and they strove to make as much money as they could. In 1918, what has since been called the "Prohibition Era" began when a widespread movement to curb people's use of alcohol—which was seen as a destructive force in society—resulted in the passage of the Eighteenth Amendment to the U.S. Constitution. This amendment prohibited or banned the "manufacture, sale, or transportation of intoxicating liquors," and the Volstead Act, passed a year later, defined the prohibited liquors as those with more than a 0.5 percent alcohol content. Although most Americans initially supported it, Prohibition was eventually repealed due to the government's inability to enforce it (some claimed the amendment and act had actually caused more crime and corruption than they prevented) and to changing attitudes nationwide (see Chapter 7).

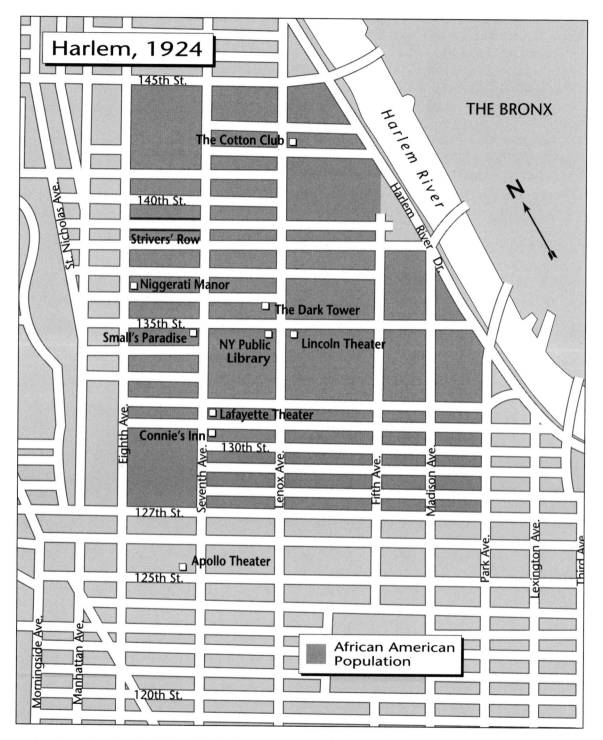

Harlem in the 1920s. *(Map by XNR Productions, Inc.)*

At the same time, however, there was a mood of rebellion in the air. The devastation and bloodshed of World War I had caused some people to turn away from their old values and seek meaning—and also entertainment—in different ways and places than they ever had before. One of these places was Harlem, the center of the vibrant African American culture that had begun to fascinate many whites from other parts of New York City as well as other American and European cities. The old stereotypes about black people still existed, but now people of color were being viewed in a positive light. Before, African Americans had been stereotyped as having loose sexual mores and violent, animalistic natures; in the 1920s, they were viewed as delightfully natural and uninhibited, freed from the restrictions that kept white people in line. (Meanwhile, of course, blacks were still subject to widespread racism and discrimination, and the majority of the African American population still lived in poverty.)

"Harlemania" takes off

The cultural blossoming that took place during the Harlem Renaissance happened partly because of the new interest that white intellectuals, publishers, and patrons of the arts were taking in African American culture. But their interest, and that of many other more ordinary white people, extended even further: it reached into Harlem itself. Suddenly, it had become fun and fashionable for whites to venture into the heart of the African American community—especially very late at night, perhaps after attending a musical show on Broadway—and frequent nightclubs where the very best in black music and dance could be heard and seen. Some of these white visitors actually mingled with black people, but the majority stuck to the clubs with "whites only" policies. That meant that the only black people seen in the clubs were the performers.

The actual residents of Harlem were also enjoying its after-dark sights, sounds, and sensations in clubs and speakeasies (illegal bars or saloons) that catered to blacks and at the rent parties that were a popular form of entertainment for ordinary folks. The leading figures of the Harlem Renaissance were divided in their attitudes toward Harlem's thriving nightlife. Some celebrated and embraced it—like poet

Langston Hughes (1902–1967; see biographical entry), who referred to it often in his work. Some scorned it, or at least avoided mentioning it. Members of the Talented Tenth, for example, disapproved of anything they thought would make black people look bad: bathtub gin (a cheap, homemade liquor popular during Prohibition) and gyrating bodies on dance floors were not their style.

A'Lelia Walker, heiress to the fortune of Madame C.J. Walker, hosted interracial parties at her home on Striver's Row. *(Underwood & Underwood/ Corbis-Bettmann. Reproduced by permission.)*

A'Lelia Walker's Dark Tower

There were a few places, however, where these two worlds overlapped. One such place was a townhouse home on Striver's Row (a neighborhood that was home to Harlem's richest residents). The home belonged to A'Lelia Walker, the flamboyant heir to the fortune of her mother, Madame C. J. Walker, who had made millions selling hair and skin care products to African Americans. In 1928 A'Lelia opened the multi-story Dark Tower, which was part literary gathering place, part nightclub. Visitors could listen to the latest jazz and blues, sung and played by some of Harlem's most gifted performers; There was also a salon, decorated with poems by Langston Hughes and Countee Cullen painted on the walls. The salon was the setting for talk about literature, art, and other lofty topics. For a few years Walker's home was *the* place to be and to be seen; guests ranged from struggling young black writers and Broadway performers to wealthy white New Yorkers and members of European royalty.

The glamorous Savoy Ballroom

Another exciting place to be was the Savoy Ballroom, a glamorous club that opened in March of 1926 and offered twelve continuous hours of dancing every day. The Savoy featured a magnificent marble staircase, a cut-glass chandelier, and a huge dance floor made of polished mahogany wood. It had room for four thousand guests. Customers paid a fifty-cent entrance fee on weeknights, or seventy-five cents on weekends, to do the Lindy Hop or the Shim Sham to the music of bands led by jazz greats such as Fletcher Henderson (1898–1952) and Joe "King" Oliver (1885–1938). Here, whites who were in the habit of "going uptown" to Harlem mingled with those black Harlemites who could afford the costs of entrance, food, and drinks.

The Cotton Club and other hot spots

There was no such mingling at several of Harlem's best-known and biggest nightclubs—most of them located on or near "Jungle Alley," or 133rd Street. These were nightclubs where white people could watch blacks perform in a carefully created atmosphere of "primitive" exoticism without actually interacting with them. The most famous of these was the Cotton Club, located at 142nd Street and Lenox Avenue. Owned by a white gangster and bootlegger (someone who sells illegal liquor) named Owney Madden, the club opened in 1923. It presented Harlem's biggest, most impressive floor shows and was unyielding in its policy of keeping blacks out; even the great jazz composer and bandleader W.C. Handy (1873–1958) was once turned away at the door. Guests were greeted by a doorman and ushered into a big, horseshoe-shaped room fitted out with "jungle" decor and enough seating, arranged in tables on two tiers, for seven hundred people. Patrons were discouraged from loud talk and had to keep their liquor bottles in their pockets, rather than on the floor (during the years of Prohibition, liquor was illegal, so patrons of restaurants and bars brought their own bottles and tried to keep them out of sight). They could enjoy a menu of fried chicken and barbecued ribs or fancier dishes, all of it sold at very high prices. There was a glittering, incredibly athletic, fast-paced two-hour floor show every evening, featuring a main act as well as numbers performed by the Cotton Club's celebrated chorus line (made up of young women who had to be under twenty-one, at least five feet six inches tall, and light-skinned). The club's featured acts included, at various times, singers Ethel Waters (1896–1977;

A performance by the Cotton Club's celebrated chorus line.

(© Bettmann/CORBIS. Reproduced by permission.)

see biographical entry) and Adelaide Hall (1901–1993), dancers Earl "Snakehips" Tucker (1905–1937) and Clayton "Peg Leg" Bates (1902–1998), and bands led by Duke Ellington (1899–1974; see biographical entry) and Cab Calloway (1907–1994). During his tenure, Ellington was able to persuade the club to relax its whites-only rule, but black guests were still given the least desirable, most out-of-the-way seats.

Not quite as fancy as the Cotton Club, Connie's Inn was also not quite as strict about not allowing black patrons. It featured a red canopy, very high prices (which meant that most of its patrons were white), and the famous Tree of Hope right outside the front door: this was an old elm that was supposed to bring anybody who rubbed its bark good luck. Small's Paradise, a club frequented by many blacks, had dancing waiters and "gut-bucket" jam sessions at which musicians improvised on their instruments. "Happy" Rhone's, the first upstairs club, was very swank with its black and white decor and its waitresses (all the other clubs had only male waiters). The Clam House boasted the eccentric and entertaining piano player and singer Gladys Bentley, an avowed lesbian who often wore men's suits and was known for her risqué songs. The music and the decor at the Nest Club were both of high quality, and Pod and Jerry's Catagonia Club was especially popular with white celebrities and jazz musicians like Artie Shaw, Hoagy Carmichael, and Benny Goodman. Other well-known night spots included Barron's, Banks, Basement Brownies, the Bucket of Blood, Leroys, Haynes Oriental, and the Lybia.

Most of the clubs mentioned above catered either to wealthy whites or to blacks with enough money to afford the inflated prices. But that didn't mean that ordinary working people were left out of Harlem's nightlife. They could drop in to any one of hundreds of tiny speakeasies or "dives" located on the side streets off Jungle Alley. One of the most popular was the Sugar Cane, located on the edge of Harlem's toughest neighborhood and reached by climbing down a steep set of stairs to a basement room with space for one hundred bodies (on weekends, though, twice that many people came). These places were gritty and rough compared to the Cotton Club or Small's Paradise, but they offered racially mixed, lively crowds dancing to bands (usually made up of three instruments and a singer) on floors so crowded they led to a new expression called "dancing on a dime," which meant dancing restricted to a mere shuffling of the feet. Cocaine and marijuana were frequently in use at these clubs, which had petty gamblers, pimps, and prostitutes among their clients. Some club owners actually paid off the police so that they could stay open after 3:00 A.M., when the larger clubs closed. These smaller places were often the site of early morning performances by singers and musicians who came in after working their regular jobs.

Rent parties boost pocketbooks and spirits

Working people could also attend rent parties,
Harlem's answer to a unique economic problem. Harlem's residents paid rents that were from twelve to fifteen dollars
higher than those paid in other parts of New York, even
though their salaries were lower than those of white New Yorkers; they spent an average of 40 percent of their incomes on
rent—twice as much as their white counterparts paid for their
apartments. On Monday mornings, landlords tended to throw
the belongings of tenants who hadn't paid their rent out on
the street. That made Saturday night a popular time for rent
parties, although they were also held on other nights of the
week (especially Thursday, when those who worked as maids
usually had the night off). The money guests paid for entrance
(from ten to fifty cents), food, and cheap liquor would help the
host make his or her rent payment.

Anybody could throw a rent party, which was sometimes referred to as a "parlor social" or "whist party" to make

it sound more innocent than it actually was. All that was necessary was to have the Wayside Printer (a traveling cart equipped with printing equipment) make up some cards advertising the party's date, time, and location and distribute the cards in gathering places and to passersby. On the night of the party, the host would clear out the furniture from his or her living room and borrow some chairs from the local undertaker, set up a bar in the hallway, and prepare some food to offer guests. The menu might include boiled pigs' feet, okra gumbo (a soup or stew), hoppin' John (a mixture of pork, rice, and black-eyed peas), collard greens, ham hocks, cabbage, and sweet potato pie.

But the music was the most important part of the rent party. It might be played by a sole piano player (who would earn about five dollars a night) or by a three-piece band with a singer. The musicians would start to set up sometime after 10:00 P.M. and would usually start playing around midnight, playing jazz and blues and often making comments and wisecracks to the dancers crowded around them. ("Do it, you dirty no-gooder!") Sometimes professional musicians would show up after their regular and higher-paying jobs; they referred to rent parties as "jumps" or "shouts" and considered them good settings in which to work on their skills or try out new ideas. Among other attendees were white jazz fans and musicians who, like the famous composer George Gershwin (1898–1937), admired the work of great piano players like Fats Waller (1904–1943) or Willie "The Lion" Smith (see Chapter 4). As quoted in David Levering Lewis's book *When Harlem Was in Vogue,* Smith later recalled that "you would see all kinds of people making the party scene; formally dressed society folks from downtown, policemen, painters, carpenters, mechanics, truckmen in their workingmen's clothes, gamblers, lesbians, and musicians of all kinds."

Carl Van Vechten's parties

Much different from the Harlem rent parties—but also an important part of the Harlem Renaissance social scene—were those gatherings hosted by white literary critic and arts supporter Carl Van Vechten (1880–1964; see biographical entry) and his wife, actress Fania Marinoff, in their posh apart-

Harlem Renaissance Slang

Few Americans realize how many popular terms and expressions come from African American culture—and how many of these originated during the Harlem Renaissance period. Richly expressive and inventive, much of the period's slang has been forgotten, but some of it is still in use today, as the following sample shows.

Ain't got 'em: Has no value.

Air out: Leave or take a stroll.

Bam, down in bam: South, down South ("bam" comes from Alabama).

Bardacious: Wonderful.

Berries: Expression of approval. ("She's the berries.")

Blowing your top: Getting very angry (can also be used when something goes well).

Boogie-woogie: A kind of dancing.

Bookooing: Showing off (from the French word *beaucoup*—very much).

Bull-skating: Bragging.

Chip: To steal.

Cloaker: A liar.

Collar a hot: To eat a meal.

Collar a nod: To sleep.

Cruising: Parading, sauntering, or looking for a pick-up.

Diddy-wah-diddy: A far-off place.

Dickty or dicty: Grand, fancy.

Dig: To understand ("Do you dig?"); may come from an African word, *dega,* meaning to understand.

Dog it: To show off, to strut ("put on the dog").

Doing the dozens: To insult someone's parents (usually the mother).

Draped down: Fashionably dressed.

First thing smoking: A train. ("I'm leaving on the first thing smoking.")

Freeby, freebie: Something for nothing.

Funky: Smelly, or sexy.

Gum beater: A braggart or idle talker.

Gut bucket: A sleazy cabaret, or loud, vulgar music.

Haul bottom, haul hiney: Get moving, get busy.

Hauling: Running away.

Hincty: Snooty.

Hoof: To dance.

Hot: Wonderful.

Hunky hunk: A term of endearment for a black male.

ment on West 55th Street in Manhattan. The Van Vechtens made a point of inviting guests of all races to their parties for, as Marinoff explained, they were "engaged in a crusade to break down the color bar." Indeed, these gatherings were much enjoyed by both black and white guests. In his living room decorated in the most fashionable 1920s style—using the colors raspberry, purple, and turquoise with a wide variety

Hush mah mouf! An expression of astonishment; "mah mouf" translates as "my mouth."

I shot him lightly and he died politely: "I overwhelmed him," physically or intellectually.

Jump salty: To get angry.

Knock yourself out: Have a good time.

Lily-livered: Cowardly.

Miss Anne: A white female.

Mister Charlie, Mister Eddie: A white male.

Mule blood: Black molasses.

Naps: Kinky hair.

Now you cookin' with gas: Now you're on the right track.

Ofay: A white person (from Pig Latin for foe), sometimes shortened to fay.

Pick: To rob or gyp.

Righteous: Correct.

Righteous rags: Stylish clothing.

Rug-cutter: A person who goes to rent parties and "cuts up" the host's rugs with his feet; or a good dancer.

Russian: A southern black who has moved north in a hurry ("rushin'" to get there).

Scarf: To eat.

Sell out: To run away in fear.

Shin dig: An extremely crowded party where one's shins got kicked while dancing.

Shout: A ball or prom.

Sobbing hearted: Broken-hearted.

Solid: Perfect.

Stomp: A raucous party with dancing.

Stroll: To do something well. ("He's really strolling.")

Swap spit: To kiss.

Syndicating: To gossip.

The Big Apple: New York City.

The man: The law, the boss, whoever is in charge.

Tight: Tough or hard.

Too bad!: Wonderful.

Trucking: Strolling (also a dance step).

You're breaking me down: You're wearing me out; you're too much.

Source: The Harlem Renaissance: A Historical Dictionary for the Era, *edited by Bruce Kellner. Westport, CT: Greenwood Press, 1984.*

of accessories such as cut-glass chandeliers and oriental rugs—Van Vechten served the best bootlegged gin to a multitude of friends and acquaintances. At his parties young African American writers and performers met editors, publishers, producers, and other people with the power, money, and influence to help support their work. Singers like Bessie Smith (c. 1894–1937; see biographical entry) sometimes sang for the other guests, and poets like Langston Hughes (1902–1967; see biographical entry) recited their work. Audiences might include such famous individuals as George Gershwin, novelists Fannie Hurst and Theodore Dreiser, publisher Horace Liveright, and poet Elinor Wylie.

For More Information

Bontemps, Arna, ed. *The Harlem Renaissance Remembered*. New York: Dodd, Mead, 1972.

Emery, Lynne Fauley. *Black Dance in the United States from 1619 to 1970*. Palo Alto, CA: National Press Books, 1980.

Huggins, Nathan Irvin. *Voices of the Harlem Renaissance*. New York: Oxford University Press, 1976.

Kellner, Bruce, ed. *The Harlem Renaissance: A Historical Dictionary for the Era*. Westport, CT: Greenwood Press, 1984.

Lewis, David Levering. *When Harlem Was in Vogue*. New York: Knopf, 1981.

Major, Clarence. *The Cotton Club*. Detroit: Broadside Press, 1973.

Mapp, Edward. *Dictionary of Blacks in the Performing Arts*. Metuchen, NJ: Scarecrow Press, 1978.

Watson, Steven. *The Harlem Renaissance: Hub of African-American Culture, 1920–1930*. New York: Pantheon Books, 1995.

"... a swell time while it lasted ...": The End of the Harlem Renaissance

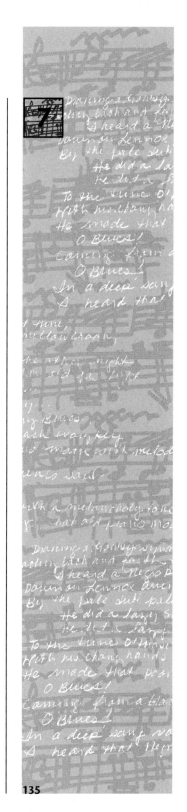

In his autobiography, *The Big Sea,* Langston Hughes (1902–1967; see biographical entry) wrote of the Harlem Renaissance: "I was there. I had a swell time while it lasted. But I thought it wouldn't last long.... For how could a large and enthusiastic number of people be crazy about Negroes forever?"

The effect of the Great Depression on the Harlem Renaissance

Just as modern-day critics and historians disagree on when exactly the Harlem Renaissance began, none can pinpoint the moment it ended. Some say that it died naturally because it did not have a strong enough foundation to last. Others say the loss of certain key people—to jobs and lives outside of Harlem or to death—triggered its demise. Still others claim that the end of Prohibition (a ban on the "manufacture, sale, or transportation of intoxicating liquors" that began with the 1918 passage of the 18th Amendment to the Constitution and ended with the repeal of the amendment in 1933 after the government was no longer able to enforce it; see Chapter 6) made "going

Most residents of Harlem enjoyed relatively good economic times during the 1920s.
(© Underwood & Underwood/CORBIS. Reproduced by permission.)

uptown" unnecessary and not so glamorous, taking Harlem out of the spotlight. But all agree that the biggest reason for the decline of the Harlem Renaissance was the dawn of the Great Depression, a period of economic downturn that caused widespread poverty and suffering for millions of Americans.

The Depression lasted from approximately 1929 (when the stock market collapsed) until the United States entered

World War II in 1941, when the demand for war-related materials and supplies created jobs and gave the economy a big boost. Throughout the 1920s the U.S. economy was weakened by a number of factors, among them (1) the tendency of many Americans to spend more money than they earned and to rely on credit to buy what they wanted; (2) an uneven distribution of wealth that put the largest part of the profits earned by big businesses into the hands of a small percentage of people; and (3) unwise lending practices by American banks.

At the same time, the stock market was growing too fast, as investors eager to get rich quick paid inflated prices for stocks. Then, toward the end of the 1920s, people began to think that they would lose the money they had invested in stocks. Large numbers of investors panicked and sold their stocks, causing the stock market "crash" and losses estimated at thirty billion dollars. The result was dismal: the production and sale of goods in the United States declined rapidly, and so did the employment rate. Soon more than fifteen million Americans (about one-quarter of the workforce) were out of work.

The Great Depression had a devastating effect on Harlem's African American community. Median family income went from $1,808 in 1929 to $1,019 in 1932, a 43.6 percent decrease in only three years. Yet migrants continued to flood into Harlem, so rents stayed high. Even though the number of black professionals had grown by 69 percent between 1920 and 1930 (according to research by sociologist Charles S. Johnson at Fisk University), those who would come of age in the 1930s faced a bleak future as black banks and businesses collapsed and the funds for education dried up.

Harlem undergoes a change

Hard economic times meant a cultural downturn as well, as Harlem began its descent from a thriving center of black life to a community beset by poverty and crime. Now only the richest people, black or white, could afford Harlem's fancy, expensive nightclubs; everybody else went to the shabbier speakeasies. Meanwhile, music fans were becoming more interested in the sophisticated sounds of "swing," and the jazz center moved south, away from Harlem and into downtown Manhattan.

The Scottsboro Boys with
their defense attorney
Sam Liebowitz (seated
front, left). Many people
felt that the accusations
against the boys were
racially motivated.
*(UPI/Corbis-Bettmann.
Reproduced by permission.)*

The Scottsboro Boys with their defense attorney Sam Liebowitz (seated front, left). Many people felt that the accusations against the boys were racially motivated. *(UPI/Corbis-Bettmann. Reproduced by permission.)*

Racism, however, seemed just as strong as ever, as
shown by the 1931 case of the Scottsboro Boys. These nine
Alabama youths, whose ages ranged from thirteen to nineteen, had been accused of raping two white prostitutes, one
of whom later reversed her story. The evidence against them
was extremely flimsy, yet eight of the nine were convicted
and sentenced to death (the youngest received life imprisonment). Many people felt that the accusations and convictions

were racially motivated. A widespread public outcry finally led to several new trials, and five of the youths were released while the other four spent long terms in prison. For blacks as well as whites concerned about civil rights, the case highlighted the fact that the battle against racism and injustice was far from over.

It's not over yet

Nevertheless, for a few years after the stock market crash, some things remained much the same as they had been during the glory years of the Harlem Renaissance. There were still accomplishments to laud and interesting things to do and see. A number of major literary works were published between 1929 and 1931, including novels by Wallace Thurman (*The Blacker the Berry*; see biographical entry), Claude McKay (*Banjo*; see biographical entry) and Langston Hughes (*Not without Laughter*; see biographical entry), poetry by Countee Cullen (*The Black Christ*; see biographical entry); and James Weldon Johnson's history of Harlem, *Black Manhattan*. In 1929 both Thurman's drama *Harlem* and the musical revue *Ain't Misbehavin'* opened on Broadway. Duke Ellington appeared with his orchestra in a short film called *Black and Tan,* and the Harmon Foundation sponsored an exhibition of works by African American artists at the National Gallery and a traveling exhibit that was viewed by 150,000 people around the United States.

Still, things had changed, and they would change even more over the next few years. The wealthy whites who had supported African American writers and other artists with money and encouragement could no longer afford to do so, or they just weren't as interested as they had been; "we were no longer in vogue," remembered Langston Hughes. In addition, conflicts and events that occurred within the ranks of the Harlem Renaissance leadership helped bring the period to a close.

"... the end of the gay times ...."

One such event was the death of heiress and hostess A'lelia Walker, whose nightclub and literary salon, the Dark Tower, had been a popular and fashionable gathering place for what Zora Neale Hurston (1891–1960; see biographical entry) called "the Niggerati" (the innovative young black writers and artists who formed the core of the Harlem Renaissance) and their followers. Walker had long suffered from high blood pressure, and she died suddenly from a heart attack on August 17, 1931. Laid out in a silver casket, her body was viewed by several thousand mourners. Her crowded funeral featured a eulogy delivered by the distinguished Reverend Adam Clayton Powell, Sr. and a performance of popular songwriter Noel Coward's "I'll See You Again" by a group called the Four Bon Bons. Walker's luxurious Long Island mansion, Villa Lewaro, had already been auctioned off, and her Harlem townhouse was leased to the city. Remembering the funeral, Hughes wrote in *The Big Sea:* "That was really the end of the gay times of the New Negro in Harlem."

But there were a few more sad events to come. The younger generation of the Harlem Renaissance was again reminded of its own mortality with the deaths of writers Wallace Thurman (1902–1934) and Rudolph Fisher (1897–1934), which occurred within days of each other in 1934. Thurman suffered from tuberculosis and other ailments, and his doctor had warned him to stop drinking alcohol. Depressed and deeply disappointed in himself (despite what other people saw as some major achievements), Thurman not only ignored his doctor's warning but went on a drinking binge that led to his death in the charity ward of a New York hospital. Fisher, a radiologist, died of cancer that may have been caused by exposure to his own x-ray equipment.

The lives of other Harlem Renaissance notables were moving in different directions as well. During the 1930s Alain Locke (1886–1954; see biographical entry) turned all of his attention to his work as a Howard University professor. In a letter to Charlotte Mason (quoted in David Levering Lewis's *When Harlem Was in Vogue*), he commented: "I know it isn't the end of the world, but it is the end of an era." W.E.B. Du Bois (1868–1963; see biographical entry) left the editorship of the financially troubled *Crisis* in 1934, after puzzling his friends with his advocacy of voluntary segregation as the only solution to racism. James Weldon Johnson (1871–1938) resigned his position as leader of the National Association for the Advancement of Colored People (NAACP) and joined the staff at Fisk University as a professor of creative writing. Charles S.

Johnson (1893–1956) and painter Aaron Douglas (1899–1979; see biographical entry) also took jobs at Fisk. Jessie Fauset (1882–1961; see biographical entry) wrote *The Chinaberry Tree* and *Comedy, American Style* before marrying and settling into life as a New Jersey homemaker.

Few of the Harlem Renaissance writers retained the glory and prominence they had once enjoyed. The immensely promising and innovative Jean Toomer (1894–1967; see biographical entry) wrote little after becoming involved with the Gurdjieff movement (which held that people could achieve higher consciousness through a balance of mind, soul, and body) and even claimed that he considered himself not black but "American, simply an American." Countee Cullen (1903–1946; see biographical entry) received little fanfare and no glowing reviews for his poems in *The Black Christ* or for his novel *One Way to Heaven,* and in 1934 he returned to DeWitt Clinton High School, where he had been a student, to teach French. Cullen remained there until his death in 1946. Claude McKay (1890–1948; see biographical entry), who had left Harlem for Europe and North Africa before the renaissance began, returned after it had ended and tried unsuccessfully to establish a magazine that would appeal to a wide spectrum of African Americans. He published two nonfiction works, the autobiographical *A Long Way from Home* (1937) and *Harlem: Negro Metropolis* (1940) and surprised his former friends by converting to Catholicism just before his death in 1948.

Hurston and Hughes continue their careers

Two notable figures who produced significant works in the post-Harlem Renaissance years were Zora Neale Hurston and Langston Hughes. Yet, due to a disagreement over shared work on a play called *Mule Bone,* these two talented people spoke to each other only once over the next few decades. *Mule Bone* was to be a three-act comedy based on a folktale collected by Hurston during her travels in the South. Wealthy patron Charlotte Mason (see Chapter 2) paid the rent on a house in New Jersey where Hurston and Hughes worked together on the play. Then, Hurston went off on a trip to Florida, and Hughes traveled to Cuba and other places in pursuit of other projects. Later, Hughes heard that Hurston was marketing *Mule Bone* as

Cover of the Playbill for _Mule Bone_ by Zora Neale Hurston and Langston Hughes. The writers had a falling out over shared work on the play and it wasn't staged until 1991, long after both authors' deaths. _(Playbill is a registered trademark. Reproduced by permission.)_

PLAYBILL®

ETHEL BARRYMORE THEATRE

MULE BONE

her own creation; her refusal to acknowledge Hughes's role caused a permanent rift between the two, and the play was not staged until 1991.

This conflict aside, however, Hurston's career thrived after 1932, when she turned away from Mason's sheltering embrace and monetary support. The publication of _Their Eyes Were Watching God_—widely regarded as her finest work and a masterpiece of American literature—came in 1937. Hurston also produced an autobiography, *Dust Tracks on a Road* (1942), and another novel, *Seraph on the Suwanee*; 1948) which were praised by critics but not very popular with readers. Finally she retired from literary pursuits to live on a houseboat and support herself with low-paying jobs. Hurston died poor in 1960 and was buried in an anonymous grave, but in 1973 writer Alice Walker—who greatly admired Hurston's work—located what she thought was probably Hurston's burial site and placed a memorial stone there.

Langston Hughes was one of few Harlem Renaissance stars to enjoy a fully successful career and public adoration until the end of his life. But this occurred after he endured some painful events, especially the ending of his relationships with both Charlotte Mason and Zora Neale Hurston. It was with deep regret that Hughes broke with Mason, who seems to have served not only as a material supporter but also as a maternal figure to him. Her idea that African American writers should produce "primitive" works finally became too limiting for Hughes, and when he told Mason that he wanted to write according to his own creative vision, not hers, and could no longer accept her support, she gave him a strong tongue-lashing and sent him on his way. Then Hughes's friendship with Hurston came to a nasty end with the conflict over *Mule Bone*. Hughes recovered his spirits somewhat during a poetry-reading tour of the Deep South and the West, and he published a volume of short stories called *The Ways of White Folk* (1934) that featured satires of various Harlem Renaissance figures, including Charlotte Mason and Carl Van Vechten. In 1932 Hughes traveled to Russia with a group of twenty young people, very few of them actors, who had been hired to appear in a Russian-produced film (to be called *Black and White*) about the problems and experiences of African Americans since the Civil War. The group was very warmly received in Moscow, but the film was never made, due partly to the participants' lack of acting ability and a bad script and partly to Russia's reluctance to offend the U.S. government.

Hughes continued to travel extensively, both overseas and in the United States, and his poetry became more politically radical as his frustrations over black people's continued suffering grew. Eventually he returned to Harlem. There, he put his talent to use in many different ways over the next several decades, writing not only poetry but also nonfiction articles, essays, and even song lyrics. By the end of his life he was revered as the best-known, and perhaps the most influential, figure in African American literature.

Writers shift their focus

As the Great Depression tightened its grim hold on the United States, novelists and other artists began turning away from the literary experimentation of the 1920s. Their focus shifted toward realism and highlighting larger social issues. Major writers like Sherwood Anderson, John Dos Passos, and Theodore Dreiser were creating works that portrayed the struggles of ordinary Americans in hard times, and their writings often revealed their leftist (the belief that society needs to change to benefit all citizens) attitudes. Many writers were even touting communism (an economic system that promotes the ownership of all property by the community as a whole) as the only solution to society's ills; both Langston Hughes and Countee Cullen, for example, supported the Communist Party's candidate in the U.S. presidential election of 1932.

The New Deal disappoints African Americans

That candidate did not win, however. The winner of the presidential race was Franklin Delano Roosevelt (1882–1945), the Democratic party candidate. He had gained the support of several groups of voters—blacks among them—who had never voted for a Democrat before. (African Americans traditionally voted Republican because the man they credited with ending slavery, President Abraham Lincoln, had been a Republican.) Roosevelt promised not only to help those hurt by the Depression but also to work for expanded civil rights for blacks. The program of reforms he sponsored, which he called the "New Deal," did indeed bring hope and jobs to unemployed, desperate Americans, but Roosevelt did not really live up to his promise of helping African Americans. He told black leaders that he could not afford to offend the "Dixiecrats," a group of powerful southern politicians whose support he needed to push his reforms through Congress and who were opposed to granting blacks more civil rights.

African Americans were very discouraged with how slowly they were moving toward full equality. It seemed that no matter how smart or talented they were or what great things they created or did, they could never prove their worth to whites. Despite the grand predictions of Alain Locke and others that black achievements would lead to recognition and respect from white America, the Harlem Renaissance had not sparked any real changes. A new spirit seemed to overtake Harlem—a spirit of disappointment—and the communal feeling that had once prevailed (the feeling of we-are-all-in-this-together) began to fade. Even the Tree of Hope outside the famous Connie's Inn (see Chapter 6), some superstitious people noted, was ailing.

A burst of anger

Disappointment led to frustration among black Americans, and frustration finally erupted into anger and violence. One of the issues that had come to disturb Harlem residents was the fact that few of the many white-owned businesses in Harlem, whose profits came from black customers, hired black employees, particularly in positions of responsibility. There were some peaceful organized protests, but finally, on March 19, 1935, the African American community expressed its rage through rioting and destruction on Harlem's Lenox Avenue. The incident was fueled by the rumored beating death of a teenager who had been roughed up by white store clerks after being caught shoplifting. In the end, three blacks were killed, thirty were injured, and more than a hundred were jailed; the approximately twenty thousand participants had caused a two-million-dollar loss to white-owned commercial property. This event suggested to many that a new, more brutal, era had begun in Harlem.

Taking stock of the Harlem Renaissance

Even at its height, the Harlem Renaissance was viewed by some as a shallow movement, in which the most privileged members of the African American community amused themselves while the less privileged continued to suffer in much the same way they always had. And there were those who said that

Lenox Avenue in the heart of Harlem in 1935.

(Corbis-Bettmann. Reproduced by permission.)

the Harlem Renaissance occurred mostly for the benefit of white people whose interest in African American culture was just a passing fad.

In the years following the Harlem Renaissance, African Americans endured trying times as they struggled to define themselves within their country's wider culture. Contemporary black writers like Richard Wright, James Baldwin, and Alice Walker have faulted some Harlem Renaissance artists for appealing to only a small segment of the black audience, but they have also admitted that the period left an artistic foundation upon which later writers, painters, and musicians could, and did, build. The innovative jazz-influenced poetry of Langston Hughes, the skillfully written and colorful short stories of Jean Toomer, the novels of Claude McKay and Jessie Redmon Fauset, the paintings of Aaron Douglas, and the music of Fats Waller and Duke Ellington—these are all real achievements. They are worth remembering, worth studying, and still enjoyable and enriching for today's readers and audiences. As critic George Kent wrote in the June 1972 issue of *Black World* magazine, the talented participants in the Harlem Renaissance "made paths through what had been stubborn thickets." For one short but thrilling decade, they created a world that had never before existed.

For More Information

Bontemps, Arna. *The Harlem Renaissance Remembered.* New York: Dodd, Mead, 1972.

Huggins, Nathan Irvin. *Harlem Renaissance.* New York: Oxford University Press, 1971.

Kellner, Bruce, ed. *The Harlem Renaissance: A Historical Dictionary for the Era.* Westport, CT: Greenwood Press, 1984.

Lewis, David Levering. *When Harlem Was in Vogue.* New York: Knopf, 1981.

Watson, Steven. *The Harlem Renaissance: Hub of African-American Culture, 1920–1930.* New York: Pantheon Books, 1995.

Biographies

Countee Cullen

Born May 30, 1903
Most sources say Louisville, Kentucky
Died January 9, 1946
New York, New York

American poet, novelist, and dramatist

"If I am going to be a poet at all, I am going to be a POET and not a NEGRO poet."

Countee Cullen.
(The Bettmann Archive/ Corbis-Bettmann. Reproduced by permission.)

One of the most promising young poets of the Harlem Renaissance, Countee Cullen was a favorite of the Talented Tenth (as defined by W.E.B. Du Bois and his followers, the most accomplished and ambitious segment of African American society) due both to his gentlemanly personal style and his highly acclaimed poetry. Cullen wished to be recognized on his own merits and struggled against being defined as a "black" poet. His writing style reflected his regard for the nineteenth-century poets of the romantic movement (romanticism was a movement in literature that promoted emotion and imagination), including John Keats (1795–1821), Percy Bysshe Shelley (1792–1822), and William Wordsworth (1770–1850). Unlike Langston Hughes (1902–1967; see biographical entry)—his chief competitor for the title of Harlem's leading poet—Cullen employed traditional verse forms like the sonnet and the ballad, and he used a formal voice instead of the blues- and jazz-influenced "street" language Hughes used. Much of Cullen's poetry does reflect his concern about racial issues, though, even if he chose to express those concerns in a more conventional way than other Harlem Renaissance writers.

A mysterious childhood

Not much is known about Cullen's earliest years. At different times in his life he stated that his birthplace was New York or Baltimore, but he was probably born in Louisville, Kentucky, in 1903 to a woman named Elizabeth Lucas. His father seems to have disappeared before or soon after his birth. Cullen was raised by a woman named Elizabeth Porter, who was probably his paternal grandmother and who was then living in Baltimore, Maryland. Porter later moved to New York City and opened a home for abandoned children. After her death in 1918, Cullen was unofficially adopted by the Reverend Frederick Asbury Cullen and his wife, Carolyn Mitchell Cullen. Reverend Cullen was the pastor of Harlem's largest congregation, the Salem Methodist Episcopal Church, and his graceful, quiet wife sang soprano in the church choir. The reverend was also a political activist who worked hard to improve the lot of black people; he was president of the Harlem chapter of the National Association for the Advancement of Colored People (NAACP) and an organizer of the Silent Protest Parade (see Chapter 1). Countee Cullen apparently loved and admired his adoptive mother and father very much and no doubt absorbed their political awareness, though he never shared their religious enthusiasm.

A high school achiever

Cullen started writing poetry while he was still in elementary school. At the mostly white DeWitt Clinton High School, he was active in student government and a member of the Inter-High School Poetry Society. He was editor of the school's literary magazine, *The Magpie,* which published his poem "I Have a Rendevous with Life" in its January 1921 issue. Even before finishing high school, Cullen was recognized as an outstanding young poet when he won a citywide poetry contest sponsored by the Federation of Women's Clubs. He graduated from DeWitt Clinton on January 26, 1922, with an excellent academic record.

Cullen soon discovered a thriving community of African American writers who met at the 135th Street branch of the New York Public Library to discuss literature and read their work, and he became a central figure in their group. Even from these early days he was described as a "perfect gentleman"; always well dressed, he had unfailing good manners and a sunny, outgoing disposition. Like W.E.B. Du Bois (1898–1963; see biographical entry), whom he worshiped, he believed in projecting a positive image as a way to gain respect. A year before his high school graduation, in an interview with the Brooklyn *Eagle* newspaper, Cullen stated: "If I am going to be a poet at all, I am going to be a POET and not a NEGRO poet." These ideals would continue to shape his approach to poetry and distinguish him from other Harlem Renaissance poets.

Harlem's promising poet

Cullen went on to study at New York University (NYU). During his sophomore year (1923), he won second prize in the Witter Bynner Poetry Contest (open to all American undergraduates) for "The Ballad of the Brown Girl." This poem is a retelling of an old, western European ballad, putting the story of a young girl who is wronged by her higher-born lover into an African American context. In Cullen's version, a brown girl who has married a white man stabs a white woman who speaks out against the interracial marriage. The husband then kills his wife; in the end, he too ends up dead. Cullen portrays the brown girl as the energetic, passionate descendent of kings, while the white people in the poem are passionless and unfeeling. "The Ballad of the Brown Girl" provides an early example of Cullen's sense of black people's alien status in society; it also illustrates his use of elements of African heritage in verse. In a *New York Times* interview he commented that even though he struggled against his racial consciousness, "it colors my writing, I fear, in spite of everything that I can do."

Over the next two years Cullen continued to develop his craft and build his reputation. In 1924 he won an honor-

 "Incident" by Countee Cullen

Once riding in old Baltimore,
Heart-filled, head-filled with glee,
I saw a Baltimorean
Keep looking straight at me.

Now I was eight and very small,
And he was no whit bigger,
And so I smiled, but he poked out
His tongue, and called me, "Nigger."

I saw the whole of Baltimore
From May until December;
Of all the things that happened there
That's all that I remember.

From On These I Stand, *Amistead Research Center, Tulane University, New Orleans, Louisiana. Administered by JJKR Associates. Reproduced by permission.*

"Heritage" by Countee Cullen

What is Africa to me:
Copper sun or scarlet sea,
Jungle star or jungle track,
Strong bronzed men, or regal black
Women from whose loins I sprang
When the birds of Eden sang?
One three centuries removed
From the scenes his fathers loved,
Spicy grove, cinnamon tree,
What is Africa to me?

So I lie, who all day long
Want no sound except the song
Sung by wild barbaric birds
Goading massive jungle herds,
Juggernauts of flesh that pass
Trampling tall defiant grass
Where young forest lovers lie,
Plighting troth beneath the sky.
So I lie, who will always hear,
Through I cram against my ear
Both my thumbs, and keep them there,
Great drums throbbing through the air.
So I lie, whose fount of pride,
Dear distress, and joy allied,
Is my somber flesh and skin,
With the dark blood dammed within
Like great pulsing tides of wine
That, I fear, must burst the fine
Channels of the chafing net
Where they surge and foam and fret.

Africa? A book one thumbs
Listlessly, till slumber comes.
Unremembered are her bats

Circling through the night, her cats
Crouching in the river reeds,
Stalking gentle flesh that feeds
By the river bank; no more
Does the bugle-throated roar
Cry that monarch claws have leapt
From the scabbards where they slept.
Silver snakes that once a year
Doff the lovely coats you wear,
Seek no covert in your fear
Lest a mortal eye should see;
What's your nakedness to me?
Here no leprous flowers rear
Fierce corollas in the air;
Here no bodies sleek and wet,
Dripping mingled rain and sweat,
Tread the savage measures of
Jungle boys and girls in love.
What is last year's snow to me,
Last year's anything? The tree
Budding yearly must forget
How its past arose or set—
Bough and blossom, flower, fruit,
Even what shy bird with mute
Wonder at her travail there,
Meekly labored in its hair.
One three centuries removed
From the scenes his fathers loved,
Spicy grove, cinnamon tree,
What is Africa to me?

So I lie, who find no peace
Night or day, no slight release
From the unremittant beat
Made by cruel padded feet

Walking through my body's street.
Up and down they go, and back,
Treading out a jungle track.
So I lie, who never quite
Safely sleep from rain at night—
I can never rest at all
When the rain begins to fall;
Like a soul gone mad with pain
I must watch its weird refrain;
Ever must I twist and squirm,
Writhing like a baited worm,
While its primal measures drip
Through my body, crying, "Strip!
Doff this new exuberance.
Come and dance the Lover's Dance!"
In an old remembered way
Rain works on me night and day.

Quaint, outlandish heathen gods
Black men fashion out of rods,
Clay, and brittle bits of stone,
In a likeness like their own,
My conversion came high-priced;
I belong to Jesus Christ,
Preacher of humility;
Heathen gods are naught to me.

Father, Son, and Holy Ghost,
So I make an idle boast;
Jesus of the twice-turned cheek,
Lamb of God, although I speak
With my mouth thus, in my heart
Do I play a double part.
Ever at Thy glowing altar
Must my heart grow sick and falter,

Wishing He I served were black,
Thinking then it would not lack
Precedent of pain to guide it,
Let who would or might deride it;
Surely then this flesh would know
Yours had borne a kindred woe.
Lord, I fashion dark gods, too,
Daring even to give You
Dark despairing features where,
Crowned with dark rebellious hair,
Patience wavers just so much as
Mortal grief compels, while touches
Quick and hot, of anger, rise
To smitten cheek and weary eyes.
Lord, forgive me if my need
Sometimes shapes a human creed.

All day long and all night through,
One thing only must I do:
Quench my pride and cool my blood,
Lest I perish in the flood.
Lest a hidden ember set
Timber that I thought was wet
Burning like the dryest flax,
Melting like the merest wax,
Lest the grave restore its dead.
Not yet has my heart or head
In the least way realized
They and I are civilized.

From On These I Stand, *Amistead Research Center, Tulane University, New Orleans, ouisiana. Administered by JJKR Associates. Reproduced by permission.*

able mention in the Witter Bynner contest for a poem called "Spirit Birth." His most eventful year, however, was 1925, when he won second prize in *Opportunity* magazine's literary contest for "One Who Said Me Nay," *Poetry* magazine's John Reed Memorial Prize for "Threnody for a Brown Girl" (threnody means song for the dead), and *Crisis*'s Spingarn medal for "Two Moods of Love." In addition, Cullen won first prize in the 1925 Witter Bynner contest (with renowned poet Carl Sandburg serving as a judge) and graduated from NYU as one of only eleven graduates that year elected to the Phi Beta Kappa honor society.

Color is published

But perhaps the most exciting event in Cullen's life that year was the publication of his first volume of poetry, *Color* (1925), which contains many of the poems for which he would be most famous. Most of these are collected in the first of the book's three sections, entitled "Color," which explores such themes as racial identity, the effects of racism on self-esteem, and the meaning of a black American's African heritage. The often-quoted "Yet Do I Marvel" is a sonnet in which the speaker accepts God's wisdom but wonders why He would be so cruel as to make a poet black and yet "bid him sing" in a world too racist to accept him. In "Incident," the speaker recalls his first encounter with racism when he was a child on a trip to Baltimore; all he remembers of the trip is a white boy calling him "nigger." "Heritage" is a long poem meditating on the speaker's attraction to the land of his ancestors, even though he feels very distant from it. The volume's other sections are "Epitaphs," with poems about poets John Keats and Paul Laurence Dunbar (1872–1906); and "Varia," featuring such titles as "She of the Dancing Feet Sings" and "To John Keats, Poet. At Springtime."

Cullen was by this time at the peak of his fame as Harlem's most promising poet. As reported in Stephen Watson's book *The Harlem Renaissance: Hub of African-American Culture, 1920–1930*, *New Negro* anthologist and Harlem Renaissance cheerleader Alain Locke (1886–1954; see biographical entry) enthused, "Ladies and gentlemen! A genius! Posterity will laugh at us if we do not proclaim him now." Meanwhile, Cullen enrolled at Harvard University to pursue a master's degree, which he received in 1926. He became assistant editor at *Opportunity,* working under the magazine's dynamic editor, Charles S. Johnson (1893–1956; see Chapter 2). Cullen began writing his own column, *The Dark Tower,* in December 1926 (it would run in *Opportunity* through September 1928), using it not only to comment on, publicize, and celebrate works by African American authors but also to articulate his own ideas about literature. One of these ideas was that black writers should not make their work too "racial," but should instead keep it as accessible as possible to white readers and thus gain wider acceptance. Although Cullen admired Langston Hughes as a poet, for example, he disapproved of those Hughes poems that exposed the darker, seedier underside of black life; some things, Cullen asserted, shouldn't be "broadcast ... to the world."

More poetry, and a wedding

In 1927 Cullen published two books: *The Ballad of a Brown Girl,* which was appearing for the first time as a separate volume; and *Copper Sun,* which contains poems on such subjects as love, religion, and African American racial heritage. One of the best poems in this volume is "From the Dark Tower," a sonnet about the black experience that depicts black people as builders of America who have not been allowed to reap the bounty they helped to sow; for now, they hide their pain behind masks, but someday they may turn from suffering to rebellion. "Threnody for a Brown Girl" centers on the death of an African American girl and the irony of honoring her with a white tombstone, since white is the color of oppression.

Cullen made an important contribution to African American literature with *Caroling Dusk: An Anthology of Verse by Negro Poets* (1927), which features contributions by most of the younger Harlem Renaissance writers. *Caroling Dusk* was one of the first anthologies to showcase the work of black poets. In his introduction to the volume, Cullen expresses his belief that black American writers have a stronger link to the American and English literary tradition than to African culture and that they should try to make their work a bridge between the races.

On April 10, 1928, Cullen found himself at the center of one of the biggest social events of the Harlem Renaissance when he married Nina Yolande Du Bois, daughter of W.E.B. Du Bois. All of Harlem's leading citizens came out for this glamorous spectacle. Thirteen hundred guests were invited to the wedding, and another thousand milled around outside the church. When it was over, though, Cullen returned to his post at *Opportunity* in New York and Du Bois went back to her teaching job in Baltimore. Two months later Cullen—who had received a fellowship from the Guggenheim Foundation that would allow him to study and write as he pleased—sailed for France with his best friend, Harold Jackman. The marriage to Du Bois was not a success, due both to the couple's basic incompatibility and to Cullen's alleged homosexuality; they were divorced in Paris in 1930. W.E.B. Du Bois remained loyal to Cullen, however, blaming his daughter for the breakup.

Literary career declines

In France, Cullen worked on the poems that were published in *The Black Christ and Other Poems* (1929), which was not highly praised by critics. Strongly evident in this volume is Cullen's continuing struggle with the problem, as he had described it in his introduction to *Caroling Dusk,* "of reconciling a Christian upbringing with a pagan inclination." It seemed that Cullen was now moving closer to Christianity. The title poem tells the story of a black man, Jim, who has rebelled against his mother's faith but who seems to achieve a mystical resurrection after being lynched. *The Black Christ* also contains some notable poems about love in which Cullen expresses a mistrust of women and a linking of love with death, a theme that critics have detected in much of his work.

By the end of the 1920s Cullen had written all of the poetry for which he would later be remembered. His only novel, *One Way to Heaven* (1932), was not well received, drawing few comments even from his most loyal supporters. Its main plot concerns a straitlaced Harlem maid named Mattie Johnson who marries a supposedly reformed gambler and con man, Sam Lucas; a subplot features Constancia Brandon, a Harlem hostess whose gatherings allow Cullen to satirize the African American community's partygoing crowd. The weak connection between these two plots, critics agreed, spoils the novel's impact.

In 1934 Cullen took a job teaching French and English at Frederick Douglass High School in Harlem, where he would stay for the remaining twelve years of his life. There he tried to nurture a new generation of African American achievers (including writer James Baldwin [1924–1987], who would later gain fame for *The Fire Next Time* and other acclaimed works), encouraging a love of poetry among his students. The last collection of Cullen's poems published before his death, *The Medea and Some Poems* (1935), features his retelling of the Medea, a tragedy by classical Greek author Euripedes, as well as "Scottsboro, Too, Is Worth Its Song," about the trial of nine Alabama youths accused of raping two white prostitutes, and "Only the Polished Skeleton," in which death is described as the final equalizer of the races. Cullen also published two collections of stories for children, *The Lost Zoo* (1940) and *My Lives and How I Lost Them* (1942), the latter featuring the author's cat, Christopher.

"... the shape of the building never emerged."

In 1939 Cullen worked with his friend Arna Bontemps (1902–1973) on adapting Bontemps's novel *God Sends Sunday* for the stage. There was talk of bringing the resulting play, *St. Louis Woman,* to Broadway, but many of Cullen's friends (especially Walter White, head of the National Association for the Advancement of Colored People [NAACP]) told him that the play was degrading to blacks and should be scrapped. Cullen disagreed and was frustrated by the delays and postponements that kept the play from being produced; it appeared on Broadway after his death.

At the time of his death—of high blood pressure and kidney failure—in January 1946, Cullen had already assembled a manuscript of poems that he wished to serve as his memorial: *On These I Stand: An Anthology of the Best Poems of Countee Cullen* appeared in 1947. At his funeral, many of the stars of the Harlem Renaissance (including Carl Van Vechten, Langston Hughes, Alain Locke, and Paul Robeson) helped to carry Cullen's coffin to its final resting place. Delivering the eulogy (reported in the Chicago *Defender* several months later), W.E.B. Du Bois noted sadly that "Cullen's career was not finished. It did not culminate. It laid [a] fine, beautiful foundation, but the shape of the building never emerged." A monument to Cullen now stands at the branch of the New York Public Library named for him. It features two busts of Cullen, one made of brown cement and reaching out to the other, which is made of white cement and fashioned in the classical Greek style, with a traditional laurel wreath around the poet's head. This design expresses well Cullen's central conflict—his desire to be judged not on the basis of his race but on the basis of his poetry.

For More Information

Baker, Houston A., Jr. *A Many-Colored Coat of Dreams: The Poetry of Countee Cullen.* Detroit: Broadside Press, 1974.

Bronz, Stephen H. *Roots of Racial Consciousness—The 1920s: Three Harlem Renaissance Authors.* New York: Libra Publishers, 1964.

Davis, Arthur P. "The Alien and Exile Theme in Countee Cullen's Racial Poems." *Phylon* (Fourth Quarter 1953): 390–400.

Ferguson, Blanche E. *Countee Cullen and the Negro Renaissance.* New York: Dodd, Mead, 1966.

Lewis, David Levering. *When Harlem Was in Vogue.* New York: Alfred Knopf, 1981.

Perry, Margaret. *A Bio-Bibliography of Countee P. Cullen, 1903–1946.* Westport: CT: Greenwood Publishing Group, 1971.

Shucard, Alan R. *Countee Cullen.* Boston: Twayne, 1984.

Watson, Steven. *The Harlem Renaissance: Hub of African-American Culture, 1920–1930.* New York: Pantheon Books, 1995.

Aaron Douglas

Born May 26, 1899
Topeka, Kansas
Died February 22, 1979
Nashville, Tennessee

American painter, illustrator, and educator

One of the most notable figures in African American art, Aaron Douglas was especially active during the Harlem Renaissance, and he is often referred to as the period's "official artist." His distinctive style of geometric symbolism (featuring flat silhouettes of human figures, muted colors, and images that are symbolic, not realistic) may be seen on many magazine covers, book illustrations and dustcovers, and advertisements from the Harlem Renaissance. Douglas also painted some impressive murals (large-scale paintings, often mounted in public places) that display his unique blend of African and modernist techniques and his interest in including elements of African American history, religion, myth, and social issues in his works. Before Douglas, no African American artist had created works so unique in style and so affirming of black identity and experience.

A determined and talented young artist

Douglas was born into a relatively large, proud, politically active African American community in Topeka, Kansas.

Aaron Douglas's distinctive artistic style brought the Harlem Renaissance to life on magazine covers, book jackets, and murals.

Aaron Douglas.
(Gibbes Museum of Art/ Carolina Art Association. Reproduced by permission.)

161

His family did not have much money (his father was a baker). Douglas's parents emphasized education and instilled a sense of optimism and self-confidence in their son. Douglas inherited his mother's fondness for drawing and painting and decided early in his life that he would like to become an artist, even though prejudice against blacks must have made this goal seem difficult to reach.

In high school Douglas took courses that prepared him to study for a fine arts degree in college. After graduation, lacking the money to enter a university, he traveled east with a friend to find a job. He spent some months working in a Detroit, Michigan, automobile factory, where he experienced racism and discrimination; in later years he remembered that he was always given the worst, dirtiest jobs in the factory. In the evenings Douglas took art classes at the Detroit Museum of Art, his first formal education in the field he had chosen.

In July 1917 Douglas moved from Detroit to Dunkirk, New York, to take another factory job he had heard about. Later that year he returned to Topeka with three hundred dollars and new clothes to wear to college. He enrolled at the University of Nebraska in Lincoln, and in a very short time he had become a star of the school's Fine Arts Department. At the same time, he was reading the works of black leader W.E.B. Du Bois (1868–1963; see biographical entry) and *Crisis,* the magazine of the National Association for the Advancement of Colored People (NAACP), and becoming aware of developments in African American politics. When the United States entered World War I (1914–18) in 1917, Douglas was eager to show his patriotism, and he joined the Student Army Training Corps.

Joining the Harlem Renaissance

After he received his bachelor's degree in fine arts in 1922, Douglas wanted to continue his studies and pursue a master's degree, but the University of Nebraska did not offer an advanced degree in fine arts. Instead he took a job teaching art at Lincoln High School in Kansas City, where he made a good living but felt artistically limited. Douglas longed for contact with other artists, especially those who shared his interest in the African American experience. At this point in time he was following with great interest the growth of what was being called the New Negro movement: the shift toward black pride and the demand for advancement and equality for African Americans.

In early 1925 the *Survey Graphic* magazine published an issue devoted to the work of writers and thinkers who were part of the blossoming of black culture now known as the Harlem Renaissance. This exciting publication—and especially editor Alain Locke's essay on the influence of African art on modern art—intensified Douglas's interest in his African American heritage and in furthering his career as an artist. At the end of the 1925 school year, Douglas headed for Harlem with the intention of stopping there only briefly before moving on to Paris, France, to study art.

Douglas was welcomed warmly into the circle of writers, artists, and other participants in Harlem's thriving, colorful cultural scene. He was dazzled by the sights and sounds of the community and thrilled to be able to meet and talk to important people like Charles S. Johnson (1893–1956), editor of *Opportunity* magazine, and even the great W.E.B. Du Bois. For his part, Du Bois was eager to encourage a young black artist to develop his talent, and he introduced Douglas to someone who would prove a major influence on his career: white artist Winold Reiss (1887–1953).

An important influence

Born in Germany, Reiss had moved to the United States as a young man and pursued an interest in creating realistic portraits of members of various ethnic groups, first Native Americans and then African Americans. His portraits of black literary figures and leaders had been featured in the special issue of the *Survey Graphic;* they showed black people just as they were, rather than making them look either just like whites or like exaggerated caricatures.

Impressed by Douglas's obvious artistic ability, Reiss gave him a two-year scholarship to study at his studio. Reiss believed strongly that an artist should draw inspiration from his or her own experience and background, and he immediately began encouraging Douglas to look into both his African heritage and the African American folk tradition for ideas and elements he could weave into his art. Reiss was himself already blending modernist trends in art—especially cubism, a style that reduces images to flat lines, planes, and angles—with elements of African art.

Douglas was strongly influenced by his teacher's style, which stressed simplicity and clarity combined with traces of European styles like Art Deco (which was based on cubism and used geometric shapes to decorate furnishings, textiles, graphic arts, and more) and cubism, as well as elements of Egyptian art. Like Reiss, Douglas began creating flat black-and-white pictures that resembled the "cut-out" patterns of German folk art. These images were not meant to render an appearance of depth or perspective (the method artists use for realistic representations).

A hard-working and busy artist

When he first arrived in Harlem, Douglas had taken a number of low-paying jobs—including work in a fabric-dyeing factory and as a waiter—to support himself, so it was a relief when Du Bois offered him work in the mailroom of the *Crisis*. The job paid sixty dollars a month and allowed the fledgling artist to study with Reiss in the mornings and work in the afternoons.

Meanwhile, Douglas's reputation as a promising young artist grew, and he began to receive requests for magazine covers and illustrations. By the end of 1925 he had done two covers for *Opportunity* magazine (both fairly realistic portraits of people) and an illustration in his own black-and-white silhouette style. This period also marked the appearance of the *New Negro* anthology, to which Douglas contributed two pieces: "Meditation," a portrait of a lounging figure in silhouette, and "Rebirth," a more complicated drawing with suns, plants, eyes, and idol heads used as symbols.

As 1926 began Douglas was busy with both his studies and his magazine assignments. For *Opportunity*'s special issue on industry in February, he drew a cover design that featured two worker figures, with structures resembling factories and smokestacks in the background. That same month he made his first appearance in *Crisis* with "Invincible Music, the Spirit of

Africa," a drawing of a drum-playing figure with his head raised; the piece resembles Egyptian art in its simple form and strong symbolism. Also in February Douglas's illustrations of Eugene O'Neill's black-themed play *The Emperor Jones* (in which actor and singer Paul Robeson [1898–1976] was then starring) were published in the white publication *Theatre Arts Monthly.*

Other notable magazine work by Douglas from 1926 includes an illustration in *Opportunity* for Langston Hughes's (1902–1967; see biographical entry) poem "To Midnight Nan at Leroy's," which recreates the feeling of a Harlem nightclub; a poster for the NAACP's Krigwa Players theater group, which appeared in the May issue of *Crisis* and features bold, African imagery in its portrayal of a seated figure with exaggerated thick lips, a dangling earring, and tribal markings on his face; and the cover of the September issue of *Crisis,* a more realistically drawn portrait of Tutankhamen (King Tut), the ancient Egyptian boy-king whose tomb had recently been discovered.

Leading artist of the Harlem Renaissance

Douglas received prizes in contests sponsored by both *Opportunity* and *Crisis* in 1926, signaling his arrival as the leading visual artist of the Harlem Renaissance. By this time he had become a full-fledged member of what writer and folklorist Zora Neale Hurston (1891–1960) called the "Niggerati," the bold, daring younger generation of Harlem Renaissance writers and artists. With Hurston, Hughes, and others, Douglas helped to produce *Fire!!,* a literary journal meant to announce a new spirit of freedom and experimentation, but which lasted for only one issue. The home Douglas had made in Harlem with his wife, Alta (who had been his high school sweetheart), became a gathering place for these friends and colleagues.

Expanding into book illustration

Nineteen twenty-seven was also a busy year for Douglas. He was still producing magazine covers and illustrations, among them the cover of the May issue of *Crisis,* for which he drew a portrait of a Mangbetu (a West African ethnic group) woman in elaborate headdress. In addition, Douglas began doing illustrations, book jackets, and advertisements for books. One of his most important assignments in this area was producing illustrations for *God's Trombones: Seven Negro Sermons* (1927), a collection of poems by NAACP leader and writer James Weldon Johnson (1871–1938).

Very modern-looking in their simplicity and flatness, the *God's Trombones* drawings provide striking examples of Douglas's trademark style. Examples include "The Creation," which shows God's hand reaching down to man and features the use of transparent circles overlapping and layered on top of each other (a device Douglas would continue to use); "The Prodigal Son," a more contemporary scene set in what appears to be a Harlem nightclub, illustrating the temptations of modern life; "Go Down Death: A Funeral Sermon," with death portrayed as an angel on a horse surrounded by circles and rays of light, and seemingly offering relief from a harsh world; and "Judgment Day," in which a black trumpeter sounds the call to receive God's judgment.

Over the next few years Douglas would produce a number of other notable Harlem Renaissance book illustrations, including the covers for Langston Hughes's *Fine Clothes to the Jew* (1927) and Wallace Thurman's (1902–1934; see biographical entry) *The Blacker the Berry* (1929) and drawings for Paul Morand's (1888–1976) *Black Magic* (1929). Douglas did the covers for four of novelist and poet Claude McKay's (1890–1948; see biographical entry) books: *Home to Harlem* (1928), *Banjo* (1929), *Banana Bottom* (1933), and *A Long Way from Home* (1937). Although he did not illustrate *Nigger Heaven* (1926), the controversial novel by white literary critic Carl Van Vechten (1880–1964; see biographical entry), he did drawings for advertisements for the book.

Studying at the Barnes Foundation

The next phase of Douglas's career would find him creating large-scale murals, but before that phase began, a significant development took place. Douglas had the opportunity to spend a year studying at the Barnes Foundation, which had been founded by eccentric white millionaire Albert Barnes (1872–1951) as a repository for his extensive collection of art.

Among the pieces in his collection were works by European modernists like Henri Matisse (1869–1954) and Pablo Picasso (1881–1973), as well as samples of African art, in which Barnes was intensely interested.

Eager to show that his foundation did not discriminate against African Americans, Barnes offered Douglas a one-year fellowship, through which Douglas was paid $125 a month to attend lectures and study the artworks at the foundation in Merion, Pennsylvania (located near Philadelphia). So during 1928 Douglas traveled to Merion every Tuesday and stayed until Friday, returning to Harlem for the remaining days of the week.

Murals depicting African American history

The next year, Douglas received his first mural-painting assignment, which came from Fisk University, a well-respected black institution in Nashville, Tennessee. He and Alta moved to Nashville for the summer of 1930 and, working with several assistants, Douglas spent the next few months creating a series of murals for Fisk's new library. The main mural is a panorama of African American history in which Douglas shows how blacks had been snatched from their African homes and transported to a new, harsh life of slavery in the United States; images of their emancipation (freedom) from slavery and their role in the building of America follow. The mural pays tribute to African Americans and their deep spirituality, their courage, and their resilience in the face of adversity.

An additional seven murals in the library's lobby illustrate the concepts of philosophy, drama, music, poetry, science, day, and night. All are done in Douglas's typical style, featuring silhouetted figures, muted colors, overlapping circles and rays of light, and storylines that are easy to follow and understand. Around the same time he was working on the Fisk University murals, Douglas also produced murals for the Sherman Hotel's College Inn Room in Chicago, Illinois, and for the Bennett College for Women in Greensboro, North Carolina. For the Bennett College mural, Douglas again drew from African American history with a portrayal of Harriet Tubman (c. 1820–1913), the dynamic black woman who helped many slaves escape to the North in the mid-nineteenth century.

A year in Paris

In 1931 Douglas was finally able to fulfill a lifelong dream as he sailed for Paris, where he planned to spend a year on intensive art studies. He rented a room in a small hotel on the Left Bank, the traditional gathering place for Parisian artists and writers. Enrolling at an art studio called the Academie Scandinave, Douglas began a program in traditional, classical drawing and painting, producing mostly figure studies drawn from live models. He worked very hard, with no time to spare for the socializing and carousing popular with other artists.

During this period a number of other African American artists were also living and working in Paris, where they found not only inspiration and training opportunities but some relief from the racism and discrimination of the United States. Artists Hale Woodruff, Augusta Savage, and Palmer Hayden (see Chapter 5) as well as writers Claude McKay, Countee Cullen, and (though not continuously) Langston Hughes formed a loose-knit group called the "Negro Colony." Douglas also had a chance to meet the famous black artist Henry Tanner (1859–1937), one of very few African American artists to achieve acclaim in the years before World War I (1914–18). Tanner advised the younger artist to continue his studies and to work with live models whenever he could.

A new mood in Harlem

By the time Douglas returned to the United States, the Great Depression (the period of economic hardship and widespread unemployment that lasted from the stock market crash of 1929 until 1941, when America entered World War II [1939–45]) was well under way. The mood in Harlem—and indeed, across the whole country—was much more gloomy than it had been during the peak years of the Harlem Renaissance. Many artists and intellectuals were beginning to look toward communism (a political system in which all property is owned by the community as a whole) as a solution to the economic and social woes plaguing the United States. Douglas was among those who thought, for at least a brief period, that communism might be the only way to bring an end to poverty and racism in America.

Aspects of Negro Life: The Negro in an African Setting by Aaron Douglas. *(Art Resource. Reproduced by permission.)*

Meanwhile, U.S. president Franklin D. Roosevelt (1882–1945) was seeking his own solutions to the country's problems. In the early 1930s his administration started the Works Projects Administration (WPA; a U.S. government agency founded in 1935, called the Works Progress Administration until 1939), a program designed to put Americans back to work by assigning them to special jobs and projects. Several Harlem Renaissance artists and writers benefited from the

WPA, including Douglas. In 1934 he was commissioned to create a series of murals for the Countee Cullen Library, the Harlem branch of the New York Public Library. Entitled *Aspects of Negro Life,* this series would later be seen as the finest achievement of Douglas's career.

Aspects of Negro Life

The first panel in the *Aspects of Negro Life* mural, titled "The Negro in an African Setting," shows two dancers performing inside a circle of tribal figures, some of them holding spears and some beating drums. Painted in soft shades of gold, brown, blue, and purple and highlighted with Douglas's trademark transparent circles and rays of light, the composition conveys a sense of excitement and energy. In the second panel, "From Slavery through Reconstruction," the history of African Americans through the years after the Civil War (1861–65) is depicted through images of toiling workers, a leader-type figure who points into the distance, and chains being broken as freedom is finally won. But there are also figures representing the departing Union Army, and others who wear the conical head coverings of the terrorist group the Ku Klux Klan (KKK). This mural is painted in shades of mauve and rose, green, blue, and brown.

The mural's third panel, "An Idyll of the Deep South," shows how African Americans lived, relaxed, and suffered when most of them were still living in the rural South. Several figures in the painting are working in the fields, while others play guitars and sing; another group of figures mourns the death of a lynched man, a reference to the widespread violence against blacks that had dominated the early twentieth century. In the final panel, "Song of the Towers," a figure with suitcase in hand flees from clutching fingers that seem to represent the rural life of toil and hardship. In the distance are skyscraper-like structures that represent the northern cities, where he may find both enjoyment and artistic achievement—depicted through the figure of a jazz musician—and the evils of industry (as black smoke billows from smokestacks). Like the other murals, these are done in muted purples, browns, and greens.

Leans toward teaching

In *Aspects of Negro Life* Douglas had created a meaningful tribute to the history, trials, and accomplishments of black people during their several centuries in the United States. Although he remained active as an artist and a teacher, Douglas would never again produce a work as original or noteworthy as those he had completed during and just after the Harlem Renaissance.

In 1937 Douglas received a fellowship from the Rosenwald Foundation, a charitable organization that benefited many African American writers and artists. This fellowship allowed him to make a tour of the southern states, visiting various black educational institutions. The next year he traveled to the Dominican Republic and Haiti, where he painted a series of watercolors depicting life in these Caribbean nations. In 1940 Douglas accepted a job at Fisk University, where he was to organize art classes and create a fine arts major, which the school did not yet have. During the first four years of his more than two decades at Fisk, Douglas taught in the spring and returned to New York in the fall to attend Teacher's College at Columbia University, where he earned his master's degree in fine arts in 1944.

In the remaining years of his life, Douglas continued to paint, and he exhibited his paintings in galleries in such cities as Baltimore, Maryland; Washington, D.C.; St. Louis, Missouri; and Los Angeles, California. He often lectured on black art and was recognized for his contributions to art education. Most of his time and energy, however, were devoted to his work and students at Fisk. In his contacts with students he stressed a thorough study of the history of art and the importance of learning artistic rules and traditions before experimenting with unconventional methods and themes. Douglas also encouraged young people to expand their knowledge of African American history, and he fostered an attitude of hope and optimism about the future. He retired from Fisk in 1966.

Douglas's distinctive artistic style brought the Harlem Renaissance to life on magazine covers, book jackets, and murals. At the time of his death in Nashville in 1979, he was universally acknowledged as a key figure in the development of African American art.

For More Information

Books

Chederholm, Theresa Dickason. *Afro-American Artists: A Bio-Bibliographical Dictionary.* Boston: Boston Public Library, 1973.

Hayward Gallery. *Rhapsodies in Black: Art of the Harlem Renaissance.* Berkeley: University of California Press, 1997.

Kirschke, Amy Helene. *Aaron Douglas: Art, Race, and the Harlem Renaissance.* Jackson: University Press of Mississippi, 1995.

Studio Museum in Harlem. *Harlem Renaissance: The Art of Black America.* New York: Abradale Press, 1994.

Watson, Steven. *The Harlem Renaissance: Hub of African-American Culture, 1920–1930.* New York: Pantheon, 1995.

Web sites

"Aaron Douglas: Works Viewable on the Internet." *Artcyclopedia.* [Online] http://www.artcyclopedia.com/artists/douglas_aaron.html (accessed June 13, 2000).

W.E.B. Du Bois

Born February 23, 1868
Great Barrington, Massachusetts
Died August 27, 1963
Accra, Ghana

Sociologist, civil rights activist, writer, and editor

W.E.B. Du Bois is considered the greatest African American intellectual and civil rights activist of the twentieth century. He was among the first to call for full and unconditional equal rights for people of color. A social scientist by education and training, Du Bois carefully documented the historical and social truths of black people's lives as well as the realities of the harsh conditions they endured. But he did not limit himself to social science, for he was also notable as a writer (of nonfiction, fiction, and poetry), an editor, and the organizer of several Pan-African Congresses that highlighted the common interests of all people of African descent. Du Bois played an important role in the Harlem Renaissance by providing guidance, inspiration, and real opportunities for talented young blacks: he opened the pages of the *Crisis*, the influential magazine he edited, to the work of the period's most promising young authors and artists.

A bright, hardworking student

William Edward Burghardt Du Bois (pronounced du-BOYCE) was born in Great Barrington, Massachusetts, a pre-

"The problem of the twentieth century is the problem of the color line."

(W. E. B. Du Bois as quoted in W. E. B. Du Bois by Mark Stafford)

W. E. B. Du Bois.
(Courtesy of the Library of Congress.)

dominantly white town with a small but long-established African American community. Du Bois's ancestors were of mixed European and African ancestry, but his family had always identified itself as black. His father, Alfred Du Bois, left soon after his son's birth, and his mother, Mary Salvina Burghardt, struggled thereafter to support herself and her son on wages she earned as a maid. But Willie (the nickname given to Du Bois by his mother) helped out with money he earned by doing odd jobs such as delivering groceries and selling newspapers. By the time he was fifteen years old, Du Bois had also become a reporter, contributing articles on Great Barrington's black community to two black newspapers, the *Springfield Republican* and the *New York Globe.*

The only African American in his high school class of fifteen, Du Bois was a brilliant student. Soon after his high school graduation, his mother died. Du Bois received a scholarship to Fisk University (one of the nation's leading black colleges) in Nashville, Tennessee. There, he studied a variety of subjects, including classical literature, German, Greek, Latin, philosophy, chemistry, and physics, and he edited the university's literary magazine, the *Fisk Herald.* At Fisk, for the first time, Du Bois experienced the brutal realities of southern racism and the Jim Crow laws (which enforced segregation or separation of blacks and whites) that kept African Americans from becoming full citizens. Du Bois reacted by rarely leaving the Fisk campus and avoiding places like movie theaters and streetcars where blacks had to sit in separate seating. Some of his friends later said that during this period of his life, Du Bois became more reserved and withdrawn—qualities that would later make him seem cold and distant.

While he was studying at Fisk, Du Bois spent his summers teaching at schools in rural black communities in eastern Tennessee. His experiences strongly influenced the course of his life. Working in schools that lacked even the most basic supplies and witnessing the harsh conditions in which the people around him lived, Du Bois developed a greater awareness of African Americans' problems and suffering. At the same time, he recognized their strength in withstanding troubles, and he appreciated the people's rich cultural tradition of songs (especially spirituals or religious songs) and stories.

A brilliant career begins

After graduating from Fisk in 1888, Du Bois went on to Harvard University, studying history and social sciences. He earned a bachelor's degree (with honors) in 1890 and a master's degree in 1891. At his 1890 commencement, Du Bois was one of only five students in the graduating class to be chosen to deliver a speech. His excellent academic record earned him a scholarship to study overseas, and he spent two years (1892–1893) at the University of Berlin in Germany, focusing on history, economics, and politics. Du Bois's money ran out before he could finish a degree, but he managed to travel throughout Europe and returned to the United States with a more global perspective than he had had before.

In 1894 Du Bois became a professor of classics at Wilberforce University, a black institution in Ohio. He stayed only a year, but during that time he met and married Nina Gomer, who would be his wife for fifty-three years (until her death in 1950). Then he returned to Harvard to complete his doctoral degree in sociology, writing his dissertation on "The Suppression of the African Slave Trade to the United States, 1638-1870." In 1896 Du Bois became the first African American to receive a Ph.D. from Harvard. The next year he became an assistant professor of sociology at the University of Pennsylvania.

While teaching at Pennsylvania, Du Bois produced a major work called *The Philadelphia Negro,* one of the first scientifically conducted social studies ever done in the United States and the first in-depth analysis of a black community. Du Bois studied the conditions of poverty, violence, and crime that plagued Philadelphia's African Americans, and he interviewed thousands of people, creating a stunningly detailed report.

Gaining fame as a scholar and activist

Among those impressed by *The Philadelphia Negro* was Horace Bumstead, the president of Atlanta University (a black institution), who offered Du Bois a job. Du Bois was to teach sociology and also direct a series of annual conferences on issues important to African Americans. Entitled *Studies of the Negro Problem,* the series was a great success and helped make Du Bois a nationally known figure.

Du Bois had long believed that if the realities of racially based hatred, discrimination, and injustice were exposed, whites would quickly take steps to end them. As time went on, however, he became more and more convinced that exposing the problem would make no difference—that only protest and activism would produce results. He was also developing a philosophy of "pan-Africanism," the belief that all people of African descent had common interests and should work together to help each other. In 1900 (not long after the tragic death of his only son, three-year-old Burghardt, of an intestinal ailment) Du Bois attended the first meeting of the Pan-African Association in Europe, at which a group of over thirty activists discussed goals similar to his. The group disbanded after two years, but Du Bois continued to believe in the tenets (principles, beliefs, or teachings) of pan-Africanism.

The Souls of Black Folk

The event that catapulted Du Bois to the forefront of African American politics and thought was the 1903 publication of his influential book *The Souls of Black Folk*. A collection of fourteen essays (some of them previously published in other places) that highlights Du Bois's intellectual brilliance as well as his passionate ideals, the book describes the damaging effects of racism, celebrates the resilience of black people, and captures what it was like to be an African American at a time when violence and discrimination against blacks had increased to astonishing levels. Du Bois described blacks as having to struggle with a kind of double consciousness: "One ever feels his two-ness, an American, a Negro; two souls, two thoughts, two unreconciled strivings; two warring ideals in one dark body, whose dogged strength alone keeps it from being torn asunder."

The Souls of Black Folk had another important aspect: it stated in bold terms the difference of opinion between Du Bois and Booker T. Washington (1865–1915), who had been the most prominent black leader of the post-Civil War period. The founder of the Tuskegee Institute, where blacks were taught practical skills to help them support themselves, Washington encouraged African Americans to put up with discrimination while slowly making economic advances. Racial equality would come not through protest and higher education, Washington argued, but through vocational training and patience. Du Bois, on the other hand, believed that blacks should demand full equal rights, and he called on the "Talented Tenth"—the best educated and most successful members of African American society—to lead the way. Compromising with whites who want to restrict black freedoms, Du Bois insisted, would never end racism and could even hold up racial progress.

This philosophical difference split the black community into two factions: many blacks remained loyal to Washington, while those with higher ambitions and less patience sided with Du Bois. In 1905 Du Bois and other like-minded activists founded the Niagara Movement, a group committed to demanding full equal rights for blacks. But Washington's influence was too great, and the Niagara Movement fell apart after four years, as its former members joined other groups.

The birth of the NAACP and the *Crisis*

One of these other groups would turn out to be the strongest and longest-lived African American organization of the twentieth century. In 1910 Du Bois joined with a group of white social workers and reformers (having decided that an interracial approach was best, to attract white financial backers) to form the National Association for the Advancement of Colored People (NAACP). Still in existence today, the organization set out to fight for equality by trying race-related legal cases, lobbying legislators (talking to senators and members of Congress to persuade them to support or block particular laws), and providing public information. The only black member of the NAACP's board of directors, Du Bois was named director of publicity and research, and he immediately founded and became editor of *The Crisis,* a magazine that would be the group's mouthpiece.

Du Bois set to work to make *Crisis* a forum for African American ideas. It served as a place for many voices to proclaim the arrival of a new spirit of pride and a new determination to resist injustice. His own writings in the magazine were bold and forceful as he led the way toward what would soon be called the New Negro movement. By 1913 the circulation of *Crisis* had grown to thirty thousand, and readers eagerly awaited the publication of each issue.

Cover of the first issue of *Crisis,* a monthly journal sponsored by the NAACP. W.E.B. Du Bois edited *Crisis* for twenty-four years.

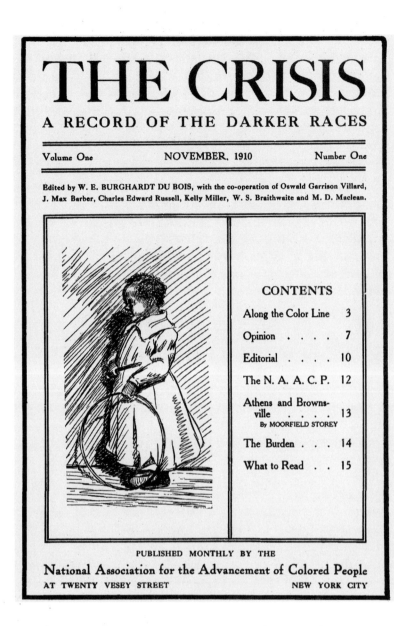

THE CRISIS

A RECORD OF THE DARKER RACES

Volume One   NOVEMBER, 1910   Number One

Edited by W. E. BURGHARDT DU BOIS, with the co-operation of Oswald Garrison Villard, J. Max Barber, Charles Edward Russell, Kelly Miller, W. S. Braithwaite and M. D. Maclean.

CONTENTS

Along the Color Line   3

Opinion   7

Editorial   10

The N. A. A. C. P.   12

Athens and Browns-
    ville   13
    By MOORFIELD STOREY

The Burden . . .   14

What to Read . .   15

PUBLISHED MONTHLY BY THE

National Association for the Advancement of Colored People
AT TWENTY VESEY STREET   NEW YORK CITY

When the United States entered World War I (1914–18), which was supposedly being fought in defense of global democratic ideals, African Americans were divided in their opinions about it. Some felt that blacks should refuse to participate in the conflict since they had been denied democratic rights in their own country, while others felt that taking part would show how loyal blacks were to the United States. At first Du Bois was opposed to the war and thought the United States should stay out of it altogether, but when the United States did become involved, he urged blacks to join the fight. He hoped that if African Americans showed they were willing to die for their country, their country would grant them the rights they had long been denied. In 1919 Du Bois traveled to France to report on the heroism of some of the thousands of black soldiers who had fought there. The issue of *Crisis* in which this story appeared sold a record-breaking 106,000 copies.

At the end of the war, the African American soldiers who had risked their lives in defense of democracy returned to a country in which racism and discrimination continued to exist. Violence against blacks—especially in the form of lynchings (or mob-type hangings of blacks)—had actually increased during the first two decades of the twentieth century. Du Bois used the pages of *Crisis* to urge returning soldiers and other blacks to continue the fight they had begun—the fight for equality. When the summer of 1919 brought a bloody series of race riots (see Chapter 1) as blacks reacted to earlier violence perpetrated against them, some blamed Du Bois for stirring up anger with his passionate and defiant words.

An important role in the Harlem Renaissance

With the 1920s came the cultural explosion known as the Harlem Renaissance, a period of great creative achievement that Du Bois, through his insistence on black pride and accomplishment, helped to begin and continued to nurture. In addition to simply inspiring the young black writers, artists, and performers of the Harlem Renaissance through his example and his eloquent words, Du Bois gave them material support and, in many cases, personal encouragement. He opened the pages of *Crisis* to their work, hiring a sharp young writer and editor, Jessie Redmon Fauset (1882–1961; see biographical entry), as literary editor and providing a place where new writings and art could be seen by a wide audience. Du Bois also took part by founding a theatrical group, the Krigwa Players, and wrote a novel called *Dark Princess: A Romance* (1928).

The 1920s were years not only of accomplishment but of conflict for Du Bois. He often clashed with the younger generation of Harlem Renaissance writers and artists who did not share his views. Du Bois and his Talented Tenth felt that black literature, entertainment, and art should portray blacks only as accomplished and respectable; the younger members of the movement insisted on a broader representation of African American life, even if it meant exposing Harlem's seamy underside of drinking, sex, and violence.

Du Bois also carried on a battle of words with Marcus Garvey (1887–1940), the Jamaican-born black nationalist leader who had built a huge following among ordinary African Americans. Garvey delivered a strong message of black pride and championed the establishment of a separate black state. Du Bois considered Garvey a dangerous fake, so he was no doubt among those greatly relieved when Garvey was convicted of mail fraud and forced to leave the United States.

Working on pan-Africanist goals

Part of the tension between Du Bois and Garvey was probably due to a major difference in the men's personalities and public appeal. Garvey's flamboyance (he normally wore fancy military uniforms and plumed hats) made him popular with common people, while the usually unsmiling Du Bois was seen by many as an arrogant, condescending elitist. (Elitists are people who act snobbish or superior because of their advanced education or influential position.) Du Bois's closest friends claimed that he could be warm—and even funny—but he never showed this side of his personality to strangers. His perceived coldness kept Du Bois from gaining as many followers as Garvey or Booker T. Washington.

All through the 1920s Du Bois continued to work on his pan-Africanist goals, organizing four Pan-African Congresses between 1919 and 1927. These meetings brought together black leaders from the United States, Africa, the Caribbean, and Europe. At the first one, held soon after the end of World War I, Du Bois and the others pushed for the independence of the African colonies that had been ruled by Germany; since Germany had lost the war, the fate of these colonies was unresolved. Ultimately, the ideas of the Pan-African Congress were ignored, and the colonies were divided between the European winners of the war.

A break with the NAACP

Over the years Du Bois grew more and more disappointed as all his efforts to promote racial progress and equality seemed to fail. Meanwhile, he found himself in frequent conflict with the mostly white leadership of the NAACP, who often felt he expressed his views too strongly. He was slowly moving away from integrationism (the idea that blacks and whites must live together, with the same rights and responsibilities) and eventually expressed his belief that African Americans should depend on each other more than on white people, both economically and socially. To the NAACP, it now sounded like Du Bois was promoting segregation, and this conflicted with the group's goals. In 1934 Du Bois was forced to resign from the NAACP and to give up his editorship of *Crisis*.

That same year Du Bois returned to Atlanta University as chairman of the sociology department. In addition to teaching, he founded and edited *Phylon,* a social science journal that focused on race relations. In 1936 Du Bois took a trip abroad and had a chance to compare U.S. society with those of other countries. He was especially impressed with the communist (in which all property is owned by the community as a whole) government and socialist (in which the means of producing and distributing goods are shared by citizens of the country or owned by the government) values of the Soviet Union. Du Bois was beginning to see this kind of political system as the only kind that could overcome poverty and racism.

In 1946 the NAACP unexpectedly offered Du Bois a chance to take over his old position. The organization's leaders may have assumed that the seventy-seven-year-old Du Bois would take a less active role than he had before, but this was not the case. Instead, he quickly became as outspoken as ever, and by 1948 the NAACP voted to force his resignation. Two years later Du Bois ran unsuccessfully for the U.S. Senate as the candidate of the American Labor Party.

In conflict with the U.S. government

Throughout the 1950s Du Bois repeatedly ran into trouble with the U.S. government because of his ties to groups thought to have communist sympathies. At this point in

American history, anticommunist sentiment intensified in response to the growing strength of communist countries like the Soviet Union and China; some people were afraid that the United States might be threatened by a communist takeover. In November 1951 Du Bois was tried in a U.S. federal court for failing to register as the agent of a foreign country; this charge stemmed from his having circulated a petition to ban nuclear weapons. He was found innocent, but the experience left him with an even more negative feeling about the United States. In addition, because of his links to communist groups, Du Bois's passport—along with that of his second wife, writer Shirley Graham, whom he had married in 1951—was seized, and he was not allowed to leave the country until 1958. When his passport was finally returned, Du Bois traveled to Russia, China, and Africa.

In 1961 Du Bois decided to accept an invitation from Ghana's president, Kwame Nkrumah (1909–1972), to move to that newly independent West African country, where he would begin work on a history of Africa to be called *Encyclopedia Africana*. Before he left the United States, however, Du Bois made one last dramatic gesture: he joined the Communist Party. In his application to the organization, Du Bois stated, "I have been long and slow in coming to this conclusion, but at last my mind is settled.... Capitalism [the economic system of the United States, in which property and means of production are privately owned] cannot reform itself, it is doomed to self-destruction. No universal selfishness can bring social good to all."

A citizen of Ghana

Du Bois became a citizen of Ghana in 1963, and he died there the next year at the age of ninety-five. Revered in that country as a hero of black people, he was given a grand state funeral and buried on the grounds of Ghana's government house. The day after his death happened to be the day of the March on Washington for Jobs and Freedom, when more than two hundred thousand people gathered in the U.S. capital to peacefully demand progress for African Americans. The news of the great black leader's death spread quickly throughout the crowd, and NAACP leader Roy Wilkins made note of Du Bois's contribution to African American history, reminding those present that "at the dawn of the twentieth century, his was the voice that was calling to you to gather here today in this cause."

For More Information

Books

Hamilton, Virginia. *W.E.B. Du Bois: A Biography.* New York: Crowell, 1972.

Lewis, David Levering. *W.E.B. Du Bois: Biography of a Race, 1868–1919.* New York: Henry Holt, 1993.

Moore, Jack B. *W.E.B. Du Bois.* Boston: Twayne, 1981.

Rampersad, Arnold. *The Art and Imagination of W.E.B. Du Bois.* Cambridge, MA: Harvard University Press, 1976.

Rudwick, Elliott. *W.E.B. Du Bois: Voice of the Black Protest Movement.* Urbana: University of Illinois Press, 1982.

Stafford, Mark. *W.E.B. Du Bois.* New York: Chelsea House, 1989.

Web sites

Reuben, Paul P. "Chapter 9: Harlem Renaissance—W.E.B. Du Bois." *PAL: Perspectives in American Literature—A Research and Reference Guide.* [Online] Available: http://www.csustan.edu/english/reuben/pal/chap9/dubois.html (accessed on March 23, 2000).

Edward Kennedy "Duke" Ellington

Born April 29, 1899
Washington, D.C.
Died May 24, 1974
New York, New York

American bandleader, composer, and pianist

"After hearing [piano player Harvey Brooks] I said to myself, 'Man, you're just going to have to do it.'"

Duke Ellington.
(AP/Wide World Photos, Inc. Reproduced by permission.)

Celebrated as one of the most important musicians and composers in the United States, Edward Kennedy "Duke" Ellington was an innovator in the field of jazz, a musical form that emerged during the first two decades of the twentieth century. His popularity spanned from the 1920s to the middle of the 1970s, and many of his most famous compositions were written after the Harlem Renaissance had ended. Nevertheless, it was during this exciting period in African American cultural history that Ellington's career had its roots. In his dignified and polished manners, his high standards, and his pride in black history and accomplishments, he seemed to embody the ideals of the New Negro Movement.

A secure and nurturing upbringing

It is often noted that the success Ellington achieved during his lifetime had much to do with the security and positive values provided by his parents. He was born in Washington, D.C., to James Edward Ellington, a butler with a part-time catering business who was able to purchase his own home, and

Daisy Kennedy Ellington. Ellington's parents gave him both warm emotional support and the courage and optimism to believe he could achieve anything he wanted. The values of ambition, pride, and achievement were also evident in Washington D.C.'s strong African American community of black professionals.

Ellington seems to have inherited his polite, cultured demeanor from his father, who was famous for his elegant manners and speech. But, as he noted in an article in the *Washington Post* in 1969, he was also influenced by his eighth-grade English teacher, Miss Boston, who encouraged her students to speak and behave properly and to take pride in themselves. "Your responsibility," Miss Boston would tell them, "is to command respect for the race."

A late-blooming interest in music

Nicknamed "Duke" by a schoolmate because he was always so well dressed, Ellington showed little interest in music as a young boy. When he was seven years old he took piano lessons, but he was not really interested in playing; by the time he reached junior high school, he had quit the lessons. At this time he was more interested in art, and he enrolled in the Armstrong Manual Training School with the intention of becoming a commercial artist after graduation. But when Ellington was fourteen, something happened to change his life's course.

While his family was vacationing in Asbury Park, New York, Ellington heard about a Philadelphia piano player named Harvey Brooks with a great command of the ragtime music that had become so popular. (A precursor to jazz, ragtime combined elements of white popular music with syncopated rhythms that originated in Africa.) On his way back to Washington, Ellington stopped in Philadelphia and visited Brooks, whose music dazzled him. As reported in a biography of Ellington by John Edward Hasse, he later recalled: "When I got home I had a tremendous yearning to play. I hadn't been able to get off the ground before, but after hearing him I said to myself, 'Man, you're just going to have to do it.'"

Learning from older musicians

His interest in art now replaced by a passion for music, Ellington spent his teen years listening to and learning from the many talented piano players who made up Washington's active, diverse music scene. One of his biggest influences was Oliver "Doc" Perry (1885–c. 1961), a popular black bandleader of the 1910s and 1920s. Formally trained and personally refined but also very versatile in what and where he played, Perry took the young Ellington under his wing and coached him not only in reading music and other technical skills but also in developing a professional attitude toward performing. Ellington would later refer to Perry as his "piano parent."

Another Washington musician whose example Ellington followed was Louis N. Brown (1889–1974), who played ragtime and popular music for dances and parties but also directed church choirs; he seemed to move easily between fancy and casual settings, performing for rich people one day and poor people the next. During his own career, Ellington also refused to limit himself to any one kind of venue or audience.

Ellington learned about music theory and composition from Henry Lee Grant, a well-educated, multitalented composer, conductor, choir director, concert pianist, and teacher. In addition, Grant helped to instill in the younger musician a sense of pride in black music.

A career gathers steam

Inspired by the example of these older musicians, Ellington was soon ready to begin his own career. He wrote his first composition, "Soda Fountain Rag," when he was sixteen. Two years later he formed his first band, Duke's Serenaders, with bass and saxophone player Otto Hardwick and trumpeter Arthur Whetsol; these three musicians would form the core for Ellington's later, more famous group, the Duke Ellington Orchestra. The Serenaders had their first engagement at the True Reformers Hall, located close to Ellington's parents' home. They quickly became popular, performing first at "hops" or dance parties and eventually for embassy receptions and other fancy gatherings (and changing their name to Duke's Washingtonians).

In July 1918 Ellington was financially secure enough to start a family, and he married Edna Thompson. The next year, the couple's son Mercer (who would grow up to be a musician himself) was born. Meanwhile, the Washingtonians were playing a wide variety of engagements and attracting an enthusiastic following. In March of 1923 Ellington decided to try his luck in New York, where talented African Americans with artistic ambitions—whether in writing, music, theater, or the visual arts—were gathering to take part in what would later be called the Harlem Renaissance.

The Duke in New York

The Harlem music scene was more exciting and more competitive than that of Washington, and Ellington felt he must do all he could to set his band apart from the others. Focusing on playing dance music that would appeal to a wide range of tastes, they played first at a popular nightclub called Barron's, then moved to the Hollywood Club (which soon became the Kentucky Club). Under the name the Duke Ellington Orchestra, they also began making recordings of their music; by 1927 they had made more than sixty records.

The swelling popularity of Ellington's band propelled them to the best venue in all of Harlem: the famous Cotton Club. Beginning in 1927, the group played there for thirty-eight months, and during that period Ellington established himself solidly as a jazz leader. Typically, the band would open the club's big floor show (which featured a variety of singers and dancers) with a major number, then perform songs at several intervals during the course of the evening.

Creating the "Big Band" sound

Appearing in an elegant white tuxedo, Ellington led his ten musicians (their number later expanded to twelve)—all attired in satin-trimmed, beige tuxedos—in helping to create what would come to be known as the "big band" sound. This style (also made famous by Fletcher Henderson's orchestra [see Chapter 4] and other groups) featured multiple players of various instruments (instead of just one of each) who performed

Duke Ellington at the piano rehearsing with Louis Armstrong in 1946.
(AP/Wide World Photos, Inc. Reproduced by permission.)

carefully orchestrated compositions. A big band usually included trumpet, saxophone, clarinet, bass, guitar, and drums, and in the case of the Ellington band it also featured the imaginative piano playing of its leader.

In addition, Ellington's orchestra became famous for its distinctive "jungle" sound, which featured the use of mutes (a kind of plug placed in a horn instrument to alter its sound) and growls (a sound imitating an animal's growl or roar) in keeping with the Cotton Club's wild, "primitive" atmosphere. Although popular as a place where patrons could hear the exciting music invented by African Americans, the Cotton Club's whites-only policy meant that the only blacks white patrons were likely to see were either serving drinks and food or performing on stage. The handsome, elegant, well-mannered Ellington managed to get the club to relax its racist policy somewhat during his tenure there, but the clientele remained mostly white.

While performing at the Cotton Club, Ellington's band grew more and more popular. They made nearly two hundred recordings, were featured on radio shows, and made appearances on Broadway (playing, for example, for *Show Girl* in 1929) and on film (including *Check and Double Check* in 1930). Some of Ellington's most memorable songs were penned during this period, among them "Black and Tan Fantasy" (1927), "Creole Love Call" (1928), "Mood Indigo" (1930), and the longer work *Creole Rhapsody* (1931).

The 1930s and 1940s: A period of great achievements

With the arrival of the Great Depression in the late 1920s and early 1930s, fewer people could afford to patronize expensive places like the Cotton Club, and a new, grimmer mood began to replace Harlem's gaiety. In search of different opportunities, Ellington left the Cotton Club in 1931, adding a talented singer named Ivie Anderson and taking his band on a series of tours to such cities as Boston, Chicago, Philadelphia, Denver, Kansas City, Toledo, Cleveland, St. Louis, and Indianapolis. In 1933 they traveled to London, where they were pleasantly surprised by the passion for jazz shown by European music lovers. During this period Ellington wrote some of his best-known songs, including "It Don't Mean a Thing (If It Ain't Got That Swing)" (1932) and "Sophisticated Lady" (1933). Another European tour followed in 1939, with stops in France, Belgium, Norway, Sweden, and the Netherlands.

The late 1930s and early 1940s were years of great creativity and accomplishment for Ellington. His grief over the death of his beloved mother in 1935 inspired a well-received extended piece called "Reminiscing in Tempo," which, along with "Symphony in Black" were more complex, emotional works than the usual big band jazz fare. Other popular songs from this period include "Jack the Bear," "Concerto for Cootie," and "Portrait of Bert Williams," the last a tribute to a famous figure (a star of the early black theater; see Chapter 4) from African American cultural history.

A new friend and collaborator

Another important development at this time was the addition to the band of Billy Strayhorn, a young pianist, arranger, and composer who would become Ellington's close friend and collaborator. Strayhorn wrote one of the Ellington band's best-known songs, "Take the 'A' Train," which provided listeners with directions on how to get to Harlem by subway. After Strayhorn's death at the age of fifty-one, Ellington composed a tribute to his friend, "And His Mother Called Him Bill" (1967).

January 1943 marked a milestone in Ellington's career: he and his band made their debut appearance at New York's prestigious Carnegie Hall. The performance included both dance numbers and Ellington's longer, more ambitious pieces. One of these was *Black, Brown, and Beige,* which he intended as a chronicle of the history and cultural strength of African Americans; one particular section, titled "Come Sunday," evokes the memory of slaves maintaining their worship and love of God despite their painful existence. Over the next five years Ellington and his band would perform six more times at Carnegie Hall.

On his way home from another European tour in 1950, Ellington wrote "A Tone Parallel to Harlem"—one of his many tributes to the center of African American life—which premiered in January 1951 at a benefit concert for the National Association for the Advancement of Colored People (NAACP). By now, jazz had moved into its modern period, and the big band and swing sounds that Ellington had helped to popularize were being moved aside in favor of "be bop," a jazz style that featured more complex harmonies and rhythms. Cast somewhat adrift by this shift, Ellington continued to do what he had always done, and his efforts were still admired by many music fans.

The Sacred Concerts

During the 1960s and 1970s Ellington was revered as a key figure in the development of jazz, and he received many awards and tributes. But he was not content to rest on his good reputation, and he and his orchestra kept up a busy schedule of concerts, radio broadcasts, film appearances, recording, and touring. In 1965, distraught over Strayhorn's serious illness, Ellington wrote an extended, religious-themed composition entitled "In the Beginning God," into which he wove his earlier "Come Sunday" and a variety of other pieces.

This work debuted in San Francisco in September and in New York at the Fifth Avenue Presbyterian Church three months later as "The Sacred Concert." The program was very well received and would be followed by two more Sacred Concerts, one performed in 1968 at the Cathedral of St. John the Divine in New York and one at Westminster Abbey in London in 1973, six months before Ellington's death. Although music critics are divided on the quality of the works featured in these concerts, Ellington considered them the best work he had ever done.

In 1973, while hospitalized for influenza and fatigue, Ellington learned that he had lung cancer. Although he left his band the following year, he continued to play the piano, even when confined to a hospital bed. He died in May 1974, mourned by jazz fans all over the world who recognized the value of a great talent that had first flowered during the Harlem Renaissance.

For More Information

Books

Charter, Samuel B., and Leonard Kunstad. *Jazz: A History of the New York Scene.* Garden City, NY: Doubleday, 1962.

Dance, Stanley. *The World of Duke Ellington.* New York: Da Capo, 1981.

Gammond, Peter, ed. *Duke Ellington: His Life and Music.* New York: Da Capo, 1977.

Hasse, John Edward. *Beyond Category: The Life and Works of Duke Ellington.* New York: Simon & Schuster, 1993.

Southern, Eileen. *The Biographical Dictionary of Afro-American and African Musicians.* Westport, CT: Greenwood Press, 1982.

Tucker, Mark. "The Renaissance Education of Duke Ellington." In *Black Music in the Harlem Renaissance.* Edited by Samuel A. Floyd, Jr. Knoxville: University of Tennessee Press, 1990, pp. 111–27.

Ulanov, Barry. *Duke Ellington.* New York: Da Capo, 1975.

Periodicals

Teachout, Terry. "Just as Spiritual, It Turns Out, as He Was Cool." *New York Times* (5 December 1999): Part Two, pp. 39–40.

West, Hollie I. "The Duke at 70." *Washington Post* (27 April 1969): sec. K, pp. 1, 9–10.

Web sites

Duke Ellington Biography. [Online] http://www.duke.edu/~bwj1/bio.html (accessed February 24, 2000).

Edward K. "Duke" Ellington.[Online] http://www.schirmer.com/composers/ellington_bio.html (accessed February 24, 2000).

Jessie Redmon Fauset

Born April 27, 1882
Camden County, New Jersey
Died April 30, 1961
Philadelphia, Pennsylvania

American editor and novelist

Fauset played an important role in the Harlem Renaissance not only through her own writing (including four novels, short stories, poems, essays, and articles) but through her efforts to support the work of other black writers. As literary editor of *Crisis*—a magazine sponsored by the National Association for the Advancement of Colored People (NAACP)—she recognized and promoted the talent of such Harlem Renaissance stars as Langston Hughes (1902–1967), Claude McKay (1890–1948), Countee Cullen (1903–1946), and Jean Toomer (1894–1967; see biographical entries on these authors). Fauset's own novels have been criticized as too narrowly focused on the prim, proper world of the black middle class—the environment in which Fauset had been raised. But critics have praised her for confronting such issues as "passing" (light-skinned blacks posing as whites), for exploring the intense color consciousness—and color prejudice—that exists within African American society, and for exposing the trials of women who try to break out of the limited roles assigned to them.

> Jessie Redmon Fauset felt strongly that black writers were best qualified to describe the African American experience, and she set out to prove this herself.

A member of the black middle class

Born in Camden Country, New Jersey (located just outside of Philadelphia, Pennsylvania), Fauset was the seventh child born to Redmon Fauset, an outspoken minister of the African Methodist Episcopal Church, and Annie Seamon Fauset. After her mother's death, Fauset's father married a widow with three children, and the couple went on to have three more children together.

Fauset would later be described as an "O.P."—a member of one of the families that made up the upper-crust, black "Old Philadelphia" community—but this was only partly true. Her family was old, with proof that its ancestors were in the United States as early as the 1700s. They were well respected and cultured, but they were certainly not wealthy. Fauset still faced racial prejudice when she attended Philadelphia's public schools. She graduated with honors from the city's elite High School for Girls (where she was probably the only black student) in 1900.

Fauset hoped to enroll at the exclusive Bryn Mawr College, but rather than admit a black student, the college arranged for her to receive a scholarship to Cornell University in Ithaca, New York. There she excelled, studying classical languages (Latin and Greek) as well as French and German and receiving the coveted honor of election to Phi Beta Kappa (an organization that recognizes high academic achievement).

Teaching high school French

Extremely intelligent and efficient and keenly interested in literature, Fauset wanted to pursue a career in publishing, but in the early part of the twentieth century such positions were not open to black women. She returned to Philadelphia to look for a teaching job, but her race prevented her from teaching in the city's public schools. Instead, Fauset taught in a Baltimore junior high for one year, then became a French teacher at Washington, D.C.'s prestigious M Street High School (its name was later changed to Paul Dunbar High School), where that city's thriving African American community sent its best students.

Fauset would spend the next fourteen years in this position, while traveling to Europe every summer and working on an advanced degree in Latin and French. She received her master's degree from the University of Pennsylvania in 1919 and that same year accepted an invitation from W.E.B. Du Bois (1868–1963; see biographical entry) to become an editor at the *Crisis* magazine in New York. Fauset's relationship with Du Bois dated back to 1903, when, soon after her father's death, she had written the famous black leader a letter. The two had continued to correspond, and Fauset had developed a deep and reverent admiration for Du Bois.

An influential literary editor

Fauset was initially assigned to edit the *Brownies' Book,* a magazine designed to encouraged black children to take pride in their heritage. She wrote the short poem that appeared in the magazine every month and that declared its intent: "To children, who with eager look / Scanned vainly the library shelf, and nook, / For History or Song or Story / That told of Colored People's glory,— / We dedicate the Brownies' Book." During the course of this magazine's somewhat short life—it was published from January 1920 to December 1921—Fauset not only edited contributors' work but wrote countless signed and unsigned poems, stories, and articles.

With the demise of the *Brownies' Book,* Fauset became literary editor at *Crisis,* making what may have been her greatest contribution to the Harlem Renaissance. Responsible for choosing the poetry and fiction that would appear in *Crisis,* Fauset soon showed that she had a keen eye for talent. She was among the first editors to spotlight the work of the up-and-coming generation of black writers, thus bringing their work to the attention not only of the magazine's readers but of publishers on the lookout for promising literary talent.

As early as 1921, Fauset recognized the talent of Langston Hughes, publishing his early, great poem "The Negro Speaks of Rivers." She also nurtured the careers of poets Claude McKay and Countee Cullen and novelist Jean Toomer, offering good advice along the way on how best to polish their writing. At the same time, Fauset was busy with her duties as Du Bois's trusted assistant: she made his travel arrangements, edited his speeches, ran *Crisis* when he was traveling, and defended him to those put off by his remote air and gruffness. In addition,

Fauset's home became a place of shelter and literary exchange for Harlem Renaissance writers and other artists, whose boldness and daring must sometimes have contrasted with her own impeccable manners and properness.

A well-received first novel

Fauset was moved to begin writing fiction after reading *Birthright* (1922), a novel about black characters and issues by T.S. Stribling (1881–1965), a white author. Fauset felt strongly that black writers were best qualified to describe the African American experience, and she set out to prove this herself. Her first novel, *There Is Confusion,* was published in 1924 by Boni & Liveright (the company that had also just published Jean Toomer's important novel *Cane*). This landmark event—the almost-unheard-of publication of a black woman novelist's work by a major white publishing company—was to be marked by a dinner in Fauset's honor at the Civic Club. As discussed in Chapter 2, the dinner turned out to have a much broader purpose and effect.

In *There Is Confusion,* Fauset carefully recreates the gracious but often pretentious milieu of the black middle class, a world in which she had lived all her life. The novel's central character is Joanna Marshall, the daughter of a successful black businessman who longs to "amount to something." Joanna's ambition and class consciousness alienate her from her boyfriend, medical student Peter Bye, who is also bitter about the fact that the wealthy white branch of his family has cut all ties with his own racially mixed branch.

Joanna's friend Maggie Ellersley is in love with Joanna's brother Philip but runs away to marry an older man (who turns out to be a gambler) after Joanna makes it clear that she considers working-class Maggie socially inferior to the Marshall family. Meanwhile, Peter goes off to Europe to fight in World War I and forms a friendship with his white cousin, whom he has met by chance and who is later killed in battle. Maggie and Philip are also reunited in Europe, and when Peter returns to the United States, he and Joanna are married. Joanna gives birth to a son, and Peter refuses an offer by the white Byes—who have been left without a male heir—to raise the boy as their own.

There Is Confusion earned good reviews in the white press, and black critics were even more enthusiastic—especially those who agreed with Du Bois that African American authors should portray blacks as morally upright and honorable. In the decades since its publication, the novel has been faulted for its confusing structure (featuring two separate plotlines and shifts in time) and weak characters. Nevertheless, *There Is Confusion* does provide interesting perspectives on the limited options available to women in the 1920s, the discrimination faced by urban blacks in the North, and the complications caused by a racially mixed heritage.

Plum Bun praised as her finest work

Soon after the publication of *There Is Confusion,* Fauset spent several months traveling in Europe and North Africa, visiting Italy, France, Austria, and Morocco. She continued to work at *Crisis* until 1926, and the next year—despite her wish to find a job in publishing—she became a French teacher at DeWitt Clinton High School in New York City, a position she would hold for the next seventeen years. In 1928 Fauset married Herbert Harris.

The novel considered Fauset's finest work, *Plum Bun,* appeared in 1929. The title comes from the traditional nursery rhyme "To market, to market / To buy a plum bun, / Home again, home again, / Market is done"; Fauset also structured the novel around the rhyme. The first section, "Home," takes place in Philadelphia and introduces Angela Murray, a young, light-skinned black woman who fears her race will prevent her from attaining the love and success she desires. Angela's dark-skinned sister, Virginia, on the other hand, is secure in her identity as an African American. In "To Market," Angela moves to New York after the deaths of her parents. She studies painting, passing as white and making a number of friends, including Anthony Cross, who is also hiding his true racial identity (which is biracial) and Rachel Powell, a confident young black woman. "Plum Bun" details Angela's affair with a wealthy white student, Roger Fielding, whose feelings for Angela turn out to be shallow.

In "Home Again," Angela is beginning to lose her romantic illusions and has learned more about herself and the need for honesty in her relationships. *Plum Bun*'s conclusion,

Jessie Fauset (left) with Langston Hughes (center) and Zora Neale Hurston (right) at Booker T. Washington's grave at the Tuskegee Instititute in 1927. *(Schomburg Center for Black Culture. Reproduced by permission.)*

"Market Is Done," concerns Angela's anger when her friend Rachel is passed over for a scholarship because she is black and Angela's decision to publicly reveal the truth about her own racial identity. Anthony also chooses to embrace his black identity, and he and Angela marry.

Very positive reviews of *Plum Bun* appeared in the leading publications including the *New Republic* and the *New York*

Times. The novel was proclaimed superior to Fauset's first novel in successfully illuminating such themes as the necessity of accepting one's true identity, the importance of family and roots, and the limits of gender roles. Yet critics have continued to point out the narrowness of Fauset's vision and the class consciousness her characters reveal: all of the whites in the novel are mean and violent, the lower-class blacks are aimless and in need of direction, and the middle- and upper-class blacks are attractive, dignified, and morally superior.

Last two novels not as successful

Fauset's last two novels did not receive as much critical acclaim as her first two, perhaps because her wish to support herself as a novelist had led her to write what she thought would appeal to a majority of readers. Despite its flaws, *The Chinaberry Tree* (1931) has value as a detailed document of black middle-class life. In an introduction to the novel, the well-known white author Zona Gale (1874–1938) wrote that the book would introduce Americans to "a great group of Negroes of education and substance who are living lives of quiet interests and pursuits." Set in the small New Jersey town of Red Brook (and containing almost no white characters), *The Chinaberry Tree* centers on Laurentine Strange, the daughter of a wealthy white man and his black former servant. The novel follows Laurentine's efforts to achieve acceptance (for she has long been ostracized by her community) and respectability.

In her last novel, *Comedy: American Style* (1933), Fauset again focuses on the damaging effects of color consciousness and passing. The central character is Olivia Cary, a light-skinned African American who desperately wishes to be white and whose family suffers for her obsession. She has three children: two—Christopher and Teresa—who are light-skinned like herself, and one—Oliver—who is darker like his father. Olivia's rejection of Oliver leads to his suicide, while Teresa's decision to pass as white leaves her emotionally dead. Only Christopher embraces his black identity, while Olivia is finally completely isolated as she lives apart from her family in a fantasy world. Through the character of Phebe Grant, a black woman with strong self-esteem who marries Christopher, Fauset suggests that the values of acceptance, hard work, honesty, and loyalty will lead to happiness.

In the remaining decades of her life, Fauset published no more fiction, despite rumors that she was working on a fifth novel. She and her husband lived with Fauset's sister in Harlem from the time of their marriage until the sister's death in the early 1940s. They moved to Montclair, New Jersey, and lived quietly until Harris's death in 1958, after which Fauset went to Philadelphia to live with her stepbrother. She died of heart disease in 1961.

For More Information

Books

Christian, Barbara. *Black Women Novelists: The Development of a Tradition, 1892–1976.* Westport, CT: Greenwood Press, 1980.

Huggins, Nathan Irvin. *Harlem Renaissance.* New York: Oxford University Press, 1971.

Lewis, David Levering. *When Harlem Was in Vogue.* New York: Knopf, 1981.

McLendon, Jacquelyn Y. *The Politics of Color in the Fiction of Jessie Fauset and Nella Larsen.* Charlottesville: University Press of Virginia, 1995.

Sylvander, Carolyn Wedin. *Jessie Redmon Fauset: Black American Writer.* Troy, NY: Whitston, 1981.

Watson, Steven. *The Harlem Renaissance: Hub of African-American Culture, 1920–1930.* New York: Pantheon Books, 1995.

Periodicals

Johnson, Abby Arthur. "Literary Midwife: Jessie Redmon Fauset and the Harlem Renaissance." *Phylon* (June 1978): 143–53.

Langston Hughes

Born February 1, 1902
Joplin, Missouri
Died May 22, 1967
New York, New York

**American poet, short story writer, novelist,
playwright, autobiographer, and nonfiction writer**

Probably the most famous and celebrated of all African American poets, Langston Hughes had a career that spanned five decades. He produced a wide variety of literary works from novels, plays, and short stories to children's books, translations, and anthologies. But it is for his poetry—with its gripping, vivid images and plainspoken, jazz- and blues-influenced language—that he is most remembered. And the Harlem Renaissance, the period in which he began his career, simply would not have been the same without him.

A rootless childhood

Born in 1902 in Joplin, Missouri, Hughes was of mixed Native American, French, and African heritage, but his family was identified as black. His father, James Nathaniel Hughes, was born in Oklahoma but moved to Joplin in 1899; he had not been allowed to take the bar examination (the test that qualifies those who have studied law to become practicing attorneys) in his own state due to his race. Langston's mother, Carrie, who came from a distinguished and financially secure

"[Let the] smug Negro middle class ... turn from their white, respectable, ordinary books to catch a glimmer of their own beauty."

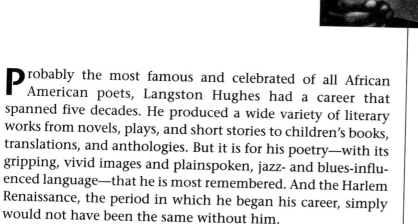

Langston Hughes.
(The Bettmann Archive/Newsphotos, Inc./Corbis-Bettmann. Reproduced by permission.)

Kansas family, was an imaginative person who liked to write poetry and perform dramatic monologues.

In 1903, after four years of marriage and the births of two children (the first died; Langston was the second), frustrated by the poverty and racism he seemed unable to escape in the United States, James Hughes left his family and moved to Mexico. He established himself there as an attorney, bought land, and was able to send money back to his wife, but Carrie refused to join him. Instead, she traveled from city to city in search of jobs, sometimes taking young Langston with her and sometimes leaving him with her mother, Mary Langston, in Lawrence, Kansas. A gentle and proud woman who ran a boarding house for University of Kansas students, Mary exerted a strong and positive influence on her grandson.

Around 1907, during one of his sojourns with his mother, young Hughes entered a library for the first time and fell instantly in love with reading. In his autobiography, *The Big Sea* (1940), he recalled, "[Even] before I was six, books began to happen to me, so that after a while there came a time when I believed in books more than people—which, of course, was wrong."

Already a poet

After the death of his grandmother in 1910, Hughes lived briefly with her friends, the Reed family. During this time he got his first job, cleaning the lobby and restrooms in an old hotel near his school. (Later in his life, he would write a poem called "Brass Spittoons" about this experience.) In 1914 he went to live with his mother and her new husband, Homer Clark, and his new stepbrother, Gwyn, in Lincoln, Illinois. The family stayed for one year and then moved to Cleveland, Ohio.

Hughes then entered Cleveland's Central High School, where he spent four successful years. He was on the school's track team, often made the monthly honor roll, and served as editor of the yearbook. He also began to write poetry and publish his work in the *Belfrey Owl*, a school publication. His style already showed the influence of the famous African American poet Paul Laurence Dunbar (1872–1906; see Chapter 3) as well as white poets Carl Sandburg (1878–1967) and Walt Whitman (1819–1892).

Hughes had spent much of his early childhood on the move as his mother sought out work or left him in the care of others. In some of the schools he had attended he had been the only black student, and sometimes he had been ridiculed. But Hughes had a soft-spoken, agreeable nature and a handsome face; he had learned how to adapt himself to new situations, and people usually liked him. These qualities would continue to help him in adult life. But there was also a part of Hughes that he shared with no one, and even his closest friends found him a little mysterious.

High school and beyond

Between his junior and senior years of high school, Hughes spent an unhappy summer living with his father in Mexico. He found his father's outlook depressingly negative, and he was happy to return to the United States. Sometime during Hughes's senior year, he wrote a poem called "When Sue Wears Red," about a girl he had seen at a dance. Later, critics would praise this poem as the first by any poet to celebrate the beauty of a black woman. It was an early example of Hughes's distinctive and already confident voice.

The next summer Hughes produced a poem that was to become perhaps his most famous. In July 1920 he traveled by train to visit his father again in Mexico. While crossing the Mississippi River to St. Louis, Missouri, Hughes wrote fifteen lines on the back of an envelope. Finished in a quarter of an hour and dedicated to black leader W.E.B. Du Bois (1868–1963), this poem, titled "The Negro Speaks of Rivers," tells in clear, plain language of the important and deeply spiritual role that rivers—including the Nile in Egypt, the Congo in Africa, and the Mississippi in the United States—have played in the lives of black people. When it was published a year later, the poem gained notice as a simple yet elegant expression of pride in the spirituality and endurance of black peoples throughout the world.

Having graduated from college, Hughes lived with his father for a year. They disagreed about what he should do next: James Hughes wanted his son to attend a European university to avoid the racism of the United States, but Hughes finally convinced him that he should go to Columbia University in

"The Negro Speaks of Rivers" by Langston Hughes

I've known rivers:
I've known rivers ancient as the world
and older than the flow of human
blood in human veins.
My soul has grown deep like the rivers.
I bathed in the Euphrates when dawns
were young.
I built my hut near the Congo and it
lulled me to sleep.
I looked upon the Nile and raised the
pyramids above it.
I heard the singing of the Mississippi
when Abe Lincoln
went down to New Orleans, and I've
seen its muddy
bosom turn all golden in the sunset.
I've known rivers:
Ancient, dusky rivers.
My soul has grown deep like rivers.

From Selected Poems of Langston Hughes, Vintage Books, 1990. Copyright © 1994 by the Estate of Langston Hughes. Reproduced by permission of Alfred A. Knopf, a Division of Random House, Inc. In the British Commonwealth by Harold Ober Associates Incorporated.

New York City, where he promised to study engineering. Meanwhile, Hughes had sent samples of his writing to Jessie Fauset (1882–1961; see biographical entry), the literary editor of the prominent black publication *Crisis* (see Chapter 1). Two of his poems and a children's play were published in *Brownies' Book,* a magazine for young people produced by the staff of *Crisis*, and in June 1921 "The Negro Speaks of Rivers" appeared in *Crisis*. Thus, Hughes's reputation as a promising poet arrived in New York a little ahead of him.

" ... this rise of dreams and beauty"

Arrive he did, though, later in the summer of 1921, on a steam-driven ship he'd boarded in Mexico. In his autobiography Hughes describes the excitement of this arrival: "There is no thrill in all the world like entering, for the first time, New York harbor, coming in from the flat monotony of the sea to this rise of dreams and beauty." Deeply interested in the goings-on in Harlem, Hughes enrolled for the fall term at Columbia University. Although he managed to keep up acceptable grades, he spent more time attending Broadway shows—especially the wildly popular *Shuffle Along* (see Chapter 4), which he saw over and over again—than worrying about school. But Hughes did pursue his interest in literature and writing by attending lectures and poetry readings at the 135th Street branch of the New York Public Library. There he met another young poet named Countee Cullen (1903–1946; see biographical entry), who was to become a close friend and rival.

After finals in the spring of 1922, Hughes dropped out of Columbia and began to spend all of his time in Harlem, taking odd jobs to support himself and writing some of the best poems of his career. During the winter of 1923, he produced "The Weary Blues," about a piano player in a Lenox Avenue nightclub who moans in the language of the blues about his loneliness and troubles but who finally seems to achieve peace through his own music. Written in a nontraditional form (despite Hughes's use of rhyme), this poem brilliantly captures the spirit of Harlem's nightlife and people as well as the strength and richness of African American culture. This was not the side of black life that Du Bois and his Talented Tenth (the most accomplished and ambitious segment of African American society) wanted writers to portray, but Hughes was committed—then and for the rest of his career—to celebrating the ordinary scenes and people around him.

A journey to Africa

In the spring of 1923, Hughes left New York for a period of sea travel, serving as a cook's assistant on a freighter that would take him to Africa for the first time. The ship docked in such cities as Dakar (Senegal) and Lagos (Nigeria), and the young writer exulted in reaching, as he wrote in his autobiography, "My Africa, Motherland of the Negro Peoples! And me a Negro! Africa! The real thing." By late 1923 Hughes was back in the United States, but he soon shipped out again on another freighter, only to resign from his job in Europe shortly thereafter. In the spring of 1924 he was living in Paris and working as a busboy in a nightclub where French music fans went to hear the exciting jazz that had been brought over from the United States by African Americans.

In Paris, Hughes received a visit from Alain Locke, who had read and admired Hughes's work in *Crisis* and asked him for some poems to include in the *Survey Graphic* issue on black writers (see Chapter 2) that Locke was then busy putting together. Hughes and Locke traveled to Venice, Italy, together, but after Hughes was robbed of his money and passport the two parted company. Hughes finally managed to get a job on a ship bound for the United States, and he arrived back in New York with twenty-five cents in his pocket and a sheaf of new poems. Soon after his arrival, he attended a benefit party for the National Association for the Advancement of Colored

People (NAACP), where he met white writer-critic—and booster of African American culture—Carl Van Vechten (1880–1964; see biographical entry) for the first time. Van Vechten would later help Hughes get his first volume of poetry published. Another important relationship Hughes formed during this period was with poet Arna Bontemps (1902–1973). They shared a strong, lifelong friendship and worked on many projects together.

The Weary Blues is published

In 1925 Hughes won the top poetry prize for "The Weary Blues" in the annual contest sponsored by *Opportunity* magazine (see Chapter 2). At the awards dinner, he ran into Van Vechten, who asked him if he had enough poems to publish as a book; Hughes subsequently sent Van Vechten all of the poems he had ready for publication. Meanwhile, Hughes was living with his mother in Washington, D.C., and working as a busboy at the Wardman Park Hotel. One evening the famous white poet Vachel Lindsay (1879–1931), who was scheduled to give a poetry reading at the hotel later, went into the restaurant for dinner. Hughes left three of his poems near Lindsay's plate, and at the poetry reading that night Lindsay read Hughes's poems along with his own and announced that he had discovered a talented black busboy-poet. Lindsay told Hughes that he should keep writing and try to get his work into print.

Meanwhile, Van Vechten had already sent Hughes's poems to his own publisher, Alfred A. Knopf, who agreed to publish them in a volume to be titled *The Weary Blues,* with an introduction written by Van Vechten. Besides the title poem, the volume includes "Mother to Son," spoken in black dialect by a mother who encourages her son to continue struggling up the staircase of life; "Negro," a sorrowful but proud poem about all the roles (slave, worker, singer, etc.) that blacks have played in American life; and "Troubled Woman," whose central figure is bent and hurt but not crushed by adversity.

The Weary Blues, which appeared in 1926, received positive reviews from many major publications, including the *New York Times,* the *Washington Post,* and the *New Republic.* It also received a few negative ones (most notably from London's

Times Literary Supplement). Members of the conservative Talented Tenth found Hughes's gritty realism distasteful and bound to give whites the wrong impression about black people. But in *Crisis*, Jessie Fauset claimed that Hughes had written more "tenderly, understandingly, and humorously about life in Harlem" than any other poet. And Hughes defended his own aims—and the viewpoint of his fellow younger Harlem Renaissance writers—in an important essay, "The Negro Artist and the Racial Mountain," published in the *Nation* in June 1926. "Let the blare of Negro jazz bands and the bellowing voice of Bessie Smith singing blues," wrote Hughes, "penetrate the closed ears of the colored near intellectuals until they listen and perhaps understand . . . ." Let the "smug Negro middle class . . . turn from their white, respectable, ordinary books to catch a glimmer of their own beauty."

"Mother to Son" by Langston Hughes

Well, son, I'll tell you:
Life for me ain't been no crystal stair.
It's had tacks in it,
And splinters,
And boards torn up,
And places with no carpet on the floor—
Bare.
But all the time
I'se been a-climbin' on,
And reachin' landin's,
And turnin' corners,
And sometimes goin' in the dark
Where there ain't been no light.
So, boy, don't you turn back.
Don't you set down on the steps
'Cause you finds it's kinder hard.
Don't you fall now—
For I'se still goin', honey,
I'se still climbin',
And life for me ain't been no crystal stair.

Living at "Niggerati Manor"

It was during this period that Hughes befriended the wealthy white Spingarn family, several members of which were active in supporting and promoting African American culture. Arthur Spingarn became Hughes's lawyer (which he would remain throughout the rest of Hughes's life) and Arthur's sister-in-law Amy offered to pay for his education. So in early 1926 Hughes entered Lincoln University, a black college located in Pennsylvania.

When classes let out that summer, he returned to New York and moved into a boarding house on 136th Street—dubbed "Niggerati Manor" by writer Zora Neale Hurston (1891–1960; see biographical entry). The house was already occupied by his friend Wallace Thurman (1902–1934; see biographical entry) and others active in the Harlem Renaissance. Inspired by all the social and cultural electricity around him, Hughes plunged into activities such as producing the one-issue magazine *Fire!!* (along with Thurman, Hurston, painter Aaron Douglas, and other friends) and attending parties at the homes of black millionairess A'Lelia Walker and Carl Van Vechten. In the fall, he returned to his studies at Lincoln.

Another book of poetry, and a new "Godmother"

The next year Hughes's second volume of poems was published. *Fine Clothes to the Jew* (1927) features even more details of everyday life in poor and working-class Harlem, with poems that speak not just of nightclub music but of storefront churches, low-paying jobs, gambling, fights, drinking, and prostitution. Again, Hughes writes in the language and rhythms of the streets, creating a style that seems plain and simple but is actually carefully crafted. He seems to strive for honesty above all else but also maintains his compassion for the subjects of his poems such as the speaker in "Mulatto," who has a black mother and an uncaring white father: "My old man died in a fine big house. / My ma died in a shack. / I wonder where I'm gonna die, / Being neither white nor black?" Like Hughes's first volume, this one was praised by many critics but faulted by those who claimed it painted an ugly picture of African American life.

Hughes was still a student at Lincoln when, on a weekend trip to New York, he met an elderly white woman named Charlotte Mason (1854–1946). He found this wealthy widow (who had recently become fascinated by black culture) charming, informed, delightfully modern in her outlook, and very appreciative of his work. She offered to support Hughes financially so that he could continue to write without having to worry about making money; meanwhile, she insisted on remaining anonymous and on being called only "Godmother". With Mason's support, Hughes was able to finish a novel, *Not Without Laughter,* which was written before his 1929 graduation from Lincoln and published in 1930.

Not Without Laughter

Hughes intended in *Not Without Laughter* to portray a typical black family in Kansas, where he had lived as a child, but he did not use his own family as a model. Whereas Hughes's grandmother had been the proprietor of a boarding house, the novel's Hager Williams (grandmother of young Sandy Williams) washes white people's clothes for a living. Hager's children include Anjee (Sandy's mother), who works as a maid while eagerly anticipating the visits of her rambling, guitar-playing husband Jimboy' Tempy, who is living what she considers a "respectable" middle-class life and avoids her family; and Harriett, a vibrant young woman who has dropped out of school to work as a waitress and who wants to become a blues singer. The novel recounts the various struggles and misadventures of the characters, especially Sandy's growing awareness of racism and his attempt to find his own place in the world. At the end of *Not Without Laughter,* Hager has died and Harriett, now a successful performer, promises to give Sandy money to finish his education.

"Dream Variation" by Langston Hughes

To fling my arms wide
In some place of the sun,
To whirl and to dance
Till the white day is done.
Then rest at cool evening
Beneath a tall tree
While night comes on gently,
  Dark like me—
That is my dream!
To fling my arms wide
In the face of the sun,
Dance! whirl! whirl!
Till the quick day is done.
Rest at pale evening....
A tall, slim tree....
Night coming tenderly
  Black like me.

At the time of its publication, *Not Without Laughter* received mixed reviews, and it is not now considered a very successful novel. Although Hughes created a rich, detailed portrait of African American family life and struggles, he failed to bring his themes to life, and the novel's central figure, Sandy, seemed to some critics more a symbol of racial progress than a well-developed character.

Two painful breakups

By early 1930 Hughes had experienced many successes, but he would endure a time of pain and loss as two important relationships ended. Hughes had greatly admired Charlotte Mason and deeply appreciated her help; she had given him many opportunities—not only to work free from worries about money but to enrich himself culturally. Yet as time went by it became clear to Hughes that the two differed profoundly in their ideas, for Mason believed that black people provided America's link to the "primitive" and should produce only works that reflected this primitivism. Hughes felt too limited by this idea; he wanted to write according to his own interests and vision, not according to someone else's ideas about how or what he should write. Mason was very angry and hurt when Hughes told her that he valued her friendship but could no longer accept her money, and she refused to speak with him again. Hughes was apparently very upset about his break with Mason, even to the point of feeling physically ill. He found relief only after a period of travel and work on various other projects.

One of his earlier projects, however, would lead to the breakup of another friendship. Financed by Mason, Hughes had worked with Zora Neale Hurston on a play called *Mule Bone,* a comedy that was based on a folktale Hurston had collected during her travels in the South. The play was almost finished when Hughes and Hurston parted company, with Hughes supposedly planning to finish polishing the final act. Sometime later, though, Hughes learned that Hurston was promoting the play as her own creation. An attempt at reconciliation between the two friends failed, and they only rarely spoke to each other for the rest of their lives. *Mule Bone* would not be produced until 1991.

A tour of the South

After a period of travel in the southern United States and in Haiti, Hughes applied for a grant from the Rosenwald Foundation (a charitable organization that gave writers and other artists money for projects) so that he could go on a poetry-reading tour of black colleges throughout the South. He received a thousand-dollar grant and started on his trip in the fall of 1931. After successful appearances before enthusiastic audiences in North Carolina, Louisiana, Arkansas, and at Tuskegee Institute in Alabama, Hughes ended his tour in San

Francisco, California, at the home of a wealthy white friend named Noel Sullivan.

Traveling through the Soviet Union

Like many young authors and intellectuals of his time, Hughes had become interested in socialism (a political system in which the means of producing and distributing goods are shared by the community or owned by the government) as a possible answer to social injustice. He was eager to experience firsthand the Communist (having an economic system that promotes the ownership of all property by the community as a whole) society that had been established in Russia since the 1917 revolution that had toppled that country's traditional czarist (pronounced ZARR-ist) system. (A czar was a ruler who wielded absolute, or unlimited, power over the Russian people.)

Hughes got his opportunity in 1931, when he joined a group of twenty African Americans whom the government of the then-Soviet Union had invited to Moscow to produce a film about the African American experience. Sometime after their arrival in Moscow, the project was abandoned, and most of the participants returned to the United States. Hughes, however, stayed to travel around the Soviet Union. One of the people he met during his trip was Arthur Koestler, a Hungarian-born British writer who would later write a novel called *Darkness at Noon* that was critical of the Soviet system. Hughes also spent some time touring Asia, stopping in Shanghai, China, and Tokyo, Japan, where he was questioned by the police as a suspicious person and finally sent out of the country.

Hughes returned to the United States in 1933 and moved into Noel Sullivan's home, Ennesfree, in Carmel, California. There he worked on a set of short stories that were published as *The Ways of White Folk* in 1934. This collection includes the stories "Home," about a talented violinist who creates resentment after returning to his hometown from Europe and who is eventually killed, and "The Blues I'm Playing," about a black pianist's conflict with her white patron (a thinly veiled portrayal of Hughes's breakup with Mason).

As the 1930s went on and the nation struggled in the midst of the Great Depression—a severe economic downturn that seemed to take an even higher toll on black people—Hughes became more outspoken about his social concerns, expressing in his poetry a rejection of both the capitalism that formed the backbone of the American economy and the Christianity that was a traditional part of both white and black American life. (Capitalism is a system of government based on private ownership and a free market system.) The poems he wrote during this period include "Goodbye Christ" and "The Ballad of Roosevelt"; the latter expresses a poor family's wait for financial assistance from U.S. president Franklin D. Roosevelt (1882–1945).

Hughes undertook a number of different projects and assignments during these difficult years: he wrote a play, *Mulatto* (based on one of his short stories), that ran on Broadway for a year, and he served as a correspondent for the Baltimore *Afro-American* newspaper during the Spanish Civil War (1936–39). This conflict between Spain's Socialist government and the Nationalist Party, led by Francisco Franco, who staged a military takeover, attracted the attention of many liberal-minded American writers—such as fiction writer Ernest Hemingway, playwright Lillian Hellman, and critic Malcolm Crowley—who traveled to Spain to support the cause of the socialists with their presence.

An active later life

Over the next several decades Hughes continued to write poetry while also pursuing his interest in drama and other genres. In 1939 he founded the New Negro Theatre in Los Angeles, California; that same year he wrote a script for a Hollywood movie called *Way Down South* and worked on his autobiography, *The Big Sea*, which was published in 1940. After receiving a Rosenwald Fellowship to write historical plays, Hughes founded the Skyloft Players in Chicago in 1941, and they produced his play *The Sun Do Move* the next year. Also in 1942, Hughes's *Shakespeare in Harlem* was published. This volume of poems paints a bleak picture of Harlem, highlighting the poverty, frustration, and bitterness that had overtaken it since the glorious days of the Harlem Renaissance. *Shakespeare in Harlem* received mixed reviews from critics, but then and for the remainder of his life Hughes continued to be known as the century's leading African American poet.

During World War II (U.S. involvement began in 1941 and ended in 1945), Hughes, who had moved back to New York, wrote slogans and verses to help sell war bonds, which people bought as a way of helping the government raise money for the war effort. He also started writing a weekly column for the *Chicago Defender,* in which he introduced a folksy character named Jesse B. Semple (later changed to Simple), who served as a mouthpiece for Hughes's political commentary and satire. This character became very popular, and Hughes would later publish several volumes of stories about him (including *The Best of Simple,* 1961). Alberta K. Hunter, a female version of Simple created by Hughes, made her appearance in a volume of poems called *One Way Ticket,* which was dominated by a humorous, ironic tone.

"What happens to a dream deferred?"

In 1951 Hughes produced *Montage of a Dream Deferred,* a book-length poem that contains some of his most powerful statements about racism and warnings about where black people's continuing frustrations could lead. In the part of the poem called "Harlem," Hughes asks "What happens to a dream deferred?"—suggesting that instead of just fading away it may eventually explode. Hughes's history of social protest and interest in communism during the 1930s caused problems for him later on, when a decidedly anticommunist sentiment overtook the United States in the 1950s. He was called to testify before Senator Joseph McCarthy's House Committee on Un-American Activities in 1953. Hughes answered all questions mildly and politely, declined to point a finger at anyone else, and distanced himself from the radical poems he had written earlier in his life.

In the remaining years of his life, Hughes continued to publish books, to make recordings of his own poetry, and to lecture—both in the United States and abroad—on black history and culture. In May 1967 he died quietly in New York after a short illness that many of his friends had known nothing about. Hughes was given a grand funeral that ended with the playing of Duke Ellington's "Do Nothing Until You Hear from Me," and then a small group of friends gathered to join hands and recite his early, celebrated poem "The Negro Speaks of Rivers" as his body was wheeled into a crematorium. Among his final poems, published in *The Panther and the Lash* (1967), was one called "Frederick Douglass," in which Hughes suggests that the freedom and equality dreamed of by the great African American leader may still be attainable.

For More Information

Books

Barksdale, Richard K. *Langston Hughes: The Poet and His Critics.* Chicago: American Library Association, 1977.

Berry, Faith. *Langston Hughes: Before and Beyond Harlem.* Westport, CT: Lawrence Hill, 1983.

Bloom, Harold, ed. *Langston Hughes: Comprehensive Research and Study Guide.* Broomall, PA: Chelsea House, 1999.

Emanuel, James. *Langston Hughes.* New York: Twayne, 1967.

Haskins, James L. *The Life of Langston Hughes: Always Movin' On.* Trenton, NJ: Africa World Press, Inc., 1993.

Hill, Christine. *Langston Hughes: Poet of the Harlem Renaissance.* Hillside, NJ: Enslow Publishers, 1997.

Hughes, Langston. *The Big Sea: An Autobiography.* New York: Knopf, 1940.

Meltzer, Milton. *Langston Hughes.* Brookfield, CT: Millbrook Press, 1997.

O'Daniel, Therman B. *Langston Hughes: Black Genius.* New York: Morrow, 1971.

Rampersad, Arnold. *The Life of Langston Hughes.* Volume 1: *1902–1941: I, Too, Sing America.* New York: Oxford University Press, 1986.

Rampersad, Arnold. *The Life of Langston Hughes.* Volume 2: *1947–1967: I Dream a World.* New York: Oxford University Press, 1988.

Wagner, Jean. *Black Poets of the United States from Paul Laurence Dunbar to Langston Hughes.* Urbana: University of Illinois Press, 1973.

Web sites

Bonvibre's Phat African American Poetry Book. [Online] http://www.math.buffalo.edu/~sww/poetry/hughes_langston.html (accessed on January 4, 2000).

Zora Neale Hurston

Born January 7, 1891
Eatonville, Florida
Died January 28, 1960
Fort Pierce, Florida

American short story writer, autobiographer,
novelist, and folklorist

A major figure in twentieth-century African American literature, Zora Neale Hurston had a sharp wit and a vibrant
personality that made her seem a natural part of the Harlem
Renaissance. Stephen Watson, author of *The Harlem Renaissance*, describes her as "outrageous, unpredictable, and head-
strong." Though probably best known as the author of *Their
Eyes Were Watching God* (1937), Hurston was also a dedicated
collector of African American folklore and one of the first writers to incorporate this rich resource into her own work. During
the Harlem Renaissance she published several memorable
short stories and honed the skills that would come to fruition
in later years, when her novels and nonfiction works appeared.
Her independent spirit and significant accomplishments made
her both a model and a source of inspiration to later generations of black writers.

"Jump at de sun"

Hurston was born in the all-black town of Eatonville,
Florida, located about five miles from the larger city of Orlando.

One of the most
memorable figures of the
Harlem Renaissance, Zora
Neale Hurston had a wit
and a vibrancy that
epitomized the Harlem
Renaissance.

Zora Neale Hurston.
*(Photograph by Carl Van
Vechten. Reproduced by
permission of the Estate of Carl
Van Vechten.)*

She was the fifth of eight children born to Lucy Ann Hurston, who had been a country schoolteacher, and John Hurston, a carpenter and Baptist preacher who served as mayor of Eatonville for three terms. Hurston noted in her autobiography, *Dust Tracks on a Road* (1942), that her mother treated her as a special child and encouraged her to "jump at de sun" and try to realize her dreams. Sometimes scolded by her father for her sassiness, Hurston was imaginative and curious and liked to spend time at the local country store, listening to the blues music and colorful stories played out and told by the townsfolk who gathered there.

But this comfortable life ended when Hurston was nine years old; her mother died and Hurston was sent off to attend school in a different town. Her father remarried, and Hurston didn't get along with his new wife. At fourteen she began a life of wandering, working first as a maid and then as a wardrobe assistant for a traveling theatrical company. She attended school only intermittently until she finally enrolled at Morgan Academy in Baltimore, from which she graduated in June 1918. That fall, Hurston entered Howard University in Washington, D.C., then the country's leading black college. Over the next six years, she took courses while supporting herself as a manicurist in a barber shop. It was during this period that she met Alain Locke (1886–1954), a professor of philosophy at Howard and soon to be one of the most influential older leaders of the Harlem Renaissance.

A promising short story writer

Hurston also began writing short stories. One of these, "John Redding Goes to Sea," about a protagonist who longs to travel to faraway places, was published in the 1921 issue of *Stylus,* Howard's literary magazine. Thanks to Locke, the story came to the attention of sociologist Charles S. Johnson (1893–1956), the editor of the important black publication *Opportunity.* Johnson recognized Hurston's talent and encouraged her to move to New York City and join the other young black writers and artists who were gathering there. In January 1925 Hurston arrived in Harlem with, as she recalled in her autobiography, "$1.50, no job, no friends, and a lot of hope."

Soon Hurston's writing—as well as her lively personality—would make her a full-fledged and popular member of the Harlem Renaissance scene. She entered several of her works in *Opportunity*'s first literary contest and made a splashy appearance at the awards dinner in May when she accepted a second-place prize for a short story, "Spunk," (which would later appear in *Opportunity* and in Locke's *New Negro* anthology) and a play, "Color Struck," as well as honorable mentions for two other works. And it was at this dinner that Hurston met two important new friends: Fannie Hurst, a well-known white author, and Annie Nathan Meyer, one of the founders of Barnard College. Hurst soon offered Hurston a job as her secretary and chauffeur, and Meyer arranged for a scholarship so that Hurston could study anthropology at Barnard.

In the fall of 1925 Hurston entered Barnard College. She was the school's only black student. Among her teachers was the famous German-born American anthropologist Franz Boas (1858–1942), who was impressed by this dynamic young woman and saw her as the perfect person to collect the still-ungathered folklore of African American culture. Hurston's studies, and especially her contact with Boas, led her to view her past and her heritage differently than she had before—to see it as something very special that might interest other people. In *Dust Tracks on a Road,* she wrote: "It was only when I was off in college, away from my native surroundings, that I could see myself like somebody else.... I had to have the spy-glass of anthropology to look through."

Gaining friends and a patron

Meanwhile, Hurston had become a popular member of the younger crowd of Harlem Renaissance writers and artists, many of whom congregated at the boarding house that Hurston (known for her witty remarks) jokingly called "Niggerati Manor." She was particularly famous for her ability to tell vivid stories, complete with authentic dialect and accents. White patrons who were drawn to Harlem found Hurston very entertaining (especially those at the parties given by critic and Harlem Renaissance enthusiast Carl Van Vechten [see Chapter 2], which Hurston often attended). In fact, some of Hurston's friends felt she consciously aimed to please white listeners and friends. Langston Hughes (1902–1967; see biographical entry) remembered in his autobiography, *The Big Sea,* that she knew how to "represent the Negro Race" and be "a perfect 'darkie' [a derogatory term for black people] ... naive, childlike, sweet." In his novel *Infants of the Spring,* a fictional portrayal of the real lives and adventures of the younger Harlem Renaissance crowd, Wallace Thurman (1902–1934; see biographical entry) cast Hurston as a character named Sweetie May Carr, who was known more "for her ribald wit and personal effervescence than for any actual literary work. She was a great favorite among those whites who went in for Negro prodigies."

As Hurston's studies at Barnard came to an end, Boas helped her get a fourteen-hundred-dollar scholarship from the Carter G. Woodson Foundation, which she used to fund a folklore-gathering trip into the southern United States. This trip was not too successful, though, because Hurston had not yet learned how to blend in with and talk to the people she interviewed; she spoke with an educated, East Coast accent that made southern blacks feel uncomfortable. Meanwhile, Hurston married Herbert Sheen in May 1927, but the marriage did not last long due to Hurston's devotion to her career above all else.

In September 1927 Hurston met Charlotte Mason (1854–1946), the wealthy white woman with a deep interest in African American culture who had already become a patron of several Harlem Renaissance writers and artists (including poet Langston Hughes and artists Miguel Covarubbias [1904–1957] and Richmond Barthé [1901–1989]). Impressed by Hurston, Mason offered to support her while she conducted her anthropological work, and in December the two women signed a contract. Hurston would receive two hundred dollars a month as well as a movie camera and a Ford automobile; she was to travel in the South and collect folklore, then report back to Mason with all the materials she had gathered.

Collecting folklore and establishing a literary career

Hurston spent the next three years traveling—mostly in Alabama and Florida—and collected a huge amount of folklore, including songs, stories, and a careful record of the slang and figures of speech used by southern blacks. But these were also frustrating years, as Hurston failed to get any of the material published and began to doubt her ability as a writer. She also went through a painful breakup with her good friend Langston Hughes after the two had worked together on a play called *Mule Bone,* which was based on one of the folktales Hurston had collected. Hughes was deeply angered and upset when Hurston tried to get the play published as her own creation. The two friends parted company and spoke to each other only rarely for the rest of their lives.

Hurston's contract with Mason ended in 1931, but Mason continued to give her money for another year. In early 1932 Hurston went to work at Rollins College in Winter Park, Florida, where she was to create an African American arts program. Plagued by illness and a lack of money, she returned briefly to New York but finally went back to her hometown of Eatonville, Florida. This period of confusion and frustration came to an end in 1933 with the appearance of Hurston's short story, "The Gilded Six Bits," in *Story* magazine, an event that gave her literary career a much-needed boost. Considered one of Hurston's finest stories, "The Gilded Six Bits" concerns a young rural black couple whose happiness is temporarily disrupted by a slick city-dweller who appears in their small community. The story's well-developed characters and skillfully rendered dialect attracted the attention of the Lippincott publishing company, whose editors asked Hurston if she had written a novel. She had not, but she went right to work on one, and the result was *Jonah's Gourd Vine,* which was published by Lippincott in 1934.

Based on the lives of Hurston's parents, *Jonah's Gourd Vine* tells the story of Alabama-born John "Buddy" Pearson, the son of a former slave and, most probably, her white owner. Pearson ends up marrying three wives in succession but is unable to remain faithful to any of them. He experiences a number of ups and downs as he pursues careers as a carpenter and a preacher. Finally he seems to have achieved a happy marriage and successful life, but while returning from a business trip he has an affair with a young woman he meets on the train, and he dies before reaching home. Praised for its rich language and emotional power, *Jonah's Gourd Vine* sold well, though many critics and readers of the time failed to note the racial themes that were at its core.

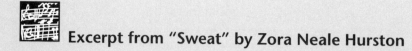

Excerpt from "Sweat" by Zora Neale Hurston

It was eleven o'clock of a Spring night in Florida. It was Sunday. Any other night, Delia Jones would have been in bed for two hours by this time. But she was a washwoman, and Monday morning meant a great deal to her. So she collected the soiled clothes on Saturday when she returned the clean things. Sunday night after church, she sorted them and put the white things to soak. It saved her almost half a day's start. A great hamper in the bedroom held the clothes that she brought home. It was so much neater than a number of bundles lying around.

She squatted in the kitchen floor beside the great pile of clothes, sorting them into small heaps according to color, and humming a song in a mournful key, but wondering through it all where Sykes, her husband, had gone with her horse and buckboard.

Just then something long, round, limp and black fell upon her shoulders and slithered to the floor beside her. A great terror took hold of her. It softened her knees and dried her mouth so that it was a full minute before she could cry out or move. Then she saw that it was the big bull whip her husband liked to carry when he drove.

She lifted her eyes to the door and saw him standing there bent over with laughter at her fright. She screamed at him.

"Sykes, what you throw dat whip on me like dat? You know it would skeer me—looks just like a snake, an' you knows how skeered Ah is of snakes."

"'Course Ah knowed it! That's how come Ah done it." He slapped his leg with his hand and almost rolled on the ground in his mirth. "If you such a big fool dat you got to have a fit over a earth worm or a string, Ah don't keer how bad Ah skeer you."

"You ain't got no business doing it. Gawd knows it's a sin. Some day Ah'm gointuh drop dead from some of yo' foolishness. 'Nother thing, were you been wid mah rig? Ah feeds dat pony. He ain't fuh you to be drivin' wid no bull whip."

"You sho is one aggravatin' nigger woman!" he declared and stepped into the room. She resumed her work and did not answer him at once. "Ah done tole you time and time again to keep them white folks' clothes outa dis house."

Mules and Men and other works

Hurston's new reputation as an accomplished writer led to the publication of the collected folktales and other materials that she had always called her "story book." *Mules and Men* was published in 1935 and featured an introduction by Franz Boas, who

He picked up the whip and glared down at her. Delia went on with her work. She went out into the yard and returned with a galvanized tub and sit it on the washbench. She saw that Sykes had kicked all of the clothes together again, and now stood in her way trucculently, his whole manner hoping, praying, for an argument. But she walked calmly around him and commenced to re-sort the things.

"Next time, Ah'm gointer kick 'em outdoors," he threatened as he struck a match along the leg of his corduroy breeches.

Delia never looked up from her work, and her thin, stooped shoulders sagged further.

"Ah ain't for no fuss t'night Sykes. Ah just come from taking sacrament at the church house."

He snorted scornfully. "Yeah, you just come from de church house on a Sunday night, but heah you is gone to work on them clothes. You ain't nothing but a hyprocrite. One of them amen-corner Christians—sing, whoop, and shout, then come home and wash white folks' clothes on the Sabbath."

He stepped roughly on the whitest pile of things, kicking them helter-skelter as he crossed the room. His wife gave a little scream of dismay and quickly gathered them together again.

"Sykes, you quit grindin' dirt into these clothes! How can ah git through by Sat'day if Ah don't start on Sunday?"

"Ah don't keer if you never git through. Anyhow, Ah done promised Gawd and a couple of other men, Ah ain't gointer have it in mah house. Don't gimme no lip neither, else Ah'll throw 'em out and put mah fist up side yo' head to boot."

Delia's habitual meekness seemed to slip from her shoulders like a blown scarf. She was on her feet; her poor little body, her bare knuckly hands bravely defying the strapping hulk before her.

"Looka heah, Sykes, you done gone too fur. Ah been married to you fur fifteen years, and Ah been takin' in washin' for fifteen years. Sweat, sweat, sweat! Work and sweat, cry and sweat, pray and sweat!"

praised the book as helping readers understand "historically the character of American Negro life." Although everyone agreed that *Mules and Men* was important as a work of anthropology, some African American and other critics faulted Hurston for giving it too light and carefree a tone and avoiding the issue of racial conflict.

Hurston spent the next few years touring with several musical revues that were based on the folktales she had gathered, including *Sun to Sun* (produced in Florida), *The Great Day*, and *Singing Steel* (both of which appeared in Chicago). She was offered a fellowship to pursue a doctoral degree in anthropology at New York's Columbia University, but the work and study schedule proved too restrictive so she turned it down. In the fall of 1935 Hurston joined the Federal Writers Project of the newly created Works Progress Administration (WPA; a U.S. government agency founded in 1935, called the Works Progress Administration until 1939, designed to give out-of-work Americans a new start), and the next year she received a Guggenheim fellowship to collect folklore in the West Indies. Hurston published the results of her work in *Tell My Horse* (1938). After her return to the United States, she began writing a novel that would become her best-known and most acclaimed work, *Their Eyes Were Watching God*, which was published in 1937.

An African American classic

The story of a woman who finds happiness by following her own heart rather than her society's expectations, *Their Eyes Were Watching God* has come to be seen as a masterpiece of African American literature. The central character is feisty Janie Woods, who tells the story of her life to a friend, recounting her marriages to three husbands: the first a middle-aged farmer; the second a handsome and ambitious man who takes her to live in Eatonville, Florida; and finally Tea Cake Woods, a migrant farmworker who makes her happy until he contracts rabies and she is forced to kill him in self-defense. Although she is married to Tea Cake for only eighteen months, Janie lives a complete, emotionally satisfying life during that period and feels fulfilled. The novel was praised for its warm and richly descriptive portrayal of southern black people and life, and particularly for the character of Janie, a strong, passionate, and independent woman. More than thirty years later, *Their Eyes Were Watching God* was championed by contemporary African American author Alice Walker, who credited Hurston with inspiring her own work.

In the fall of 1939 Hurston became a drama instructor at North Carolina College for Negroes in Durham. She also married Albert Price III, a man at least fifteen years younger than she was (they would divorce four years later), and finished her next book, *Moses, Man of the Mountain* (1939). This novel is a retelling of the biblical story of Moses, who led the enslaved Hebrews out of Egypt and into the Promised Land of Canaan. Hurston shaped her novel as an allegory (a symbolic representation) of African American oppression by whites. Though not considered as solid a literary achievement as her previous novel, *Moses* highlights Hurston's command of African American speech and folklore as well as her interest in conveying the history of African Americans in an unusual way.

Remembered as "A Genius of the South"

Hurston spent a short period from late 1940 to early 1941 living in California with a wealthy friend, Katharine Mershon, and working on her autobiography, *Dust Tracks on a Road,* which was published in 1942. The book sold well and even won an award for contributing to better race relations. It provides an entertaining, flattering view of Hurston and is not considered entirely accurate in its facts.

At this point Hurston began to be courted by magazines such as the *Saturday Evening Post* and *Reader's Digest* for contributions. Some of the pieces she wrote for them proved controversial, though, because she seemed to suggest that blacks and whites could not live together harmoniously and should be segregated.

During the last two decades of her life Hurston continued to write but did not publish much, especially after the appearance of her final novel, *Seraph on the Suwanee,* in 1948. This novel centers on white characters (Hurston wanted to show that black writers could convey white life and people in their works), including Arvay Henson, a poor woman who gradually develops a sense of self-worth. Hurston continued to live mostly in Florida, and especially enjoyed traveling up and down the Halifax and Indian rivers on her houseboat *Wanago.* But as time went by she found it increasingly difficult to support herself, and by 1950 she was forced to take a job as a maid. Over the next ten years she survived by borrowing money from friends and working for short periods as a librarian, a reporter, and a substitute teacher.

Hurston had experienced poor health for many years, and in October of 1958 she had a stroke and was forced to enter the Saint Lucie Country Welfare Home, which provided long-term care for low-income people. She died on January 28, 1960, and was buried in an unmarked grave in an all-black cemetery called the Garden of Heavenly Rest in Fort Pierce, Florida. Some of Hurston's old friends took up a collection to pay for her funeral, at which the minister declared that Hurston had been wealthy despite her poverty: "The Miami paper said she died poor. But she died rich. She did something." Nearly twenty years earlier, Hurston had written in her autobiography that she had indeed "touched the four corners of the horizon."

Hurston's works were largely overlooked until the 1970s, when African American and other writers and readers began to rediscover them. A key figure in this rediscovery was novelist and poet Alice Walker, who admired Hurston's writing and independent spirit and who cited Hurston as an influence on her own work. In 1973 Walker made a pilgrimage to Florida to try to find Hurston's grave. After a long search she located what she believed to be the unmarked grave, and there she placed a marker engraved with Hurston's name and a line from a poem by Harlem Renaissance writer Jean Toomer: "A Genius of the South."

For More Information

Bloom, Harold, ed. *Zora Neale Hurston*. Broomall, PA: Chelsea House, 1986.

Hemenway, Robert. *Zora Neale Hurston: A Literary Biography*. Chicago: University of Illinois Press, 1977.

Howard, Lillie P. *Zora Neale Hurston*. Boston: Twayne, 1980.

Hurston, Zora Neale. *Dust Tracks on a Road*. Philadelphia: Lippincott, 1942.

Karanja, Ayana I. *Zora Neale Hurston: The Breath of Her Voice*. New York: Peter Lang Publishers, 1999.

Lester, Neal A., ed. *Understanding Zora Neale Hurston's* Their Eyes Were Watching God*: A Student Casebook to Issues, Sources, and Historical Documents*. Westport, CT: Greenwood Press, 1999.

Lyons, Mary E. *Sorrow's Kitchen: The Life and Folklore of Zora Neale Hurston*. Scribner Book Company, 1990.

Porter, A.P. *Jump at de Sun: The Story of Zora Neale Hurston*. Minneapolis, MN: First Avenue Editions, 1992.

Watson, Steven. *The Harlem Renaissance: Hub of African-American Culture, 1920–1930*. New York: Pantheon Books, 1995.

Yanuzzi, Della. *Southern Storyteller*. Hillside, NJ: Enslow Publishers, 1996.

Yates, Janelle. *Zora Neale Hurston: A Storyteller's Life*. Staten Island, NY: Ward Hill Press, 1992.

Nella Larsen

Born April 13, 1891
Chicago, Illinois
Died March 30, 1964
New York, New York

American novelist

In the course of only a few years Nella Larsen produced two of the most accomplished novels of the Harlem Renaissance, and she was considered one of the period's most promising authors. Her work reflects her own experiences as a biracial person (she was the daughter of a white mother and a black father), focusing on the issues of identity and belonging that she and others of mixed racial heritage faced. Larsen is credited with moving away from casting the biracial individual as a "tragic mulatto," a common practice in nineteenth-century novels, and achieving more complex portrayals. Critics also praise her sensitive explorations of the problems of women (especially black women) in search of fulfillment.

Nella Larsen struggled all her life with the question of where she belonged— in the black world or the white.

Nella Larsen.
(Courtesy of Beineke Rare Book and Manuscript Library.)

Caught between the black and white worlds

Not much is known about Larsen's early life. She was born in 1891 in Chicago, Illinois, to a Danish-American mother and a black father born in the Caribbean islands or West Indies. Her father died when she was two years old, and her mother soon married a white man of Danish ethnicity, like herself. Larsen grew up entirely surrounded by white people, including a half-sister whom she would later claim was embarrassed to have a biracial sibling.

It seems likely that as Larsen grew older she felt a need to associate with African Americans, for after finishing high school in Chicago she enrolled at Fisk University, one of the country's leading black schools. She attended Fisk from 1909 to 1910 but apparently felt uncomfortable in that all-black world and transferred to the University of Copenhagen in Denmark, where she studied science. Living in a society that was mostly segregated, Larsen was struggling with the question of where she belonged—in the black world or the white.

A nurse and librarian

Larsen returned to the United States in 1912 and entered a nursing course at Lincoln Hospital in New York City. After spending one year as a supervising nurse at Tuskegee Institute (the black trade and agricultural school founded by African American leader Booker T. Washington [1856–1915] in Alabama), Larsen worked for several years as a nurse at Lincoln Hospital and for the New York City Department of Health. In 1921 she became a New York Public Library assistant, and two years later she completed the library's training course to become a librarian. She worked as a children's librarian at the 135th Street branch in Harlem from 1924 to 1926.

Meanwhile, back in May of 1919, Larsen had married a physicist named Elmer Imes and had become active in the Harlem social scene, even though she had a reserved personality and cultivated manners that made her seem standoffish. Her library work gave her easy access not only to the excellent black cultural material housed in the Schomburg Collection at the 135th Street branch but to the literary activities—such as book readings and discussions—that took place there. Always an avid reader and book collector, Larsen decided that she too would like to try her hand at writing.

A highly praised first novel

In January 1926 Larsen resigned her library position and devoted herself to the development of her writing skills;

she started with short stories and then began working on a novel. Larsen's efforts were encouraged by two Harlem Renaissance leaders known for their support of promising black writers, Walter White (1893–1955; a black novelist himself and a top official of the NAACP) and Carl Van Vechten (1880–1964; a white critic, novelist, photographer and booster of African American culture). When Larsen finished her novel, Van Vechten sent the manuscript to his own publisher, Alfred A. Knopf. It was accepted and published as *Quicksand* in 1928.

Written in only six weeks (though Larsen claimed she had been thinking about it for five months), *Quicksand* concerns a restless, complex protagonist named Helga Crane who is, like her creator, the daughter of a Danish-American mother and a black father. The book chronicles Helga's search for happiness and satisfaction, beginning with her education in Chicago by a white uncle and her time spent teaching at Naxos, a small all-black school in the South. Impatient with the hypocrisy she witnesses there (and unconsciously in love with the school's principal), Helga returns to Chicago, where she meets a rich black woman who helps her find a job and a place to stay in Harlem. There, Helga experiences the comfortable, insulated life of the African American middle class, a life that she soon finds too limited and unsatisfying.

Next, Helga travels to Denmark to stay with her aunt and uncle. She meets a handsome, rather arrogant Danish painter who wants to marry her, but after two years she grows tired of being treated like an exotic curiosity. Helga returns to Harlem, where she feels desperate and lost until she has a religious experience in a storefront church. She marries the church's pastor, the overweight, uneducated Reverend Pleasant Green, and moves with him to Alabama, where she begins a seemingly endless cycle of childbearing. At the end of *Quicksand,* Helga is pregnant with her fifth child and seems unlikely to escape from the isolated, physically exhausting situation she has chosen.

Praise for *Quicksand,* then and now

At the time of its publication, *Quicksand* received positive reviews from publications both black (such as *Crisis, Opportunity,* and the *Amsterdam News*) and white (including the *New York Times* and the *Saturday Review of Literature*). Larsen's psychologically complex portrait of a woman caught between two races was praised by conservative critics like W.E.B. Du Bois—who, in a review in *Crisis* (quoted in David Levering Lewis's *When Harlem Was in Vogue*), called the novel "on the whole the best piece of fiction that Negro American has produced since the heyday of [nineteenth-century African American writer Charles] Chesnutt"—as well as more liberal ones like Alain Locke.

Later critics have continued to laud Larsen's depiction of Helga, especially her feelings of alienation and loneliness and her struggle to maintain her self-esteem. Still, many reviewers have found the novel's ending weak due to its ambiguity: is the reader supposed to see this conclusion as a tragedy, or is it the fate Helga has really been seeking all along?

Passing also earns acclaim

Larsen won the Harmon Foundation's (an organization founded to recognize and support black achievers in several categories) bronze medal for literature in 1928, and the next year proved even more eventful. In 1929 she became the first African American woman to receive a Guggenheim Foundation fellowship for creative writing, and her novel *Passing* was published. This novel focuses on the practice of light-skinned African Americans "passing" as white in order to attain acceptance and material security, and it explores the costs of such deception.

Passing features two contrasting main characters, both of them light-skinned black women: Irene Redfield (from whose perspective the story is told) is married to Brian, a successful—though restless and dissatisfied—black doctor, and enjoys a comfortable if somewhat dull life in Harlem; her old friend Clare Kendry, who pretends to be white, has married a jolly but racially prejudiced white man in order to avoid a life of poverty. Irene and Clare meet by chance, and Clare begins to make frequent visits into Harlem, drawn in by the warmth and familiarity of the black community but always fearing that her husband will discover her real identity. Just as Clare's husband bursts into a Harlem party, Clare falls seventeen floors from the window of the apartment where the party is being held. She may have fallen or taken her own life, but it is strongly suggested that she was pushed by Irene, who had felt threatened by the mutual attraction between Clare and Brian.

Once again, Larsen provides a modern, skillfully written perspective on an old issue, that of passing and the toll it takes on those who choose to hide their true racial identity. Larsen portrays the self-doubt, confusion, and loneliness experienced by those who pass and explores such themes as the hypocrisy and pretentiousness of the black middle class (who enjoy a comfortable existence while ignoring the suffering of less privileged blacks) and the dangers of both risk-taking and security-seeking behaviors. Critics responded to *Passing* much as they had to *Quicksand,* praising Larsen's narrative skill and grasp of character while faulting the novel's ambiguous ending, which leaves the readers very much in doubt about the author's real message.

Time in Europe leads to break with literary life

In 1930, funded by her Guggenheim fellowship, Larsen left for Spain and France, where she intended to work on several new writing projects. Just before her departure, she had to defend herself against a charge of plagiarism (claiming someone else's work as one's own) regarding her short story "Sanctuary." Although Larsen successfully cleared herself of guilt, the incident seems to have depleted her self-confidence. Her time in Europe was also marred by problems in her marriage. She started two novels while living overseas, but neither was ever completed.

After returning to the United States, Larsen attempted to salvage her marriage by moving to Nashville, Tennessee, where her husband was teaching. Apparently, she continued to write, but she did not publish anything else. In 1933 she was divorced from Elmer Imes and returned to New York. This time Larsen moved not to Harlem but to Greenwich Village, a community located closer to downtown Manhattan that was popular with artistic people. For a short time she associated with other writers, but eventually Larsen dropped out of the literary scene.

With the death of her former husband in 1941, Larsen was left without the financial support she had been receiving from him. She returned to nursing, working for the next twenty years as a night nurse and supervising nurse in various Manhattan hospitals and leading a very quiet life. She died at the age of seventy-two, just before the revival of interest in Harlem Renaissance writers that took place during the 1960s. Recognizing her as a significant talent, many critics and readers regret that Larsen produced only two novels in her short writing career.

For More Information

Books

Christian, Barbara. *Black Women Novelists: The Development of a Tradition, 1892–1976*. Westport, CT: Greenwood Press, 1980.

Doyle, Sister Mary Ellen. "The Heroines of Black Novels." In *Perspectives on Afro-American Women.* Edited by Willa Johnson and Thomas Green. Washington, DC: ECCA Publishers, 1975, pp. 112–25.

Fuller, Hoyt. Introduction to *Passing,* by Nella Larsen. New York: Collier, 1971, pp. 10–24.

Hill, Adelaide C. Introduction to *Quicksand,* by Nella Larsen. New York: Collier, 1971, pp. 9-17.

Huggins, Nathan Irvin. *Harlem Renaissance.* New York: Oxford University Press, 1971.

McLendon, Jacquelyn Y. *The Politics of Color in the Fiction of Jessie Fauset and Nella Larsen.* Charlottesville: University Press of Virginia, 1995.

Sato, Hirako. "Under the Harlem Shadow: A Study of Jessie Fauset and Nella Larsen." In *Harlem Renaissance Remembered.* Edited by Arna Bontemps. New York: Dodd, Mead, 1972.

Periodicals

Tate, Claudia. "Nella Larsen's Passing: A Problem of Interpretation." *Black American Literature Forum* (Winter 1980): 142–46.

Thornton, Hortense. "Sexism as Quagmire: Nella Larsen's *Quicksand.*" *CLA Journal* (March 1973): 285–301.

Washington, Mary Helen. "Nella Larsen: Mystery Woman of the Harlem Renaissance." *Ms.* 9 (December 1980): 44-50.

Alain Locke

Born September 13, 1886
Philadelphia, Pennsylvania
Died June 10, 1954
New York, New York

American philosopher, educator, editor, and writer

The most memorable achievements of the Harlem Renaissance did not just spring into life by magic. The movement's young writers and artists were nurtured and encouraged by a number of older figures, the most important of whom was writer-educator Alain Locke. A highly educated philosophy professor with a passionate dedication to both preserving African American culture and encouraging bold new art, Locke served as a kind of midwife (someone who aids in the birthing process) of the Harlem Renaissance. Through his work as a writer and editor—especially of the influential anthology *The New Negro: An Interpretation*—he also served as a proud voice explaining to a broad audience the background and aims of the Harlem Renaissance.

Parents instilled early values

Locke was the descendent of a family of educated, free African Americans (they had been freed from slavery even before the end of the Civil War [1861–65]) who had been living for several generations in Philadelphia, Pennsylvania.

"All of us probably expected too much of the Negro Renaissance, but its new vitality of independence, pride, and self-respect, its scoff and defiance of prejudice and limitations were so welcome and heartening."

Alain Locke.
(Courtesy of the Library of Congress.)

They were part of the black community referred to as the "O.P." ("Old Philadelpha" families). His grandfather, Ishmael Locke, had been an educator and school administrator, and his father, Pliny, had earned a law degree at Howard University (the nation's leading black college) and taught at the Philadelphia School of Pedagogy (pronounced PEDD-uh-GOE-jee; the profession of teaching).

Locke's mother, Mary, a teacher at the Philadelphia Institute for Colored Youth, encouraged her only child to appreciate literature, to study piano and violin, and to practice good manners. Although they were not wealthy, the Lockes were members of a comfortably middle-class black community, and they always stressed the values of education and good behavior. Later in life Locke would describe his family's properness through the image of his grandmother wearing a sunbonnet and gloves to hang laundry.

A slight-statured, book-loving, intelligent boy who often suffered from ill health, Locke excelled at his studies early on. He graduated second in his class from Philadelphia's Central High School and first in his class from the Philadelphia School of Pedagogy. Locke entered Harvard University in 1904, where he developed an interest in philosophy and studied under American philosopher William James (1842–1910), whose ideas about the benefits of living in a pluralistic society (one that recognizes the value of all the different groups of which it's made) influenced his own thinking.

An outstanding student of philosophy

In 1907 Locke graduated from Harvard with high honors and a bachelor's degree in English and philosophy. That same year he became the first African American—and the last for the next sixty years—to be chosen as a Rhodes scholar, a program that allows outstanding graduates the chance to attend England's elite Oxford University. From 1907 to 1910 Locke studied at Oxford, where he experienced racism and felt isolated until he became friendly with a group of African students. He was known as a very intellectual, studious person with a warm personality, a good sense of humor, and an elegant way of dressing.

After leaving Oxford, Locke went to Germany's University of Berlin for a year of study in philosophy, then to Paris for another year at the College de France. For the rest of his life Locke would make frequent visits to Europe. He maintained a deep love of European culture that existed alongside his appreciation for African American traditions.

Returning to the United States in 1912, Locke spent six months traveling around the southern states, looking for a job in a black university. A white person with Locke's impressive record and credentials would have been hired quickly by any leading white institution, but Locke's race limited his opportunities. During his travels throughout the South, he witnessed more hostility toward blacks than he ever had in Philadelphia or Europe, and he also grew even more interested in the dynamic cultural expressions of African Americans.

In 1912 Locke became an assistant professor of English and an instructor in philosophy and education at Washington, D.C.'s Howard University, where he would remain employed (except for a short period in the late 1920s) for the next forty years. He took a very active role in educating his students about their heritage, while simultaneously stressing the value of learning about Western European culture and languages.

Although Locke's obvious brilliance and great energy made him popular with students, he could sometimes be overbearing and rather straitlaced. He did, however, encourage his students to express themselves freely, and in 1916 he founded a literary magazine called *Stylus* so that students would have a place to publish their work. Locke returned to Harvard that same year to work on his doctoral dissertation (which centered on the idea that values are not absolute but shaped by an individual's cultural background and surroundings), and he earned his Ph.D. in 1918. He was the first African American to receive a doctoral degree in philosophy from Harvard.

Recognizes black talent

As the 1920s began, Locke was among the first to sense a shift in how African Americans felt about themselves and about their role in American society. His work as an educator had brought him into contact with many talented young people, and he sensed that a cultural blossoming was under way. Locke made frequent visits to Harlem, where he would often be seen walking quickly along in an elegant suit, always carrying a tightly furled umbrella. He became a friend and supporter of many of the young writers and artists who were in New York in search of like-minded people and material success. Among those who would, over the years, benefit from Locke's influence and support were: poets Langston Hughes (1902–1967; see biographical entry) and Countee Cullen (1903–1946; see biographical entry); short story writers Zora Neale Hurston (1891–1960; see biographical entry) and Rudolph Fisher (1897–1934); novelist Jean Toomer (1894–1967; see biographical entry); and classical singer Roland Hayes (1887–1977).

Meanwhile, Locke was still teaching at Howard University, where he stirred up controversy by pushing administrators to offer courses on race relations and to establish a national black theater. This tension led to Locke's dismissal from Howard in 1924, soon after his return from a sabbatical (a period of study that is usually spent away from a professor's university) in North Africa. Locke would return to Howard in 1928, but for these few years he had the time and freedom to devote himself to the Harlem Renaissance.

As a shining example of the Talented Tenth (black leader W.E.B. Du Bois's term for the upper crust of African American society), Locke shared their conviction that African Americans could promote racial progress through their abilities and accomplishments. Unlike Du Bois, however, Locke felt that black writers and artists could help their race most by producing a broad spectrum of high-quality art, not just works that cast a positive light on African Americans. He also believed passionately that the richest sources for inspiration lay in the African American folk tradition—the treasure trove of stories and music that blacks had produced during their several centuries in the United States.

Through articles written for various publications, anthologies of black literature he edited, and his own complex network of personal connections—especially with wealthy or influential whites who were interested in African American culture—Locke served as a kind of talent or press agent for the younger generation of Harlem Renaissance writers, actors, musicians, and visual artists. Always on the lookout for new talent, he gave his young friends advice on how to further their careers, and he introduced them to people who could help them reach their goals. Most important, though, was Locke's role as the editor of *The New Negro* anthology.

The New Negro: The core of the Harlem Renaissance

Considered one of the most important books published during—and about—the Harlem Renaissance, *The New Negro: An Interpretation* had its start at a special dinner organized by *Opportunity* editor Charles S. Johnson (1893–1956; see Chapter 2). Supposedly planned as a celebration to mark the publication of Jessie Redmon Fauset's (1882–1961; see biographical entry) first novel, *There Is Confusion,* the dinner held at New York's downtown Civic Club on March 21, 1924, was really a way to introduce new talents like Jean Toomer and Countee Cullen to the white publishers and patrons who could help bring them recognition.

Among those in attendance was Paul Kellogg, editor of the *Survey Graphic* magazine, who wanted to put together a special issue showcasing the work of African American writers and artists. Kellogg asked Locke to edit the issue, which was to "express the progressive spirit of contemporary Negro life," and Locke accepted the assignment with enthusiasm. Published in March 1925, the result was a collection of poems, stories, essays, and art by thirty-four contributors (four of them white, the rest black) that blended African American folk influences with modern voices. The public's response was overwhelming. The issue was the most popular in the *Survey Graphic*'s history, with an estimated readership of forty thousand; it had to be reprinted twice. By the end of the year the publishing company of Albert and Charles Boni had put out a bound, expanded version of the *Survey Graphic* issue under the name *The New Negro: An Interpretation.* This anthology still stands as the clearest expression of the ideas that lay at the core of the Harlem Renaissance, ideas that were described by Locke in his introduction to the volume and in the four essays he contributed.

Locke's introduction announced the arrival of a "New Negro" and a bold, confident new stage in African American history. Just as the circumstances of so many blacks had been changed by the migration from the South to the North and the shift from rural to urban life, ideas about what black people were like and what they could do also had to change. Old stereotypes were being destroyed, and African Americans were beginning to take their rightful place in American society. They would no longer accept the view of themselves as a "problem," but would instead take pride in themselves and be full participants in their nation's democracy.

This would be achieved, Locke asserted, through "the revaluation by white and black alike of the Negro in terms of his artistic endowments and cultural contributions, past and prospective." Locke grandly predicted that this exciting young generation of black writers and artists would serve as "the advance guard of the African peoples in their contact with twentieth century civilization," and he said that all of this was happening in Harlem, "the laboratory of a great race-welding," where blacks from all parts of the world came together to do great things.

Although the significance and value of *The New Negro* anthology was immediately recognized, its promises were not so easily or so quickly realized. As the 1920s drew to a close, the Harlem Renaissance was also winding down. Locke returned to Howard University in 1928 and began to devote more of his time to his teaching responsibilities than to his friends in Harlem. The next year saw the American stock market crash and resulting economic decline that marked the beginning of the Great Depression (the period of economic hardship and widespread unemployment that lasted from the stock market crash of 1929 until 1941, when the United States entered World War II [1939–45]). The hoped-for improvement in race relations and in the status of blacks through artistic achievement had not come about, and African Americans had many decades of struggle still ahead. In an article in *Phylon* in 1950, Locke noted, "All of us probably expected too much of the Negro Renaissance, but its new vitality of independence, pride, and self-respect, its scoff and defiance of prejudice and limitations were so welcome and heartening."

After the Harlem Renaissance

During the remaining decades of his life, Locke maintained his position as a leading black scholar and thinker. He continued to write critical essays and, until 1942, edited an annual review of black literature for *Opportunity*. He served as a visiting professor at the universities of Wisconsin and California and the City College of New York, lectured across the United States and throughout Latin American, traveled to Europe and Africa, and served on various editorial boards. In 1933 Locke was commissioned by the American Association of Adult Education (AAAE) to evaluate adult education centers in Harlem and Atlanta, and in response to the lack of attention to black issues he found there, he established the Association of Negro Folk Education (ANFE) in 1935. Locke was elected president of the AAAE in 1945.

In 1951 Locke received a grant from the Rockefeller Foundation to produce a work summarizing his studies of African American culture. His work on this project was interrupted when he was hospitalized for a heart ailment. He retired from Howard University in 1953 and moved to New York City. Locke's health then declined steadily, and he died in June of 1954. His colleague Mary Just Butcher finished his final book, *The Negro in American Culture*, which was published in 1956.

For More Information:

Books
Alain Locke: Scholar and Educator. New York: Chelsea House Publishers, 1995.

Harris, Leonard. *The Philosophy of Alain Locke: Harlem Renaissance and Beyond.* Philadelphia, PA: Temple University Press, 1991.

Huggins, Nathan Irvin. *Harlem Renaissance.* New York: Oxford University Press, 1971.

Lewis, David Levering. *When Harlem Was in Vogue.* New York: Knopf, 1981.

Linnemann, Russell J., ed. *Alain Locke: Reflections on a Renaissance Man.* Baton Rouge: Louisiana State University Press, 1982.

Locke, Alain, ed. *The New Negro: An Interpretation.* 1925. Reprint: Scribner, 1997.

Watson, Steven. *The Harlem Renaissance: Hub of African American Culture, 1920–1930.* New York: Pantheon, 1995.

Periodicals
Long, Richard A. "Alain Locke: Cultural and Social Mentor." *Black World* (November 1970): 87–90.

Claude McKay

Born September 15, 1890
Sunny Ville, Jamaica
Died May 22, 1948
Chicago, Illinois

Jamaican-born American poet, journalist, essayist, and novelist

O ne of the most talented and respected younger writers of the Harlem Renaissance, Festus Claudius McKay, better known as Claude McKay, set himself apart from his colleagues by spending most of the 1920s living outside the United States. His radical political views and scorn for those he saw as compromising their own ideals meant that he was only a reluctant member of the New Negro movement, as Harlem's era of artistic and cultural growth was then called. Nevertheless, McKay wrote some of the period's best poetry and one of its most revealing novels, and he was much admired not only by his contemporaries but by later generations of writers and thinkers. Although McKay's poetry features traditional rhyme schemes and forms, especially the fourteen-line sonnet, it is filled with revolutionary ideas and a strong sense of the injustice that African Americans had endured for centuries. In fact, McKay's poem "If We Must Die" was probably the strongest statement against racism that had appeared up to that time, and many consider its publication the event that marked the beginning of the Harlem Renaissance.

"All my life I have been a troubadour wanderer, nourishing myself mainly on the poetry of existence."

Claude McKay.
(Courtesy of the Library of Congress.)

A Jamaican mountain childhood

Although he later came to be known as an African American literary figure, Claude McKay was originally from Jamaica. His birthplace was a little town called Sunny Ville, located in the hilly country of Jamaica's Clarendon Parish. McKay was the youngest of eleven children born to Ann Elizabeth Edwards McKay and Thomas Francis McKay. Theirs was a stable, land-owning, literate family in which education was highly valued. Thomas McKay was a descendent of West Africa's Ashanti ethnic group, and he taught his children to take pride in their heritage. He told them African folktales as well as stories about slavery and the ways whites had mistreated blacks.

Nevertheless, Jamaica was still a British colony in the late 1800s, and the youngest McKay grew up with a deep love for British culture and especially for the English literary tradition. He began writing poems even before he became a teenager, casting them in the same forms as the famous nineteenth-century British poets John Keats (1795–1821) and Percy Bysshe Shelley (1792–1822). At this early stage in his development, McKay was lucky to have access to the minds and libraries of two influential people: his older brother Uriah, a schoolteacher, and a white Englishman named Walter Jekyll, who had traveled to Jamaica to study the local folklore, especially the songs and tales of the area. Jekyll encouraged McKay to read the works of many British authors, but he also urged him to use the rich Jamaican speech patterns in his own writing. So McKay's earliest poems took the shape of formal verse laced with island dialect.

A new awareness of racism

When he was seventeen McKay received a government scholarship to become a cabinetmaker's apprentice in another small town, but two years later he left this position and moved to Jamaica's capital, Kingston. There, he became a police officer and spent an unhappy ten months experiencing racial prejudice for the first time in his life. He saw that black prisoners were treated much more harshly than others and that blacks were confined to the most low-paying jobs while whites and those of mixed racial heritage were given definite advantages.

Having felt, as he later wrote in his autobiography, "a most improper sympathy for wrongdoers," McKay returned to his country home and to writing poetry. With the help of Jekyll, who found a London publisher, McKay's poems were published in *Songs of Jamaica* and *Constab Ballads* in 1912. The first volume, a book of verse describing life in rural Jamaica, reflects McKay's appreciation for the landscapes and proud, self-confident people of his childhood. *Constab Ballads* chronicles McKay's disillusioning experiences in Kingston; these poems express the hatred that racism stirred in him and his longing for the mountains of home.

Arriving in America

Soon after these books were published, McKay became the first black Jamaican to receive a medal from his native country's Institute of Arts and Sciences. Later in 1912, he moved to the United States to attend Alabama's Tuskegee Institute, the famous school for African Americans founded by the great black leader Booker T. Washington. McKay stayed for only two months; a transfer to Kansas State College, where he intended to study agriculture, was no more successful in holding his interest.

In 1914 McKay moved to New York City. (He did not become a naturalized U.S. citizen until 1940.) He worked at a number of jobs, in kitchens and bars, as a porter, a fireman, and as a waiter on a Pullman (passenger train) car. McKay also tried his hand, though unsuccessfully, at running a restaurant and was even married for six months; his wife returned to Jamaica, and he never saw the daughter he had fathered. All this time, as he noted in his autobiography, *A Long Way from Home*, "I waded through the muck and scum with one objective dominating my mind." He wanted to be a poet.

A historic publication

McKay's literary efforts were finally rewarded when, in 1917, *Seven Arts*, a leading avant-garde magazine of literature and politics, published two of his poems—"The Harlem Dancer" and "Invocation"—under the pen name Eli Edwards.

This was the first time since the days of the celebrated black poet Paul Laurence Dunbar (1872–1906; see Chapter 3) that the work of an African American had appeared in a journal produced by whites. Written by a black author with a definite racial consciousness and expressing a feeling of alienation from mainstream American culture, these poems seemed to signal that a change was coming. Only a few years after their publication, the Harlem Renaissance began.

Meanwhile, McKay's strong sense of equality and justice had led him to seek out like-minded individuals who were interested in the concept of socialism (the belief that the best political system is one in which the means of producing and distributing goods are shared by all citizens or controlled by the government). Prominent among these new friends was Max Eastman, an attractive, soft-spoken white man with an aristocratic air and a sympathetic attitude toward the plight of blacks in America. Eastman was the editor of the radical magazine, the *Liberator,* and in 1919 McKay's poems started appearing there. The most famous of these was undoubtedly "If We Must Die," a statement of resistance to hatred and violence that would become a symbol of the new spirit embodied in the Harlem Renaissance.

"If We Must Die": A new spirit of outrage

The summer of 1919 had been a terrifying time for African Americans, as hatred and rage erupted in brutal clashes between blacks and whites in several American cities; this "Red Summer of Hate" (see Chapter 1) followed several decades when lynchings (hangings without a legitimate charge or trial) of blacks had become frighteningly commonplace in both the northern and southern United States. McKay had been traveling around the country while working his railroad job, and he later recalled that he and his fellow workers were scared by all they had heard and read about the violence; newspapers "were morbid, full of details of clashes between colored and white, murderous shootings and hangings." Despite his fear, the poem McKay wrote in response to it all was full of courage and defiance: "If we must die, let it not be like hogs," pleads the speaker; instead, let us behave "like men ... / Pressed to the wall, dying but fighting back!" (See p. 10.) Once again, McKay had achieved something that seemed to stand for the spirit of the Harlem Renaissance (even though Alain Locke thought the poem too radical to include in his *New Negro* anthology, which showcased the work of the movement's leading writers and artists) as well as for resistance to oppression of any kind. A copy of "If We Must Die" was found in the pocket of a white American soldier killed during World War II; McKay found this particularly gratifying because it meant that the poem was "just what I intended it to be ... universal."

A talented but restless poet

McKay was not satisfied with his success on the American literary scene and longed to leave the United States, so in 1919 he traveled to Europe. He spent a year in London, working on a socialist publication called the *Worker's Dreadnought* and publishing nearly two dozen poems in the *Cambridge Magazine*. McKay's infatuation with British culture was tarnished during this period by his discovery that racism also thrived in the British Isles. He did, however, find a London publisher for his poetry, and *Spring in New Hampshire* appeared in 1920. It was the first volume of McKay's poems written in standard English rather than Jamaican dialect, and it includes many of the poems that would also later appear in his acclaimed *Harlem Shadows* (1922).

Returning to the United States in 1921, McKay accepted Eastman's offer of a job as assistant editor of the *Liberator.* His colleagues admired his work (the magazine's circulation increased by sixty thousand readers during his tenure there), but he was deeply disappointed when Eastman turned down his suggestion to devote ten percent of the periodical's space to African American issues, since blacks made up ten percent of the U.S. population at the time. Eastman claimed that such a practice would cause too many of the magazine's white supporters to stop reading it.

McKay's continuing frustration with the slow rate of progress for African Americans led him to form a short-lived alliance with Jamaican-born black nationalist leader Marcus Garvey (1887–1940; see Chapter 1). Inspired by Garvey's advocacy of black unity, McKay published a few hard-hitting articles in *Negro World,* the publication of Garvey's United Negro

"Harlem Shadows" by Claude McKay

I hear the halting footsteps of a lass
In Negro Harlem when the night lets fall
Its veil. I see the shapes of girls who pass
To bend and barter at desire's call.
Ah, little dark girls who in slippered feet
Go prowling through the night from
    street to street!
Through the long night until the
    silver break
Of day the little gray feet know no rest;
Through the lone night until the last
    snow-flake
Has dropped from heaven upon the
    earth's white breast,
The dusky, half-clad girls of tired feet
Are trudging, thinly shod, from street
    to street.
Ah, stern harsh world, that in the
    wretched way
Of poverty, dishonor and disgrace,
Has pushed the timid little feet of clay,
The sacred brown feet of my fallen race!
Ah, heart of me, the weary, weary feet
In Harlem wandering from street
    to street.

From Selected Poems of Claude McKay, *by Claude McKay. Twayne Publishers, Inc. Copyright © 1953.*

Improvement Association (UNIA), but later broke with the organization.

Harlem Shadows establishes McKay

In 1922 Harcourt published *Harlem Shadows*, the volume that firmly established McKay as one of the strongest voices of the Harlem Renaissance. It includes many of his most famous poems, among them the title poem, "The Harlem Dancer," "If We Must Die," "The Lynching," and "The Tropics in New York." In "The Tropics in New York," the speaker longs for the lushness and warmth of his island home. "The Lynching" ends with a dramatic image of young white witnesses to the senseless hanging of a black American: "And little lads, lynchers that were to be, / Dance round the dreadful thing in fiendish glee." The volume's title poem centers on a fragile young black woman forced into prostitution by poverty. *Harlem Shadows* is infused with the anger and rebelliousness that blacks were beginning to express in the 1920s, and it also reflects the sense of alienation that had always made McKay feel like a restless "guest" rather than a full-fledged member of society. Several critics have noted that it wasn't just white society that shut out McKay; he also felt uncomfortable in the African American community.

Moving on again

This restlessness spurred McKay to move on again. In 1923 he left his job at the *Liberator* and traveled to Russia, where he planned to attend the Communist Party's Fourth Congress. At this event Communist sympathizers (those who believe in an economic system that promotes the ownership of all property by the community as a whole) from all over the world gathered in a country ruled by a Communist government. McKay was thrilled by the warm welcome he received from the Russian people, who viewed him as a distinguished black poet and an omen of good luck: "Never in my life," he wrote in his autobiography, "did I feel prouder of being an African, a black...." He met with some important Russian leaders during his stay, and he delivered a speech on racism in the United States and how even American socialists had failed to overcome it.

By the end of 1923 McKay had become disenchanted with Russia and had made his way to Paris, France, where he earned money as an artists' model. For the next nine years he wandered throughout Europe—writing when he could and living and working variously as a valet, a domestic, and a movie extra in France, Germany, Spain, and Morocco. McKay experienced a life of intensity and adventure, but he also endured bouts of serious illness and times when he had little or no money. Throughout this period his writing shifted from poetry to fiction as he produced three novels and a collection of short stories.

Home to Harlem is a hit

The first of McKay's three novels was his most celebrated. Published in 1928, *Home to Harlem* concerns two main characters: Jake is streetwise, uneducated, and fun-loving, but also honest and moral; Ray is serious, intellectual, and pessimistic. The two become friends when Jake runs away from the army (after learning that, because of his race, he would not be allowed to fight) and returns to Harlem. They work together on the railroad and enjoy the pleasures of Harlem while Jake searches for the prostitute who has won his love and Ray struggles with his identity. McKay's novel was praised for its treatment of racial issues and its realistic descriptions of Harlem scenes and people, which were seen as more authentic than those created by white author Carl Van Vechten in his novel *Nigger Heaven* (see Chapter 3). But not everybody liked *Home to*

Excerpt from *Home to Harlem* by Claude McKay

"Good old New York! The same old wench of a city. Elevated racketing over you' head. Subway bellowing under you' feet. Me foh wrastling round them piers again. Scratching down to the bottom of them ships and scrambling out. All alongshore for me now. No more fooling with the sea. Same old New York. But the ofay faces am different from those ovah across the pond. Sure they is. Stiffer. Tighter. Yes, they is that ... But the sun does better here than over there. And the sky's so high and dry and blue. And the air it—O Gawd it works in you' flesh and blood like Scotch. O Lawdy, Lawdy! I wants to live to a hundred and finish mah days in New York."

Jake threw himself up as if to catch the air pouring down from the blue sky. . . .

"Harlem! Harlem! Little thicker, little darker and noisier and smellier, but Harlem just the same. The niggers done plowed through Hundred and Thirtieth Street. Heading straight foh One Hundred and Twenty-fifth. Sapdes beyong Eighth Avenue. Going, going, going Harlem! Going up! Nevah befoh I seed so many dicky shines in sich swell motorcars. Plenty moh nigger shops. Seventh Avenue done gone high-brown. O Lawdy! Harlem bigger, Harlem better ... and sweeter." (pp. 25–26)

From "Zeddy," in Home To Harlem, *by Claude McKay. Northeastern University Press, 1987. Copyright (c) 1928 by Harper & Brothers. Copyright renewed (c) 1955 by Hope McKay Virtue. Reproduced by permission.*

Harlem. W.E.B. Du Bois and his Talented Tenth (Du Bois's term for the highest-achieving segment of African American society) claimed it showed black people in a bad light; Du Bois went so far as to say that after reading the novel he felt "distinctly like taking a bath."

More accomplished works of fiction

Despite such criticisms, *Home to Harlem* won the Harmon Foundation's gold medal for literature, and it was the first novel by a black writer to become a bestseller. (It was reprinted five times in two months.) None of McKay's subsequent books was as successful, though all received positive reviews. *Banjo*

(1929) continued McKay's exploration of black identity through the story of three black sailors who congregate on a beach in France; each character has a different viewpoint and faces different issues. In *Banana Bottom* (1933), a young black girl who has been raped is taken out of her Caribbean island community by a white missionary couple. After being educated in Britain, she returns to the island to embrace her own culture and heritage. *Gingertown* (1932) is a collection of twelve short stories set in both Harlem and Jamaica. The volume includes "Near-White," about a black woman who passes as white; "Highball," in which a successful black entertainer who has married a white woman still feels excluded from the white world; and "The Strange Burial of Sue," about an unfaithful wife who is defended, after her death, by both her husband and her lover against the minister who tries to condemn her.

A return to Harlem

By 1934 McKay found himself longing to return to the United States but penniless. His old friend Max Eastman took up a collection to pay for McKay's return voyage. Back in Harlem, the author continued to express his independent and defiant spirit. He hoped to found a new magazine that would appeal to all segments of the African American community, not just the educated elite, but this dream never came true. Nor was he able to establish the black writer's guild he had envisioned.

Three years after his return to the United States, McKay wrote his autobiography, *A Long Way from Home* (1937), followed three years later by *Harlem: Negro Metropolis,* a collection of essays on Harlem. Between these two publications, he met Ellen Tarry, a children's book author of mixed racial heritage and a strong Catholic faith. She became a major influence on McKay.

In 1941 McKay was working in a shipyard when he suffered a stroke. He recovered, but this turned out to be just the first in a string of illnesses that would plague him for the remaining seven years of his life. In 1944 he converted to Catholicism and moved to Chicago, where he took a job teaching at the Catholic Youth Organization. He died in May of 1948 of heart failure. At the time of his death, McKay had removed himself from the literary scene, and his work was not as appreciated as it had been during the Harlem Renaissance. He had not even been able to find a publisher for his *Selected Poems*. (They were finally published five years after his death.) The volume's previously unpublished poems reflect his travels in the late 1920s and early 1930s, especially during the time he spent in Russia and Spain. One poem in particular, "St. Isaac's Church, Petrograd," expresses a renewed awareness of God that anticipates his later conversion to Catholicism.

A troubadour wanderer

During his lifetime McKay had an uneasy relationship with other African American writers, and he scorned the idea that he belonged to any organized literary movement. But in the decades following his death—and especially during the 1960s, when the African American artists of the Black Arts movement were exploring and celebrating their racial identity—McKay's work was much read and quoted. A new generation admired his spirited independence, his bitter denunciations of racism, and his belief that black people should think of themselves as a group unified by common interests. Yet McKay remains an essentially solitary figure; as he said about himself in his autobiography, "All my life I have been a troubadour wanderer, nourishing myself mainly on the poetry of existence."

For More Information

Books

Bone, Robert A. *The Negro Novel in America*. New Haven, CT: Yale University Press, 1958.

Cooper, Wayne, ed. *The Passion of Claude McKay*. New York: Schocken, 1973.

Cooper, Wayne, ed. *Claude McKay: Rebel Sojourner in the Harlem Renaissance*. Baton Rouge: Louisiana State University Press, 1996.

Gayle, Addison, Jr. *Claude McKay: The Black Poet at War*. Detroit: Broadside, 1972.

Giles, James R. *Claude McKay*. New York: Twayne, 1976.

Hathaway, Heather. *Caribbean Waves: Relocating Claude McKay and Paule Marshall*. Bloomington: Indiana University Press, 1999.

Huggins, Nathan Irvin. *Harlem Renaissance.* New York: Oxford University Press, 1971.

Kellner, Bruce, ed. *The Harlem Renaissance: A Historical Dictionary for the Era.* Westport, CT: Greenwood Press, 1984.

Lewis, David Levering. *When Harlem Was in Vogue.* New York: Knopf, 1981.

McKay, Claude. *A Long Way from Home.* 1937. Reprint. New York: *New York Times* and Arno Press, 1969.

Tillery, Tyrone. *Claude McKay: A Black Poet's Struggle for Identity.* Amherst: University of Massachusetts Press, 1992.

Bessie Smith

Born April 15, 1894
Chattanooga, Tennessee
Died September 26, 1937
Clarksdale, Mississippi

American blues singer and songwriter

"Nobody messed with Bessie."

Bessie Smith.
(The Bettmann Archive.
Reproduced by permission.)

Some music fans and critics consider Bessie Smith the greatest and most influential blues singer of all time. Her powerful and dramatic style set a standard that other singers followed, and her self-assurance, distinctive personality, and sometimes wild lifestyle made her one of the most flamboyant characters of the Harlem Renaissance. Evident in the many recordings she made (most of which have been reissued since her death) are the raw emotion and underlying spirituality she brought to her music. As reported in *Here Me Talkin' to Ya* by Nat Shapiro and Nat Hentoff, guitarist Danny Barker said that Smith had the same effect on her listeners as the most talented southern preacher: "She could bring about mass hypnotism. When she was performing you could hear a pin drop."

An early start in entertaining

Smith was one of seven children born to an impoverished, part-time Baptist preacher and his wife in Chattanooga, Tennessee. After the deaths of her parents, she was raised by her older sister Viola and much influenced by her brother Clarence, a born entertainer himself who encouraged his little sister to learn to sing and dance. With another brother, Andrew, young Bessie performed for pennies on the street corners of Chattanooga. In 1912 Clarence helped her get a job as a dancer with his own employer, Mose Stokes's Traveling Show, one of many black music-and-comedy revues that moved around the South entertaining African American audiences.

During this period Smith sometimes appeared with a blues singer named Gertrude "Ma" Rainey. The first woman to sing the blues on stage, Ma Rainey would come to be known as the "Mother of the Blues." Over the next few years Smith performed in a number of shows. In one show she was kicked out of the chorus line for being too dark-skinned—even though the show's theme was "Glorifyin' the Brown-skinned Girl." Smith appeared again with Rainey, who no doubt influenced her own singing style, in the *Rabbit Foot Minstrel Show*.

Became a leading blues singer

In 1918 Smith teamed with another singer named Hazel Green, and the next year she was starring in her own show, *Liberty Belles*. By 1920 she was well established in the southern states as a leading blues singer. This form of music—forged from a unique blend of elements, including rhythms brought by slaves from Africa, African American spirituals (religious songs), and western European folk music—had been gathering momentum in the first two decades of the twentieth century. As the Harlem Renaissance began, the blues also came into its own as a style of music enjoyed by black and white listeners alike.

The eagerness of music recording companies to benefit from the growing popularity of the blues resulted in a new "race record" industry to capture the voices of dynamic black performers. This industry initially overlooked Smith's considerable talent, as she was first rejected by the Black Swan Phonograph Corporation, which chose to feature singer Ethel Waters (1896–1977; see biographical entry) instead. Okeh Records also turned down Smith, but only a few weeks later, in February of 1923, she signed a contract with Columbia Records.

Popular as a recording artist and performer

Paid $125 for each song she recorded, Smith cut her first record on February 16, 1923. It featured "Downhearted Blues" on one side and "Gulf Coast Blues" on the other and was a huge hit, selling 780,000 copies in six months. Billed by her record company as the "Empress of the Blues," Smith soon became Columbia's bestselling artist. Her contract, however, contained no royalty agreement, meaning that she had no claim to the profits earned from record sales. As a result, Smith earned only $28,575 from the many dozens of recordings she made over the years.

The power and raw emotion of Smith's voice were immediately evident to those who heard her sing—whether in person or on records—and her equally dynamic personality made her unforgettable. The boldness and determination that shone through when Smith sang "T'ain't Nobody's Bizness If I Do" were especially admirable to black fans hungry for models of black pride and strength. She wrote some of her own songs, too, including "Back Water Blues," which was inspired by a flood that caused much damage and suffering, and "Poor Man's Blues," a lament about the disparity between rich and poor in America.

Smith continued to tour, becoming more and more popular, especially in the southern states, and earning up to two thousand dollars a week. She preferred to run her own shows, traveling with a special railroad car that could house all the performers in her troupe with space left over for her show tent and stage equipment.

"Nobody messed with Bessie..."

A husky woman with a bad temper, Smith worked hard and played hard. Her niece Ruby Walker, who worked and traveled with her, was quoted as saying: "Nobody messed with Bessie, black or white, it didn't make no difference." Smith reportedly chased away a gang of Ku Klux Klan (KKK; an organization that expresses its hatred of nonwhites [especially blacks], Catholics, and Jews through terrorism) members who tried to disrupt her show, and she once performed after having been stabbed in the side at a party the previous day. She liked

Bessie Smith, known as the Empress of the Blues, was also known as a tough woman who shouldn't be messed with.
(AP/Wide World Photos. Reproduced by permission.)

to drink alcohol, and she was sexually interested in both men and women. Smith had a stormy relationship with her second husband, Jack Gee (her first husband, Earl Love, died in 1920), and was also linked with a wealthy Chicago bootlegger (seller of illegal liquor) named Richard Morgan.

Smith usually performed for all-black audiences, with only occasional appearances before whites, and her national reputation was based mainly on her recordings. She rarely appeared in New York, but when she did she made a big splash. She made a memorable appearance at one of the famous "integrated" (attended by both black and white guests) parties hosted by the white critic and black culture supporter Carl Van Vechten (1880–1964; see biographical entry) at his swank Manhattan apartment. Smith apparently refused Van Vechten's offer of "a dry martini" (a kind of alcoholic cocktail) with the response, "Ain't you got some whiskey, man...? I don't know about no dry martinis, nor wet ones either." One of the other guests at the party was opera singer Marguerite d'Alvarez, who performed an aria (a melodic piece performed in an opera by a solo singer) and earned a compliment from Smith: "Don't let *nobody* tell you you can't sing!"

Blues style falls out of favor

In the late 1920s Smith appeared in several musical reviews, including *Mississippi Days* (1928) and *Late Hour Tap Dancers* (1929), at Harlem's leading black theaters, the Lincoln and the Lafayette. But she never lingered long in New York, always heading out on tour again. Her one foray onto the Broadway stage was disastrous: *Pansy* (1929) closed after only three performances. Smith also appeared in a film, *St. Louis Blues,* produced in 1929.

During the 1930s musical tastes shifted away from the blues toward a more sophisticated kind of singing—a type more in keeping with the *swing* or big band (created by a group of instruments rather than solo performers) sound that had overtaken jazz. Sales of Smith's records dropped, and her contract with Columbia ended in 1931. She made her last recording—for Okeh records—two years later, and she stopped touring. By the middle of the 1930s, however, Smith had begun a comeback, polishing her singing to fit the new style and broadening her range of songs. In 1936 she replaced the hot jazz singer Billie Holiday (1915–1959) at Harlem's famous nightclub, Connie's Inn.

Death came too soon

In 1937, while Smith was on tour in Mississippi with a new show called *Broadway Rastus,* the car in which she was riding collided with a truck. Her arm was nearly severed and she received massive chest injuries. Smith died at the Afro-American Hospital in Clarksdale. Over the years the rumor has persisted that Smith was first refused treatment at an all-white hospital—a common occurrence in the segregated South—but this story has never been proven true. In any case, music fans agree that one of the finest blues singers of all time had died all too soon.

Another famous singer paid a tribute to Smith in 1970. Only a few weeks before her own tragic death from a drug overdose, rock star Janis Joplin—whose rough-edged, bluesy singing style owed much to Smith's example—purchased a headstone for Smith's unmarked grave. The inscription reads "THE GREATEST BLUES SINGER IN THE WORLD WILL NEVER STOP SINGING."

For More Information

Albertson, Chris. *Bessie.* New York: Stein & Day, 1972.

Harris, Sheldon. *Blues Who's Who: A Biographical Dictionary of Blues Singers.* New Rochelle, NY: Arlington House, 1979.

Harrison, Daphne Duval. *Black Pearls: Blues Queens of the 1920s.* New Brunswick, NJ: Rutgers University Press, 1988.

Oakley, Giles. *The Devil's Music: A History of the Blues.* New York: Harcourt Brace Jovanovich, 1978.

Shapiro, Nat, and Nat Hentoff. *Here Me Talkin' to Ya.* New York: Rinehart, 1955.

Stewart-Baxter, Derrick. *Ma Rainey and the Classic Blues Singers.* New York: Stein & Day, 1970.

Wallace Thurman

Born August 16, 1902
Salt Lake City, Utah
Died December 21, 1934
New York, New York

American novelist, playwright, editor, essayist,
short story writer, and poet

One of the most active, energetic, and multitalented participants in the Harlem Renaissance, Wallace Thurman was considered a leader of the group of young writers and artists who formed its most daring core. In addition to his own literary works, Thurman contributed to the movement through his editorial efforts and his sometimes biting—or even bitter—criticism of its excesses. Central to his work and, indeed, to his own personal life was the issue of color-consciousness and prejudice within African American society: Thurman felt that many blacks looked down upon those among them with the darker shades of skin (including himself). Despite his impressive achievements, Thurman always doubted his own talents; his death at the age of only thirty-two made him an even more tragic figure.

Reading and writing at an early age

Thurman was born in Salt Lake City, Utah, a city with a very small African American community. His father, Oscar, left the family when Thurman was very young (Thurman met

Editor of the daring one-issue literary magazine *Fire!!*, Wallace Thurman was also a talented writer.

Wallace Thurman.
(Courtesy of the Beinecke Rare Book and Manuscript Library.)

him only once again, much later in life), and his mother, Beulah, had five other husbands during her lifetime. Thurman seems to have been more attached to his grandmother, "Ma Jack" (Emma Jackson), than to anyone else in his early life.

A nervous boy who was often ill, Thurman loved to read and developed an early sense of himself as a writer, producing his first novel at the age of ten. During his high school years he read many different kinds of books, from classic literature by authors like English playwright William Shakespeare (1564–1616), French poet Charles Baudelaire (1821–1867), and Russian novelist Fyodor Dostoyevsky (1821–1881) to works by German philosopher Friedrich Nietzsche (pronounced NEE-chuh; 1844–1900) and Austrian psychologist Sigmund Freud (1856–1939). Thurman also enjoyed watching movies, a passion he would retain all his life.

In 1919 Thurman enrolled at the University of Utah in Salt Lake City, but he soon transferred to the University of Southern California, where he planned to pursue a medical degree. Instead, he ended up following his own earlier desire to become a writer, and he left the university in 1923 without even earning his undergraduate degree. For the next year and a half he wrote a column called "Inklings" for a black newspaper and also worked at the U.S. post office, where he met another young black writer, Arna Bontemps (1902–1973), who became his close friend. Thurman then edited a magazine called the *Outlet,* but it was discontinued after six months. When Bontemps announced his plan to go to New York City and join the new literary movement developing in Harlem, Thurman decided to go with him.

Making his way in Harlem

Thurman arrived in Harlem in September 1925. At first he supported himself through odd jobs (including working as an elevator operator), but finally he went to work for a publication called the *Looking Glass;* the editor, Theophilus Lewis, could not afford to pay Thurman a salary but gave him a place to stay and food to eat. Thurman performed a number of tasks, and he did so well (he was said to be able to read eleven lines of text at once) that Lewis recommended him to the *Messenger*—a prominent black journal—for a job as literary editor.

In this position Thurman was able to promote the work of the young writers he had met since arriving in New York, among them poet Langston Hughes (1902–1967; see biographical entry), whose first published short stories appeared in the *Messenger*. While working at the *Messenger,* Thurman sometimes expressed a rebellious attitude toward the older leaders of the African American community (especially civil rights advocate and *Crisis* editor W.E.B. Du Bois [1868–1963; see biographical entry]), who he felt were more eager to imitate whites than to support and appreciate real, ordinary black people.

A leader of the younger artists

Meanwhile, Thurman was leading the kind of life that conservative people like Du Bois found offensive. Along with some of his artistic friends—including Langston Hughes, Zora Neale Hurston (1891–1960; see biographical entry), and artist Richard Bruce Nugent (1906–1987)—he was staying in the wildly decorated and always lively boarding house of Iolanthe Sydney, the proprietor of a Harlem employment agency who supported her tenants' creative efforts by letting them stay rent-free. This group of young African Americans believed they were creating something new and daring as they explored their racial heritage through their art and struck out on their own individual paths, and they saw Thurman as their leader.

A slender young man with a slightly feminine manner and a high-pitched laugh, Thurman had a rapid-fire way of talking, and what he said was often brilliant. Due to his heavy drinking, sexual confusion (he was probably homosexual and seems to have felt guilty about it), and lack of money, his personal life was usually in disarray, but he worked very hard. He believed in creating art for its own sake, rather than using it to achieve political ends such as racial equality, and he held his own and others' writing to a high standard. Despite his popularity with the friends among whom he worked and played, Thurman always felt like an outsider—an attitude that was apparently connected with his very dark skin. He believed that lighter-skinned blacks considered him and other darker-complected people inferior.

The short, bright life of *Fire!!*

Thurman's first big achievement of the Harlem Renaissance was his editorship of the daring, high-quality, but short-lived journal *Fire!!* Hughes and Nugent had come up with the idea of a publication that would showcase the spirited, and sometimes experimental, work of the period's younger writers and that would thumb its nose, so to speak, at the "proper," conservative members of the Talented Tenth (Du Bois's term for the upper crust of African American society, whose members were expected to promote racial progress through their accomplishments and respectability). Hughes and Nugent asked Thurman to edit the journal, and he dove into the project with his usual energy.

The least of Thurman's problems was the content of *Fire!!,* for all the members of the magazine's editorial board (including Thurman, Hughes, Nugent, Hurston, artist Aaron Douglas [1898–1979; see biographical entry], poet Gwendolyn Bennett, and Harvard undergraduate John Davis) would contribute work, and pieces also came from poets Countee Cullen (1903–1946; see biographical entry), Helene Johnson (1907–1995; see Chapter 3), and Arna Bontemps, along with an essay by Arthur Huff Fauset (1889–1983). *Fire!!'*s foreword announced in a poem format its bold intentions: "FIRE ... flaming, burning, searing, and penetrating far beneath the superficial items of the flesh to boil the sluggish blood / FIRE ... a cry of conquest in the night, warning those who sleep and revitalizing those who linger in the quiet places dozing."

Thurman's biggest challenge was raising the money needed to produce the high-quality publication he envisioned. He wanted *Fire!!* to be printed on slick paper that would show off the contents in their best light. Hard-pressed to collect much money from the equally impoverished members of the editorial board, Thurman borrowed one thousand dollars to publish *Fire!!,* and in the end he was personally responsible for this debt (which took him four years to pay off). His colleagues at the magazine *World Tomorrow,* where he was now working , felt sorry for him in his penniless condition and gave him a check to buy a winter overcoat.

Fire!! generates heat

The publication of *Fire!!* in November, 1926 did indeed generate the heat its creators had intended. All of the brightest stars of the Harlem Renaissance (who were then known as members of the New Negro movement) were represented, and several contributions were clearly meant to shock the magazine's more stodgy readers. Richard Bruce Nugent's impressionistic short story "Smoke, Lilies and Jade" contained references to homosexuality, and Thurman's story "Cordelia the Crude" offered an alarmingly realistic view of Harlem life, complete with rent parties, gambling, drinking, prostitution, and murder.

It's not surprising, then, that most of the Talented Tenth expressed disgust for this publication of the younger generation. The well-known African American critic Benjamin Brawley (1882–1939) reported that he had tossed *Fire!!* into the fire, and W.E.B. Du Bois was said to be offended by the mere mention of the magazine. *Fire!!* would not, however, prove to be a long-term irritation, for the journal ceased publication after one issue. Its high cost—one dollar per copy, which was very expensive in the 1920s—caused many readers to borrow *Fire!!* from friends rather than buy it themselves. Getting the magazine distributed was also a problem that its editor failed to solve; in addition, many copies were destroyed when an apartment where they were being stored caught on fire, giving a new and ironic meaning to the name *Fire!!*

A marriage and a new project

After working for some time as circulation manager at the white magazine *World Tomorrow,* Thurman was hired as an editor by the Macauley publishing company, becoming the first African American to hold such a position in a white firm. In September 1928 he surprised his friends (who believed him to be homosexual, or at least not interested in marriage) by marrying Louise Thompson. Two months later Thurman launched a new project called *Harlem: A Forum of Negro Life,* which was supposed to be a general-interest magazine with both literary works and essays and articles on a variety of topics.

This time Thurman was not financially responsible. And, unlike *Fire!!, Harlem* was not meant to shock. Among its offerings were short fiction and poetry by Hughes, poetry by Georgia Douglas Johnson (1886–1966) and Helene Johnson, essays by Alain Locke (1886–1954; see biographcal entry) and Walter White (1893–1955), illustrations and sketches by Aaron Douglas , theater and book reviews, and a guide to where to go and what to do in Harlem. This new publication proved no more successful than *Fire!!*, but at least in this case Thurman had not gone into debt to get it published.

A play about Harlem's seamy side

At the same time, Thurman was working with a white collaborator, William Jourdan Rapp (an editor of *True Story* magazine), on a play based on his short story "Cordelia the Crude." With a cast of sixty actors, most of whom were not professionals, the play—called *Harlem*—opened on Broadway on February 20, 1929. *Harlem* centers on what happens to a black family that moves from the rural South to a northern city. The parents, Pa and Ma Williams, are hardworking people with three children, two of whom work to help support the family and one, Cordelia, who gets involved with Harlem's shadiest people and activities.

Forthright in its portrayal of such topics as gambling, gang warfare, and prostitution, *Harlem* got negative reviews from some critics, especially those who represented the Talented Tenth. They claimed that Thurman's highlighting of this underside of African American life would give white society the wrong impression. Other critics, however, praised Thurman for presenting a slice of the *real* Harlem and for tackling controversial subjects head-on. The play ran for ninety-three performances, was taken on tour by three road companies, and returned for a second Broadway engagement. Thurman became a celebrity for a brief period.

By this time Thurman's marriage had collapsed, and he and Thompson became involved in a bitter battle over the financial support she would receive after their planned divorce. Thurman traveled to Hollywood to investigate the possibility of a film adaptation of *Harlem,* and there he also worked on two more plays that were to be part of the trilogy he and Rapp had envisioned. *Harlem* was to be followed by *Jeremiah the Magnificent,* based on the real-life story of Jamaican-born activist Marcus Garvey (1887–1940), a charismatic, ambitious black leader who had encouraged many ordinary African Americans to be proud of their hertitage before being imprisoned for fraud. Thurman finished this play, but it was never produced during his lifetime, and he never finished writing the third play in the trilogy, *Black Cinderella*, about a color-obsessed black couple who favor their light-skinned daughter over her darker sister.

Writes *The Blacker the Berry*

While traveling in the West, Thurman visited his mother in Salt Lake City, and he later reported to his friends that members of her church who had heard about the racy content of his popular play had prayed over him, beseeching God to turn him from his evil ways. Thurman returned to New York downhearted for two reasons: he had not been able to drum up interest in adapting his play for film, and his dispute with his wife was no closer to being resolved. He was drinking heavily, and Harlem hostesses dreaded his arrival at parties, for invariably he would end his evenings by passing out.

Thurman's mood was not much lifted by the publication of his first novel, *The Blacker the Berry,* in early 1929, for as usual he felt that his work was not up to the high standards he had set for himself. The novel takes its title from an African American folk saying, "The blacker the berry, the sweeter the juice," which Thurman uses as an ironic reference to the prejudice experienced by blacks with darker skin.

The central character, Emma Lou Morgan, is the only dark-skinned member of her family, and her parents openly favor her sister over her. She also experiences discrimination within her community of Boise, Idaho, and at the University of California. Emma Lou moves to Harlem, assuming that surely in this progressive center of black life her own lot will improve. But she is mistreated there as well and has a humiliating affair with a light-skinned man named Alva. After a disastrous attempt to lighten her skin with strong chemicals, she finally realizes that she must reject the false values of those around her and accept herself as she is.

The Blacker the Berry has often been described as an autobiographical novel, for Thurman too felt that his dark skin had prejudiced other blacks against him. Reviews of the novel at the time of its publication were mixed, but most critics now agree that although it is not of top-rate literary quality, *The Blacker the Berry* effectively portrays a problem that few African American writers were willing to confront.

Satirizing the Harlem Renaissance

Thurman's second novel, *Infants of the Spring* (1932), chronicles the experiences of a group of black writers in Harlem, all of whom closely resemble Thurman and his Harlem Renaissance friends. The novel is a satire that reveals the pretensions of these young people who think that they and their work will change the world. The story is told primarily through the character of Raymond Taylor, a writer who, like Thurman, wants to create high-quality literature that is neither decadent (in a state of moral decay or decline) nor too focused on racial issues.

Among Taylor's friends and colleagues are Dr. Parkes (modeled after Alain Locke), who tells the young writers that because of their work, "new vistas will be spread open to the entire race"; the rather mysterious poet Tony Crews (modeled after Langston Hughes); and Sweetie May Carr (modeled after Zora Neale Hurston), who is taking advantage of white people's new interest in African Americans for her own benefit. The novel ends with the suicide—carefully planned to have a dramatic effect—of the daring artist and writer Paul Arbian (modeled after Richard Bruce Nugent, although Nugent did not kill himself), who seems to embody all the faddishness of the New Negro movement.

Once again, Thurman's novel received mixed reviews. Some critics complained that *Infants of the Spring* contained too much conversation and too little action, while others praised its realism; in later years many reviewers would view the novel as a reflection of Thurman's personal bitterness and dissatisfaction. In any case, Thurman took the negative reviews to heart and continued to feel that he was not yet the writer he had hoped to become.

A third novel and two film scripts

In the course of his work at Macauley's, Thurman met a white writer named Abraham L. Furman, with whom he wrote

The Interne (1932). This novel about the training of young doctors at New York's City Hospital was intended to expose the substandard practices and behavior that went on there. Reviewers, however, found the novel poorly written and overly dramatic.

In 1934 Thurman was hired to write film scripts for the Hollywood production company of Bryan Foy, Jr., who was interested in making films about social issues. Thurman spent several months living in California and wrote two scripts, *High School Girl* (1935) and *Tomorrow's Children* (1934). The latter tale of a poor white family features a seventeen-year-old girl who supports her usually-pregnant mother and alcoholic, unemployed father, along with a number of siblings who are all either physically or mentally disabled. Social welfare authorities want to sterilize (make incapable of reproducing) the parents and daughter, but a priest intervenes to squelch this plan. The story raises the question of whether the state has the right to decide whether people may or may not have children, and it exposes the different kinds of justice available to rich and poor Americans.

" ... it all died with him."

Thurman returned to New York in May of 1934, exhausted and in ill health after many long, late nights of drinking in California. His doctor told him he should quit drinking, but he disregarded this warning and spent the month after his return in constant carousing. Many parties would end with Thurman either passing out or threatening to jump out of windows and kill himself. Finally he collapsed, and he was taken to City Hospital, the same institution he had vilified in *The Interne*. There he was diagnosed with tuberculosis (a life-threatening disease of the lungs), and he spent six months in the hospital, growing weaker and weaker with each passing day. Thurman died on December 21, 1934.

On Christmas Eve, Thurman's friends gathered for his funeral, an occasion that shocked these young people into an awareness of their own mortality. Some observers classify it among several events that marked the true end of the Harlem Renaissance. "[Thurman] was our leader," remembered writer Dorothy West in a 1970 article in *Black World,* "and when he died, it all died with him."

For More Information

Books

Henderson, Mae Gwendolyn. "Portrait of Wallace Thurman." In *The Harlem Renaissance Remembered.* Edited by Arna Bontemps. New York: Dodd, Mead, 1972.

Lewis, David Levering. *When Harlem Was in Vogue.* New York: Knopf, 1981.

Notten, Eleonore Van. *Wallace Thurman's Harlem Renaissance.* Amsterdam: Rodopi, 1994.

O'Daniel, Therman B. Introduction to *The Blacker the Berry,* by Wallace Thurman. New York: Collier, 1970.

Walden, Daniel. "'The Canker Galls ...'; Or, The Short, Promising Life of Wallace Thurman." In *The Harlem Renaissance Re-examined.* Edited by Victor Kramer. New York: AMS, 1987.

Periodicals

Haslam, Gerald. "Wallace Thurman: Western Renaissance Man." *Western American Literature* (Spring 1971): 53–59.

Perkins, Huel D. "Renaissance 'Renegade'? Wallace Thurman." *Black World* 25.4 (1976): 29–35.

West, Dorothy. "Elephant's Dance: A Memoir of Wallace Thurman." *Black World* 20.1 (1970): 77–85.

Jean Toomer

Born December 26, 1894
Washington, D.C.
Died March 30, 1967
Doylestown, Pennsylvania

American poet, short story writer,
dramatist, and essayist

With the publication of his novel *Cane* (1923), which was immediately hailed as a masterpiece of American literature and perhaps the highest achievement that any African American writer had yet attained, Jean Toomer moved to the forefront of all the promising young poets, novelists, and other artists of the Harlem Renaissance. Toomer soon turned his back on his newfound fame, however, to continue his lifelong search for inner peace, a more spiritual existence, and an identity that was universal rather than racial. Although he never achieved the brilliant career that many had foreseen for him, Toomer still stands as a brilliant author of the 1920s. *Cane* remains a major accomplishment and one of the finest works—if not the best—to emerge from the Harlem Renaissance.

A mixed-race family

Nathan Eugene Toomer (he began using the name Jean at the start of his literary career) was born in Washington, D.C., to a family of mixed European and African heritage. His maternal grandfather, Pinckney Benton Stewart Pinchback,

Jean Toomer was hailed as the country's leading "Negro writer," but instead of being proud he was dismayed. He did not wish to be viewed through the lens of race. He considered himself simply an American writer who had written about the black experience in America.

Jean Toomer.
(Courtesy of the Library of Congress.)

had been a Republican lieutenant governor of Louisiana who was of mixed heritage and openly identified himself as black. Toomer's mother, Nina Pinchback, had defied her family's objections to her marrying Nathan Toomer, the illegitimate son of a former slave and her wealthy white owner. Light-skinned enough to hide his African American heritage, Nathan abandoned his young family soon after the birth of his son, and Jean Toomer saw his father only once thereafter.

Toomer spent his early boyhood under the roof of his domineering grandfather—whom he both admired and rebelled against—and his gentle but strong-willed grand-mother. The Pinchbacks lived a life of luxury in their big house on Bacon Street, located in a quiet, all-white neighborhood, with a garden tended by a former slave. But Grandfather Pinchback's gambling habit led to a decline in the family's fortunes, and eventually they were forced to move to Brooklyn, New York, where Nina was living with her new white husband.

Feeling neither black nor white

At this point in his life Toomer was introduced to the world of books and imagination by his Uncle Bismarck, who shared a nightly ritual of reading with his intelligent young nephew. Toomer spent many hours in the public library, but he also liked the outdoors and enjoyed sports, especially swimming and sailing.

After Nina died unexpectedly in 1909, the Pinchbacks' fortune declined even more, and they were forced to move into a low-income, all-black neighborhood in Washington, D.C. Toomer entered Paul Dunbar High School, attended by the brightest students of Washington's thriving African American community, but he did not feel comfortable in his new environment: he had experienced life in both the white and the black worlds, and he did not know where he belonged. A feeling of alienation and a yearning for a more meaningful existence would stay with Toomer for the rest of his life.

Years of wandering

In 1914 Toomer enrolled at the University of Wisconsin, intending to study agriculture, but he left after only one semester. Over the next four years he attended four more colleges, including the Massachusetts College of Agriculture, the American College of Physical Training (located in Chicago), the University of Chicago, and City College of New York. Toomer never earned a degree, but he continued to read and study many great literary works, such as those by playwrights George Bernard Shaw (1856–1950) and Henrik Ibsen (1828–1906), poet Walt Whitman (1819–1892), and novelist and poet Johann Wolfgang von Goethe (1749–1832). After finally leaving college, Toomer moved around a lot, working for short periods as a bodybuilder and physical education teacher, a welder, and a car salesman; at one point he even took up the life of a hobo (homeless person), hitching rides on passing trains.

Toomer was living in New York City in 1919 and spending time in Greenwich (pronounced GREN-itch) Village—a neighborhood that attracted many artistic people—when he came into contact with some members of the "Lost Generation," a group of writers (including poet Hart Crane [1899–1932] and critic Malcolm Cowley [1898–1989]) who felt alienated from the modern world and who tried in their work to stress art and human values over materialism and commercialism. One of these writers, a young, aspiring novelist named Waldo Frank, became Toomer's close friend. Toomer decided that he too would like to become a writer, and he began a period of learning and preparation.

Connecting with his heritage

The summer of 1921 found Toomer back in Washington, D.C., caring for his grandparents, who were both ill, and continuing to work on his writing. Then a friend of his grandfather's who was the principal of a small black school in Georgia stopped by for a visit. He said that he needed someone to take over the school's management for a short time, and Toomer volunteered for the job. In September, Toomer traveled to the small town of Sparta (located about eighty miles southeast of Georgia's capital, Atlanta) to become the temporary principal of the Sparta Agricultural and Industrial Institute.

The few months Toomer spent in Georgia proved a very important time in his life. He lived in a tiny shack among the area's poorest black population. He heard through his open window the spirituals (religious songs) and work songs they sang. He attended the lively, music-filled church services. He listened to blues music and stories. He also saw firsthand the hardships and the brutalities of racism that blacks faced, but he was moved by their dignity, their ability to spring back from setbacks, and their deep spirituality.

For the first time in his life Toomer was in touch with his own African American heritage. In a letter to white novelist Sherwood Anderson (1876–1941), whose work (including the unconventional novel *Winesburg, Ohio*) he greatly admired, Toomer wrote: "My seed was planted in *myself* down there. Roots have grown and strengthened." Those roots would grow into a great literary work that Toomer began writing that November, while on the train home from Georgia. At this point he did not envision this record of his experiences in the South as a novel; he was writing poems and short pieces of prose, which he started sending out to various publications.

Cane: A collage of images

One of the editors who received Toomer's work was Claude McKay (1889–1948; see biographical entry) of the *Liberator,* who told "Miss Jean Toomer" that "her" writing was "a little too long, not clear enough, and lacking unity." Before long, however, McKay (who soon learned that Toomer was actually a man) was publishing Toomer's submissions in the *Liberator,* and fragments of what would become *Cane* also appeared in *Dial* and other magazines. In the summer of 1922, hoping to refresh his memories and impressions of the South, Toomer took a trip to South Carolina. This time he traveled with Waldo Frank, who was also working on a novel about the area.

By early 1923 Toomer had joined together all his scattered pieces of writing to form an unusual novel, which he called *Cane* (in reference to one of the southern states' main crops, sugar cane, from which sugar is derived only after a long, difficult harvesting and production process). Frank sent the manuscript to his own publisher, Boni & Liveright, which published *Cane* in September 1923. The book was like nothing anyone had ever seen before—a kind of collage of poems, scenes, and characters loosely linked by theme and tone—and the fact that it appeared at a time when many writers were experimenting with language and form heightened its impact.

A portrait of African American life, rural and urban

Divided into three parts, *Cane* features fifteen poems, six vignettes or character sketches, seven short stories, and one play. All of these pieces convey the black experience in both the rural South and the urban North. The first section, set in the Georgia countryside, contains lyrical, sensuous, but also harshly realistic portraits of six black women. Through these female characters, Toomer explores aspects of black life, culture, and womanhood. "Karintha" concerns a young girl whose innocent beauty eventually leads her into prostitution; "Carma" is unfaithful to her husband; "Becky" is a poor white women with two mixed-race sons who is shunned by her community; "Fern" is the alienated, emotionally dead daughter of a mixed (black and Jewish) marriage; "Esther" is a prim young girl infatuated with a flashy preacher; and in "Louisa" the title character's black lover stabs her white lover and then is lynched.

Cane's second part takes place in Chicago and Washington, D.C., evoking through seven prose pieces and five poems the lives of African Americans who have migrated to the northern cities in search of greater freedom, only to face continued struggle and deferred hopes. Many of the pieces concern relationships between men and women that are damaged by racial conflict. In "Rhobert" the overwhelming desire to own property is revealed as destructive, and in "Bona and Paul" a black boy who is able to pass as white loses the love of a white girl who had been attracted to his blackness.

The unobtrusive (not really noticeable) voice of the first two sections emerges in the third as a first-person narrator: "Kabnis" features a black schoolteacher from the North who travels to rural Georgia—a journey that takes him into the dark corners of himself as he struggles with his African American heritage and identity. Kabnis recognizes the value of the rural black culture he discovers, and he wants to celebrate and preserve it. Before he can do so, however, he must come to terms with the reality of slavery, which is symbolized by the character of Father John, an elderly man who is a former slave.

From "Carma," in *Cane* by Jean Toomer

Wind is in the cane. Come along.
Cane leaves swaying, rusty with talk,
Scratching choruses above the
*   guinea's squawk,*
Wind is in the cane. Come along.

Carma, in overalls, and strong as any man, stands behind the old brown mule, driving the wagon home. It bumps, and groans, and shakes as it crosses the railroad track. She, riding it easy. I leave the men around the store to follow her with my eyes down the red dust road. Nigger woman driving a Georgia chariot down an old dust road. Dixie Pike is what they call it. Maybe she feels my gaze, perhaps she expects it. Anyway, she turns. The sun, which has been slanting over her shoulder, shoots primitive rockets into her mangrove-gloomed, yellow flower face. Hi! Yip! God has left the Moses-people for the nigger. "Gedap." Using reins to slap the mule, she disappears in a cloudy rumble at some indefinite point along the road.

(The sun is hammered to a band of gold. Pine needles, like mazda, are brilliantly aglow. No rain has ever come to take the rustle from the falling sweet-gum leaves. Over in the forest, across the swamp, a sawmill blows its closing whistle. Smoke curls up. Marvelous web spun by the spider sawdust pile. Curls up and spreads itself pine-high above the branch, a single silver band along the eastern valley. A black boy .... you are the most sleepiest man I ever seed, Sleeping Beauty ... cradled on a gray mule, guided by the hollow sound of cowbells, heads for them through a rusty cotton field. From down the railroad track, the chug-chug of a gas engine announces that the repair gang is coming home. A girl in the yard of a whitewashed shack not much larger than the stack of worn ties piled before it, sings. Her voice is loud. Echoes, like rain, sweep the valley. Dust takes the polish from the rails. Lights twinkle in scattered houses. From far away, a sad strong song. Pungent and composite, the smell of farmyards is the fragrance of the woman. She does not sing; her body is a song. She is in the forest, dancing. Torches flare ... juju men, greegree, witch-doctors ... torches go out ... The Dixie Pike has grown from a goat path in Africa.

Night.

Foxie, the bitch, slicks back her ears
   and barks at the rising moon.)

Wind is in the corn. Come along.
Corn leaves swaying, rusty with talk,
Scratching choruses above the
*   guinea's squawk,*
Wind is in the corn. Come along.

Carma's tale is the crudest melodrama. Her husband's in the gang. And it's her fault he got there. Working with a contractor, he was away most of the time. She had others. No one blames her for that. He returned one day and hung around the town where he picked up week-old boasts and rumors. . . Bane accused her. She denied. He couldnt see that she was becoming hysterical. He would have liked to take his fists and beat her. Who was strong as a man. Stronger. Words, like corkscrews, wormed to her strength. It fizzled out. Grabbing a gun, she ran from the house and plunged across the road into a canebrake ... There, in quarter heaven shone the crescent moon ... Bane was afraid to follow till he heard the gun go off. Then he wasted half an hour gathering the neighbor men. They met in the road where lamp-light showed tracks dissolving in the loose earth about the cane. The search began. Moths flickered the lamps. They put them out. Really, because she still might be live enough to shoot. Time and space have no meaning in a canefield. No more than the interminable stalks. . . Some one stumbled over her. A cry went up. From the road, one would have thought that they were cornering a rabbit or a skunk . . . It is difficult carrying dead weight through cane. They placed her on the sofa. A curious, nosey somebody looked for the wound. This fussing with her clothes aroused her. Her eyes were weak and pitiable for so strong a woman. Slowly, then like a flash, Bane came to know that the shot she fired, with averted head, was aimed to whistle like a dying hornet through the cane. Twice deceived, and one deception proved the other. His head went off. Slashed one of the men who'd helped, the man who'd stumbled over her. Now he's in the gang. Who was her husband. Should she not take others, this Carma, strong as a man, whose tale I have told it is the crudest melodrama?

> Wind is in the cane. Come along.
> Cane leaves swaying, rusty with talk,
> Scratching choruses above the
>   guinea's squawk,
> Wind is in the cane. Come along.

An original masterpiece

Cane was a hit with critics and followers of the literary scene, if not with general readers (it sold less than five hundred copies). Waldo Frank told Toomer that he was "creating a new phase of American literature," and the prominent African American critic William Stanley Braithwaite, who seldom praised any work too highly, called Toomer "a bright morning star of a new day of the race in literature." *Cane* became a symbol of black achievement, a work that proved black writers could take their place beside whites. Most other works of the Harlem Renaissance could be classified as realism, but Toomer's stood out from the rest as a modernist (nontraditional) novel similar to those by American writers Ernest Hemingway (1899–1961) and Gertrude Stein (1874–1946).

Toomer was now hailed as the country's leading "Negro writer," but instead of being proud he was dismayed. He did not wish to be viewed through the lens of race. He considered himself simply an American writer who had written about the black experience in America, and in an effort to convince others to see him this way, he began to deny his African heritage. He also began to turn away from his old friends and colleagues, who were puzzled by his attitude. Toomer would never again write about black life or experiences, and his work would never again be published by a major publishing house.

Becomes a Gurdjieff follower

In early 1924 Toomer became deeply interested in the teachings of Georgi Gurdjieff, a spiritual leader of Greek and Armenian heritage who had been living in Russia before moving to France, where he established the Institute for the Harmonious Development of Man in Fontainebleau (located just outside of Paris). Gurdjieff advocated a complicated system of psychology, philosophy, and physical movement and exercise that was supposed to help his followers achieve a balance of mind, body, and soul and reach a higher consciousness. This seemed like an answer to Toomer's lifelong quest for the deeper meaning of existence, and he joined Gurdjieff's group enthusiastically.

Toomer spent a summer in Fontainebleau, returning to New York with plans not to write but to teach Gurdjieff's principles. At first his lectures were quite popular, with many attendees drawn simply by Toomer's reputation as a talented author. Gradually, however, attendance dropped off, so Toomer moved on to Chicago. In the years that followed, he would live and promote the Gurdjieff system in Taos, New Mexico, and in Portage, Wisconsin.

Still writing, but not as successfully

Meanwhile, Toomer continued to write, but nothing he produced came close to *Cane* in artistry or originality. In fact, everything was infused with his new worldview and seemed designed to persuade others to join the Gurdjieff circle. In the late 1920s Toomer had several short stories ("Easter," "Mr. Costyve Duditch," and "Winter on Earth") as well as a novella (*York Beach*) published in literary journals. His final publication was a long poem called "Blue Meridian," which appeared in *New Caravan* in 1936. The poem presents an idealized vision of an America in which people of all races and religions come together in a new, universal human being called a "blue" man.

In 1932 Toomer married Margery Lattimer, a novelist and dedicated feminist whom he had met at the Gurdjieff community in Wisconsin. Less than a year later, she died soon after giving birth to a daughter. In 1934 Toomer married Marjorie Content and settled into life on a farm in Doylestown, Pennsylvania, where he would live for the rest of his life. Although he gave up his active role in the Gurdjieff movement at the time of his second marriage, Toomer continued to practice its tenets. Still, he seemed to lack a full sense of inner peace: he took his family to India in 1939 and spent nine months talking to various religious leaders there. Shocked and depressed by the poverty and disease he witnessed in India, Toomer returned to the United States.

Because Toomer's writing never again appeared in print, many of those who had known him assumed he had stopped writing, but this was not true. In the last decades of his life he produced novels, plays, short stories, poems, and autobiographical pieces, but all were rejected by editors as lacking literary merit. In addition to this disappointment, Toomer's health began to fail during the 1930s, and it steadily declined over the next thirty years. He died in 1967, just as critics and readers were beginning to rediscover *Cane* and praise it as a classic work not only of the Harlem Renaissance but of American literature in general.

For More Information

Benson, Brian Joseph, and Mabel Mayle Dillard. *Jean Toomer*. Boston: Twayne, 1980.

Bone, Robert. "Jean Toomer." In *The Negro Novel in America*. New Haven: Yale University Press, 1958.

Durham, Frank. *Studies in Cane*. Columbus, OH: Merrill, 1971.

Huggins, Nathan Irvin. *Harlem Renaissance*. New York: Oxford University Press, 1971.

Kernan, Cynthia Earl. *The Lives of Jean Toomer: A Hunger for Wholeness*. Baton Rouge: Louisiana State University Press, 1989.

Lewis, David Levering. *When Harlem Was in Vogue*. New York: Penguin Books, 1979.

McKay, Nellie. *Jean Toomer: Artist*. Chapel Hill: University of North Carolina Press, 1984.

O'Daniel, Therman B. *Jean Toomer: A Critical Evaluation*. Washington, DC: Howard University Press, 1988.

Turner, Darwin T., ed. *Cane* (A Norton Critical Edition). New York: Norton, 1989.

Watson, Steven. *The Harlem Renaissance: Hub of African-American Culture, 1920–1930*. New York: Pantheon Books, 1995.

Woodson, Jon. *To Make a New Race: Gurdjieff, Toomer, and the Harlem Renaissance*. Jackson: University Press of Mississippi, 1999.

Carl Van Vechten

Born June 17, 1880
Cedar Rapids, Iowa
Died December 21, 1964
New York, New York

**American literary and music critic,
novelist, photographer, and patron
of the Harlem Renaissance**

Although he is most famous as a participant in the Harlem Renaissance and a white supporter of the period's black writers, artists, and performers, Carl Van Vechten had a life-long interest in African American culture. A literary and music critic, he wrote numerous reviews of black-authored books and plays, as well as essays designed to introduce the artistic achievements of African Americans to a wider (white) audience. Even though some critics have questioned the motives behind his active role in the Harlem Renaissance (it has been said that he and other white patrons benefited more, psychologically and materially, than the artists they supported), most have agreed that his participation was important. Van Vechten's closest black friend, National Association for the Advancement of Colored People (NAACP) leader and writer James Weldon Johnson (1871–1938), went so far as to write in a letter to Van Vechten: "Has anyone ever written it down—in black and white—that you have been one of the most vital forces in bringing about the artistic emergence of the Negro in America?"

"Like Van Vechten, start inspectin'..."

From Andy Razaf's hit 1930 song, "Go Harlem"

Carl Van Vechten.
(Photograph by Carl Van Vechten. The Estate of Carl Van Vechten. Reproduced by permission.)

279

An early appreciation for black culture

Born in Cedar Rapids, Iowa, Van Vechten was raised in a family that respected and sympathized with black people, an attitude not at all common among whites in the late nineteenth century. His father was a cofounder of the Piney Woods School, the first school for African Americans in Mississippi, and young Carl was taught to address the family's two black servants as Mrs. Sercy and Mr. Oliphant, as did his parents. (It was more typical for all family members to call black servants by their first names.)

When he was about ten years old, Van Vechten went to a performance by black opera singer Sissieretta Jones (1869–1933), who was called "The Black Patti" after white opera star Adeline Patti. Later, he would be enthralled by George Walker (1873–1911) and Bert Williams (c. 1876–1922), renowned stars of the minstrel shows (music and comedy revues featuring performers in "blackface" makeup; see Chapter 4) that were very popular around the turn of the century. These experiences formed the basis of Van Vechten's deep and long-standing interest in African American culture.

Anxious to escape the confines of his small midwestern town, Van Vechten attended the University of Chicago, where he continued to attend and enjoy performances by black entertainers. He brought Carita Day, a black performer with a group called the Georgia Minstrels, to sing at his fraternity house, and every Sunday he escorted his fraternity's black housekeeper to her church, where he accompanied the choir on piano.

A young reporter and critic

Van Vechten's first job after graduation was as a general reporter for the *Chicago American*. Although he was assigned to report on a broad range of topics, he wrote about black entertainers whenever he could, sometimes supplying his own photos. In 1906 Van Vechten was hired by the *New York Times* as an assistant music critic. The next year he took a two-year leave of absence to study opera (another of his great interests) in Europe. During this period he married a friend from Cedar Rapids, Anna Snyder, from whom he was divorced in 1912.

Van Vechten returned to New York in 1909 and resumed his position at the *New York Times,* but in 1913 he moved to the *New York Press,* where he served as drama critic. During these years as a full-time journalist, Van Vechten gained a great deal of knowledge of music, theater, and dance and deepened his appreciation of black culture and artists. He was among the first to recognize the importance of jazz and blues music, and he reported on developments in African American theater (and on portrayals of black life in the white theater), publishing an essay called "The Negro Theater" (1919).

An even deeper interest awakened

After his marriage to actress Fania Marinoff, Van Vechten left his full-time job, but he continued to write essays and articles, and he published several collections of his writings on such topics as music, ballet, and cats. Van Vechten moved to a new level of interest in African Americans in the early 1920s, when he read a novel by NAACP leader Walter White (1893–1955). White's novel, *The Fire in the Flint* (1924), highlighted the horrors of southern racism. Van Vechten sought out and befriended White, who in turn introduced him to many of the talented young black writers who were gathering in Harlem, including Langston Hughes (1902–1967; see biographical entry), Wallace Thurman (1902–1934; see biographical entry), and Zora Neale Hurston (1891–1960; see biographical entry). At this time Van Vechten also met James Weldon Johnson, who would become a close and lifelong friend.

A tall, pale-haired man with protruding teeth, Van Vechten became a familiar figure in Harlem. With his trendy clothing, jangling bracelets, fancy cigarettes, and silver-plated liquor flask, he was seen not only at expensive, elegant nightclubs like the Cotton Club but in speakeasies (illegal bars) and at rent parties (held in Harlem homes as a way to raise money for rent). Other white people who were curious about Harlem or who had caught "Harlemania"—the 1920s trend, also called "Going Uptown," that made it fashionable for well-heeled whites to explore the lively music, dancing, and other delights of Harlem—called on Van Vechten as a tour guide who knew the most "authentic" places to go.

Yet Van Vechten's role in what would become known as the Harlem Renaissance extended far beyond his partygoing. Over the next few years he wrote close to two dozen articles and essays about African American writers and performers. These pieces, which were published in mainstream white publications, included an important series of articles on black culture for *Vanity Fair* magazine in 1925 and 1926. Van Vechten championed Bessie Smith (1894–1937; see biographical entry) and other blues singers; he urged black actors and actresses to break out of the traditional limitations placed upon them; and he helped to fund singer and actor Paul Robeson's (1898–1976) first concert of spirituals (African American religious songs).

In addition, Van Vechten became a kind of press agent for the black writers and intellectuals he knew, not only touting their work in print but introducing them to people who could publish or otherwise help them. For example, it was through his influence that Langston Hughes's first volume of poems, *The Weary Blues* (1926), was published by Alfred A. Knopf, Van Vechten's own publisher. At parties hosted by Van Vechten and his wife in their swank, richly decorated Manhattan apartment, black and white guests mingled freely; as Marinoff explained in an interview published in the *London Sunday Herald* in 1927, the couple was "engaged in a crusade to break down the color bar." At a Van Vechten party, guests might hear Bessie Smith perform a song or listen to Langston Hughes recite a poem, and they might bump shoulders with such diverse figures as the famed Harlem dancer Bill "Bojangles" Robinson (1878–1949; see sidebar on p. 90), composer George Gershwin (1898–1937), or novelist Theodore Dreiser (1871–1945).

A controversial novel

Van Vechten's flamboyant lifestyle had already made him something of a controversial figure when, in 1926, an event occurred to intensify this reputation. In the Spring 1926 issue of *Crisis*, Van Vechten had warned African Americans that they should be the first to draw inspiration and material from their own rich culture and not "continue to make a free gift of it to white authors who will exploit it until not a drop of vitality remains." Many who had read these words were surprised when, only three months later, Van Vechten's novel

Nigger Heaven appeared. Its author had clearly done exactly what he'd said other white writers might do: he'd used the racy, lively milieu of Harlem as the setting for his novel.

Part of the controversy caused by *Nigger Heaven* was due to its title. While Van Vechten claimed it was an ironic reference to the segregated balconies of movie theaters where black people were forced to sit (and it is also used by one of the characters as a name for Harlem itself, with its warm welcome to African Americans), many blacks were offended by his use of a racial slur. The novel's content also posed a problem for many readers—especially black ones—who cringed at the descriptions of Harlem's less reputable side, where gambling, drinking, prostitution, and illicit sex abounded. They claimed that Van Vechten was casting a negative light on black people and thus slowing up their progress toward equality.

Most commentators agree that the plot of *Nigger Heaven* is thin and its characters weak. The novel concerns a love affair between a prim librarian named Mary Love and a young, would-be writer named Byron Kasson. Consumed by doubts and self-pity, Byron has an affair with the beautiful Lasca Sartoris, who lives only for pleasure, and at the end of the novel he is wrongly arrested for shooting Lasca's new lover, Randall Pettijohn. Only about a third of the novel takes place in the nightclubs and bedrooms of Harlem; the rest is devoted to heady discussion between African American intellectuals. Many actual Harlem Renaissance figures appear in the novel under different names.

Van Vechten's defenders (including James Weldon Johnson, Langston Hughes, and Wallace Thurman) praised him for his realistic portrayal of Harlem, while his detractors (including Countee Cullen [1903–1946], Alain Locke [1886–1954], and the vast majority of black readers) agreed with W.E.B. Du Bois (writing in *Crisis*) that *Nigger Heaven* was "an affront to the hospitality of black folk and the intelligence of white." Van Vechten lost few of his closest friends, who saw in *Nigger Heaven* a reflection of its author's flamboyance as well as the same very artificial, mannered writing that characterized his other novels (he wrote seven altogether, none of them achieving as much attention as *Nigger Heaven*). But as a result of the fuss over the book, Van Vechten was banned from his favorite Harlem nightclub, Small's Paradise.

Becoming a photographer

With the arrival of the Great Depression (a severe economic downturn that began in the United States with the notorious stock market crash of 1929) at the end of the 1920s came a new mood of pessimism throughout the nation, and New York City was no exception. The once red-hot Harlem Renaissance fizzled out as the African American community struggled with unemployment and other hardships; even the rich people who had flocked to Harlem's nightclubs could no longer afford such diversions. Like others who had lived a fast-paced, gin-soaked life in the 1920s, Van Vechten turned to a more sedate existence in the years that followed. He quit drinking, smoking, and staying up all night club-hopping. And he shifted his focus from writing to photography.

In the early 1930s Van Vechten discovered that he had a talent for photography, a pastime that would bring him acclaim while allowing him to make a contribution to history. He did so through his memorable photographic portraits of a number of important figures, especially (but not limited to) African Americans. He photographed not only the stars of the Harlem Renaissance—including W.E.B. Du Bois, Claude McKay, Zora Neale Hurston, and Bessie Smith—but also famous white writers such as F. Scott Fitzgerald and Gertrude Stein and publisher Alfred Knopf. He also photographed some notable young blacks in the years before their talent was widely recognized; examples include entertainers Sammy Davis Jr. and Harry Belafonte, actress Diahann Carroll, and opera singer Leontyne Price.

During the remaining decades of his life, Van Vechten's photographs were in demand as illustrations for books and were widely exhibited. In 1933 his work was featured in an exhibition at Bergdorf Goodman (an upscale New York department store) that also included prints by the more famous photographers Edward Steichen and Man Ray. More than a hundred of Van Vechten's photographs of theater personalities were shown at the Museum of the City of New York in 1942, and his work was exhibited at the Philadelphia Museum of Art in 1951.

In the years that followed the Harlem Renaissance, Van Vechten continued to correspond with many of its participants, and he believed strongly that the accomplishments of the period, and of African Americans in general, should be celebrated and preserved. In pursuit of this aim, he established special collections (places where manuscripts, letters, and other documents would be gathered) at several universities, including Yale (the site of the largest such collection), Fisk, Howard, and the University of New Mexico. In 1955 Van Vechten received an honorary degree from Fisk for his contributions to the recognition and preservation of African American culture. He died in 1964.

For More Information

Books

Coleman, Leon. *Carl Van Vechten and the Harlem Renaissance: A Critical Assessment.* New York: Garland, 1999.

Lewis, David Levering. *When Harlem Was in Vogue.* New York: Knopf, 1981.

Lueders, Edward. *Carl Van Vechten.* New York: Twayne, 1965.

Watson, Steven. *The Harlem Renaissance: Hub of African-American Culture, 1920–1930.* New York: Pantheon, 1995.

Periodicals

Helbling, Mark. "Carl Van Vechten and the Harlem Renaissance." *Negro American Literature Forum* (July 1976): 39–46.

Web sites

"Carl Van Vechten Biography and Chronology." [Online] http://lcweb2.loc.gov/ammem/vvbio.html (accessed March 15, 2000).

Ethel Waters

Born October 31, 1896
Chester, Pennsylvania
Died September 1, 1977
Chatsworth, California

American singer, actress, and writer

Among the dynamic entertainers that people flocked to Harlem by the carload to see was Ethel Waters, a talented singer and actress who had emerged from humble beginnings to become a star of nightclubs, musical revues, Broadway shows, and, eventually, films. Waters began her career by singing the blues—the new, uniquely African American musical form that was taking the United States by storm—but her smooth, sophisticated style took her beyond that category and into the broader realm of popular music. Waters's very emotional singing style—and, later, the realism she put into her dramatic roles—made her an especially memorable performer. She was also an African American trailblazer, becoming the first black woman to perform on radio (in 1922) and the first black singer to appear on television (in 1939).

"I was never a child...."

Waters had a difficult, impoverished childhood. Her mother, Louise Anderson, was only thirteen when she gave birth to her daughter, who was the product of a rape by a local

"I had fame, but I was empty."

Ethel Waters.
(AP/Wide World Photos, Inc. Reproduced by permission.)

young white man named John Waters. (Ethel eventually took her father's surname.) Anderson found it too difficult to accept this child born of such violence, so Ethel was raised primarily by her grandmother, Sally Anderson, who lived at various times in Chester and Philadelphia, Pennsylvania, and in Camden, New Jersey. Waters's grandmother was a domestic worker who was rarely at home, and the two aunts who also lived with Waters usually ignored her and sometimes abused her. In her autobiography *His Eye Is on the Sparrow,* Waters reflected, "I was never a child. I never was coddled or liked, or understood by my family. I never felt I belonged. I was always an outsider.... Nobody brought me up."

Young Waters spent a lot of time roaming the streets, sometimes even stealing food when she was hungry. She liked school but didn't attend it regularly. At the age of five she sang in a children's program at a Philadelphia church, and this first appearance as an entertainer was a huge success. When Waters was eight years old she went to work for the first time, cleaning houses. Five years later her family pressured her into marrying a man named Merritt Buddy Pernsley, but she left him a year later.

Waters spent her teenage years working as a maid, a dishwasher, and a waitress. In 1917, she sang at a party at a neighborhood bar, Jack's Rathskeller. Two vaudeville (a kind of variety show—often touring—that featured musical, dance, and comedy acts) producers who were in the audience were impressed with her talent and hired her to perform in Baltimore. During that two-week engagement, Waters became the first female singer to perform the great blues song "St. Louis Blues" on stage. Soon thereafter, she signed on with a group called the Hill Sisters and toured the southern states as Sweet Mama Stringbean (a nickname that referred to her slenderness).

A sophisticated style emerges

For a few years Waters took a number of jobs as a singer and dancer in carnivals and on the black vaudeville circuit. Her unusual singing style made her stand out from other blues singers: instead of the kind of deep, rough singing practiced by stars like Ma Rainey (1886–1939) and Bessie Smith (1894–1937; see biographical entry), Waters sang in a light, clear, and polished voice, injecting a great deal of emotion into the music.

While on tour in Alabama, Waters received a severe leg injury in a car accident and returned to Philadelphia to recuperate. After some time she got a job singing in Barney Gordon's Saloon in Philadelphia and her performances there were so popular that she was hired in 1919 to perform at the famous Lincoln Theatre in Harlem. When that engagement was finished, Waters went on to sing at Edmond's Cellar, a seedy Harlem club that was frequented by a lot of gamblers, prostitutes, and other disreputable types. In time, however, Waters's sophisticated singing attracted a higher-quality crowd, and her reputation as a fine singer and dancer—bolstered by her appearance in a black musical comedy called *Hello 1919!*—continued to spread.

Recordings broaden her audience

Waters made the first of many recordings in 1919, when the Cardinal Company hired her to record "New York Glide" and "At the New Jump Steady Ball." Three years later Black Swan Records paid her one hundred dollars to record "Down Home Blues" and "Oh Daddy." (At the time this was a large sum to be paid for two songs.) These songs were so successful that Waters quickly cut another record with "There'll Be Some Changes Made" on one side and "One Man Nan" on the other. Over the next two years Waters made twenty-six records for Black Swan, and she went on tour with Fletcher Henderson's Black Swan Troubadours to promote her music.

Waters spent much of her time in the early 1920s traveling throughout the Midwest, the East, and the South on the Theatre Owners and Bookers Association (TOBA) circuit, gaining more and more fans both black and white. In 1924 she starred in the *Plantation Revue* in Chicago, and Ashton Stevens, a reviewer for that city's *Herald Examiner* newspaper, called her "the greatest artist of her race and generation." The next year Waters headlined at the Plantation Club in New York, where she made a hit of a song called "Dinah." She was offered a spot in the *Revue Negre* in Paris but turned it down, which gave dancer Josephine Baker (1906–1975; see sidebar on p. 82) her big break.

Next, Waters was persuaded by producer and performer Earl Dancer to try out for the white vaudeville circuit. She and Dancer formed a team and became a very successful headlining act. Waters made her first Broadway appearance in 1927 in *Africana,* which had a long run in New York and then went on tour. After the show closed Waters returned to New York and appeared as a single act in various nightclubs and shows. She married Clyde Matthews during this period and continued to make recordings (259 in her overall career) for such companies as Paramount, Vocalion, and Columbia.

Film, Broadway, and nightclub star

Waters began her movie career in 1929 with an appearance in *On with the Show,* in which she sang "Am I Blue?" The next year she was in *Check and Double Check* with Amos and Andy (a well-known white comedy duo who played black characters) and the famous bandleader and composer Duke Ellington (1899–1974; see biographical entry). Also in 1930 Waters traveled to Europe and performed in Paris and London; while still in England she underwent successful surgery to remove a vocal cord nodule (small bump or growth). Returning to New York, Waters starred in more musical shows, including *Blackbirds of 1930* in New York and *Rhapsody in Black,* which opened in Washington, D.C., but soon went on tour.

During the early 1930s Waters became the highest paid star ever to appear at Harlem's celebrated nightspot, the Cotton Club. This was where she introduced the song that would become her most famous, "Stormy Weather." White Broadway producer Irving Berlin (1888–1989) saw Waters at the Cotton Club and was so impressed that he signed her to appear in a new musical called *As Thousands Cheer.* This 1934 production was a huge success—and something of a landmark because Waters was the first black performer to appear on Broadway with an otherwise all-white cast. She received equal billing with her white costars, even when the show went on the road in the South, where comparable treatment was unheard of. *As Thousands Cheer* featured Waters singing such songs as "Heat Wave," "Harlem," and the haunting "Supper Time," sung in the voice of a woman whose husband has been lynched (hanged illegally by a mob).

For two years Waters traveled all around the United States with *As Thousands Cheer*, during which time she separated from her husband. She also appeared in a Broadway revue called *At Home Abroad* in 1935 and 1936, then toured the South with trumpet player Eddie Mallory. Another milestone was just around the corner for the entertainer: in 1939 she became the first black woman to play a lead role in a dramatic play on Broadway, appearing as Hagar in DuBose Heyward's *Mamba's Daughters*. Waters poured into this character all of the suffering, loneliness, and courage of her own mother, and audiences responded with seventeen curtain calls on opening night. The play had a long Broadway run, followed by a tour and a return New York engagement.

To California and back

Next, Waters appeared as Petunia Jackson in the play *Cabin in the Sky*, which ran for five months in New York in 1940 before heading on the road to Los Angeles and San Francisco. In Los Angeles, Waters was performing at the Orpheum Theatre when she was offered a role in a film called *Tales of Manhattan*. In 1942 she appeared in another film, *Cairo*, with white movie star Jeannette McDonald, and she bought a house in Los Angeles. The next year Waters starred in the film version of *Cabin in the Sky*, but this was her last film role for several years. At that time there were few good motion picture roles for black actors. (Some would argue that this situation remained essentially the same even at the beginning of the twenty-first century.)

Disappointed with her situation in California, Waters returned to New York, but her singing career seemed to have stalled as well. She performed at the Club Zanzibar in 1947 and gave a concert at Carnegie Hall in 1948, but for the most part she was unemployed and struggling to support herself and her mother. Waters wondered what had happened to her fame of only a few years ago. In early 1949, though, her luck changed when she was offered the part of Granny in the film *Pinky*. Waters used her own grandmother as the model for this role, and she would later claim that all of her acting was instinctive (rather than something she had learned) and based either on her own experiences or those of people she knew. She received an Academy Award nomination for this film appearance.

The Member of the Wedding

But Waters's most acclaimed stage and film role was still to come. In early 1950 she was offered the part of Berenice Sadie Brown, a cook who serves as a compassionate friend to the little girl who is the central character in Carson McCuller's play *The Member of the Wedding* (based on her 1946 novel). The play ran for 501 performances on Broadway, during which time Waters wrote (with author Charles Samuels) her autobiography, *His Eye Is on the Sparrow.* In 1953 Waters appeared in the film version of *The Member of the Wedding* and again received an Academy Award nomination for her work.

Around the same time Waters starred in a weekly television series called *Beulah* and also appeared in a one-woman show, *An Evening with Ethel Waters.* By the late 1950s she had achieved considerable success but still felt that something was missing in her life; as recounted in *Ethel Waters: Finally Home* by Juliann DeKorte, she later declared, "I had fame, but I was empty." Then Waters went to see the Billy Graham Crusade (a series of large religious meetings featuring Christian leader Billy Graham) at Madison Square Garden in New York. She experienced a kind of religious awakening, and for the rest of her life she devoted much of her time to working as a singer with Graham's organization.

In her remaining years Waters appeared in two more films (*The Heart Is a Rebel,* 1956, and *The Sound and the Fury,* 1959) and many stage revivals of *The Member of the Wedding.* She also did occasional guest spots on television and in nightclubs, and she wrote another autobiography, *To Me It's Wonderful* (1972). But her health steadily declined, and she died of cancer in 1977, remembered as a dynamic, talented performer whose career blossomed far beyond its roots in the Harlem Renaissance.

For More Information
Books

DeKorte, Juliann. *Ethel Waters: Finally Home.* Fleming H. Revell Company, 1978.

Kellner, Bruce. *The Harlem Renaissance: A Historical Dictionary for the Era.* Westport, CT: Greenwood Press, 1984.

Knaack, Twila. *Ethel Waters: I Touched a Sparrow.* Word Books, 1978.

Placksin, Sally. *American Women in Jazz: 1900 to the Present.* New York: Seaview Books, 1982.

Southern, Eileen. *Biographical Dictionary of Afro-American and African Musicians.* Westport, CT: Greenwood Press, 1982.

Waters, Ethel, and Charles Samuels. *His Eye Is on the Sparrow.* Westport, CT: Greenwood Press, 1951.

Waters, Ethel. *To Me It's Wonderful.* New York: Harper & Row, 1972.

Periodicals

Rankin, Allen. "The Three Lives of Ethel Waters." *Reader's Digest* (December 1972): 81–85.

Research and Activity Ideas

The following list of research and activity ideas is intended to offer suggestions for complementing social studies and language arts curricula, to trigger additional ideas for enhancing learning, and to suggest cross-disciplinary projects for library and classroom use.

Key Events: Make a timeline showing the major historical and cultural events that affected African Americans between the years of 1865 and 1935. Historical events might include the signing of the Emancipation Proclamation, World War I, and the Great Depression; cultural events might include the publication of Langston Hughes's poem "The Weary Blues" and Duke Ellington's arrival in Harlem.

Life in Harlem: Imagine that the year is 1925 and you are a young African American who has recently moved to Harlem from your rural home in Alabama. Write a letter to your family, describing the sights and sounds around you and explaining what your new life is like.

Landmarks and Places of Interest: Imagine you are a travel agent in the 1920s. Create a brochure that advertises

Harlem as a fun place to visit. Include a simple map that shows places of interest, such as the Cotton Club and the Tree of Hope.

Debate the Issues: Hold a debate about a controversial issue of the Harlem Renaissance, such as whether art should be used to help black people get ahead or as a means of personal expression, or whether the idea of African Americans as "primitive" is good or bad.

Discover Harlem Renaissance Art Works: Imagine that you are the curator of an art museum who is organizing an exhibit of Harlem Renaissance art works. Write and illustrate (perhaps with color photocopies of prints you have found in books or on the Internet) a booklet about the paintings and sculptures in the exhibit.

Blues vs Rock and Roll: Listen to the music of a blues singer, such as Bessie Smith. Use specific songs as examples to show how this music influenced the development of rock and roll. Look for similarities between blues and rock in both the music and the lyrics. You might also compare a rock song with a blues song to show how they are related.

Points of View: Write two magazine reviews of Aaron Douglas's mural series *Aspects of Negro Life*. In one, pretend you are a reviewer for a white publication who has little knowledge of African American history or culture. For the other, pretend you are writing for a black publication like *Crisis*. How will these two viewpoints differ? How will they be similar?

Design A Poster: Imagine that you have been hired to decorate A'lelia Walker's Dark Tower nightclub and literary gathering place. Design a large poster that celebrates the literature of the times. For example, draw Langston Hughes's poem "The Weary Blues" (or another Harlem Renaissance poem you like) as well as illustrations of the poem's content.

Produce A Skit: Write and act out a skit dramatizing either a meeting between a new arrival in Harlem and a friend who explains what is happening in the African American community, or a black soldier—perhaps a member of the famous 369th Infantry Regiment—who has recently returned to Harlem from World War I and talks about his experiences, hopes, expectations, and disappointments.

Host A "Radio Show:" Imagine that you are the host of a radio show. Tape a number of songs to introduce listeners to the music of the Harlem Renaissance. Write a script to introduce and describe each song and artist.

Where to Learn More

Books

Adoff, Arnold, ed. *The Poetry of Black America: An Anthology of the Twentieth Century*. New York: Harper and Row, 1973.

Arata, Esther S. *Black American Playwrights: 1800 to Present*. Metuchen, N.J.: Scarecrow Press, 1976.

Baker, Houston A. *Modernism and the Harlem Renaissance*. Chicago: University of Chicago Press, 1987.

Bone, Robert A. *The Negro Novel in America*. New Haven, Conn.: Yale University Press, 1958, 1970.

Bontemps, Arna. *The Harlem Renaissance Remembered*. New York: Dodd, Mead, 1972.

Brown, Sterling. *Negro Poetry and Drama. The Negro in American Fiction* (1937). Reprint: New York: Atheneum, 1969.

Case, Brian, and Stan Britt. *The Illustrated Encyclopedia of Jazz*. New York: Harmony Books, 1978.

Charters, Samuel B. *Jazz: A History of the New York Scene*. Garden City, N.Y.: Doubleday, 1962.

Christian, Barbara. *Black Women Novelists: The Development of a Tradition, 1892-1976*. Westport, Conn.: 1980.

Davis, Arthur P. *From the Dark Tower: Afro-American Writers, 1900 to 1960.* Washington, D.C.: Howard University Press, 1974.

Dictionary of Literary Biography, Vol. 51: Afro-American Writers from the Harlem Renaissance to 1940. Detroit: Gale Research, 1987.

Emery, Lynn Fauley. *Black Dance in the United States from 1619 to 1970.* Palo Alto, Calif.: National Press Books, 1972, 1980.

Floyd, Samuel A., Jr. *Black Music in the Harlem Renaissance.* Westport, Conn.: Greenwood Press, 1990.

Green, Stanley L. *Encyclopedia of the Musical Theatre.* New York: Dodd, Mead, 1976.

Harris, Sheldon. *Blues Who's Who: A Biographical Dictionary of Blues Singers.* New Rochelle, N.Y.: Arlington House, 1979.

Ham, Debra Newman, ed. *The African-American Mosaic: A Library of Congress Resource Guide for the Study of Black History and Culture.* Washington, D.C.: Library of Congress, 1993.

Haskins, James. *Black Theatre in America.* New York: Crowell, 1982.

Henri, Florette. *Black Migration: Movement North, 1900–1920.* Urbana: University of Illinois Press, 1977.

Huggins, Nathan. *Harlem Renaissance.* New York: Oxford University Press, 1971.

Huggins, Nathan, ed. *Voices from the Harlem Renaissance.* New York: Oxford University Press, 1971.

Hughes, Langston. *The Big Sea.* New York: Knopf, 1940.

Kellner, Bruce, ed. *The Harlem Renaissance: A Historical Dictionary for the Era.* Westport, Conn.: Greenwood Press, 1984.

Lewis, David Levering. *When Harlem Was in Vogue.* New York: Penguin Books, 1979.

Logan, Rayford W. and Michael R. Winston, eds. *Dictionary of American Negro Biography.* New York: Norton, 1982.

Mapp, Edward. *Dictionary of Blacks in the Performing Arts.* Metuchen, N.J.: Scarecrow Press, 1978.

Mitchell, Loften. *Black Drama: The Story of the American Negro in the Theatre.* New York: Hawthorn Books, 1967.

Oakley, Giles. *The Devil's Music: A History of the Blues.* New York: Harcourt Brace Jovanovich, 1978.

Perry, Margaret. *The Harlem Renaissance: An Annotated Bibliography and Commentary.* New York: Garland, 1982.

Southern, Eileen. *Biographical Dictionary of Afro-American and African Musicians.* Westport, Conn.: Greenwood Press, 1982.

Twentieth Century Literary Criticism, Vol. 26: Harlem Renaissance. Detroit: Gale Research.

Vincent, Theodore. *Voices of a Black Nation. Political Journalism in the Harlem Renaissance.* San Francisco, Calif.: Ramparts Press, 1973.

Wintz, Cary D. *Black Culture and the Harlem Renaissance.* Houston, Tex.: Rice University Press, 1988.

Wagner, Jean. *Black Poets of the United States from Paul Laurence Dunbar to Langston Hughes.* Urbana: University of Illinois Press, 1973.

Organizations

James Weldon Johnson Collection
    Beinecke Library, Yale University
    [Online] Available: http://www.library.yale.edu/beinecke/ycaljwj.htm

Schomberg Center for Research in Black Culture. New York Public Library.
    [Online] Available: http://www.nypl.org/research/sc/sc.html

Web Sites

The Circle Association's Weblinks to the Harlem Renaissance. [Online] Available: http://www.math.buffalo.edu/~sww/circle/harlem-ren-sites.html.

Harlem Renaissance Chronology, 1919–1938. [Online] Available: http://www.iniva.org/harlem/chron.html.

Reuben, Paul P. *PAL: Perspectives in American Literature.* Search "Harlem Renaissance." [Online] Available: http://www.csustan.edu/english/reuben/home.html.

Links to web sites on a variety of Harlem Renaissance subjects. [Online] Available: http://www.lincolnu.edu/~kluebber/harhis.htm.

Index